Entrepreneur® MENTOR SERIES

WRITING KILLER SALES PROPOSALS

Win the Bid and Close the Deal

BUD PORTER-ROTH

EP
Entrepreneur.
Press

Editorial Director: Jere L. Calmes
Cover Design: Beth Hanson-Winter
Composition and Production: Eliot House Productions

This publication is designed to provide accurate and authoritative
information in regard to the subject matter covered. It is sold with the
understanding that the publisher is not engaged in rendering legal,
accounting, or other professional services. If legal advice or other
expert assistance is required, the services of a competent professional
person should be sought.

—From a Declaration of Principles jointly adopted by a
Committee of the American Bar Association and
a Committee of Publishers and Associations

Library of Congress Cataloging-in-Publication
Porter-Roth, Bud.
  Writing killer sales proposals : win the bid and close the
deal/Bud Porter-Roth.
    p.   cm.   (Entrepreneur mentor series)
    ISBN 1-932156-71-2
    1. Proposal writing in business. 2. Selling. I. Title. II. Series.
    HF5718.5.P68 2004
    808'.066658—dc22   2003064247

Printed in Canada

11 10 09 08 07 06 05 04   10 9 8 7 6 5 4 3 2 1

TABLE OF CONTENTS

Foreword . . . . *vi*
Preface . . . . *viii*
Acknowledgments . . . . *xiii*

INTRODUCTION: **Build a Winning Proposal Process** . . . . **xiv**

CHAPTER 1: **Why Do We Write Proposals?** **1**
    What Is an RFP and Why Do I Have to Respond to It? 5
    Summary 14

CHAPTER 2: **Develop a Winning Proposal Process** **17**
    The Proposal Team 17
    Develop the Winning Strategy 22
    Features, Benefits, and Needs 24
    Outlining Your Proposal 27
    Proposal Style Sheet 33
    Proposal Activities 34
    In-House Review 39
    Schedule 42
    Postproposal Activities 46
    Proposal Disposition Activities 47
    Alternate Proposals 49
    Writing Levels 51
    Summary 55

CHAPTER 3: **Qualify the Opportunity** **61**
    Getting Started 63

Qualifying Both the Buyer and the RFP 65
Bid/No-Bid Decision 72
Summary 79

CHAPTER 4: **Evaluation Considerations and Strategies** **81**
In-House Proposal Evaluation 87
Customer Evaluation 94
Summary 99

CHAPTER 5: **Format the Proposal** **101**
Proposal Cover 101
Physical Organization of a Proposal 104
Front Matter 105
Additional Front Matter 114
Proposal Organization 117
Proposal Format 118

CHAPTER 6: **Develop and Write Your Proposal** **123**
The Executive Summary 124
Technical Section 141
Management Section 153
Pricing Section 163
The Proposal Appendixes 173
Summary 175

CHAPTER 7: **Follow the Submission
and Delivery Requirements** **177**
Submission Criteria 178
Proposal Delivery Requirements 184
Summary 188

CHAPTER 8: **Organize the Postproposal Activities** **189**
Postdelivery Considerations 189
Precontract Steps 194
Interpreting Postproposal Data 208
Summary 210

CHAPTER 9: **Print and Deliver Your Proposal** **213**
Methods of Printing 213
Specialty Printing 214
Types of Binding 223
Selecting a Printer or Reproduction Shop 226
Final Assembly 228

CHAPTER 10: **Preparing and Managing Boilerplate Files** **231**
Developing Boilerplate Files 232
Text Boilerplate Files 236
Illustration Boilerplate Files 252
Using Boilerplate Files 260
Indexing Files 262
Dissemination of Material 264
Maintenance of the Boilerplate Library 265
Summary 267

CHAPTER 11: **Developing Illustrations for Your Proposal** . . . **269**
The Art of Illustrations 270
Illustration Formats 280
Illustration Standards 282
Organization 286
Storage of Illustrations 290
Summary 291

APPENDIXES

Introduction to the Appendices 293

APPENDIX A: **General Preproposal Checklist** **294**

APPENDIX B: **Proposal Writing Checklist** **296**

APPENDIX C: **Presubmission Checklist** **298**

APPENDIX D: **Printing Checklist** **300**

APPENDIX E: **Evaluation Checklist** **301**

APPENDIX F: **Proposal Submission Checklist** **303**

APPENDIX G: **Postproposal Checklist** **304**

APPENDIX H: **Bid/No-Bid Checklist** **305**

APPENDIX I: **Proposal Status Sheet** **308**

APPENDIX J: **Cost Justification Whitepaper** **315**
Introduction 315
CJA Summary 323
Beyond ROI, Measuring Project Results 323
Conclusion 325

Index 327

FOREWORD

Perhaps you are like many of us in the business world and find the prospect of tackling a large proposal quite daunting. Perhaps you're a proposal specialist for whom creating precise answers to clients' questions and insightful plans for implementation are routine matters of the day. Regardless of your breadth of experience or level of trepidation, you'll find *Writing Killer Sales Proposals* by Bud Porter-Roth a valuable resource.

In my more than 20 years in the information technology business, I have worked for vendors of all sizes, from mighty General Electric down to operating as an independent consultant. I have participated in or directed the creation of proposals priced at a few hundred to many millions of dollars. I have helped evaluate responses for clients and participated in the decision process for selecting winning bids. Most of the time, I found myself on my own—with little more than a pile of sales brochures, a marketing boilerplate, and price lists to guide me. I can safely say, in all that time and through all of those activities, no one ever offered me a proposal-writing guide like this one.

Bud Porter-Roth has drawn on years of firsthand experience to put together a step-by-step, comprehensive game plan for playing and winning the RFP game.

Managers with overall proposal responsibility—or those of us in our own firms who find it necessary to create the entire proposal alone—will want to thoroughly study all of *Writing Killer Sales Proposals,* contents, from its early discussion of Qualifying the Opportunity, through How to Develop and Write Your Proposal, to the best way to organize Postproposal Activities.

The team member or area specialist will find the Technical Section, Pricing Section, and chapters on Formatting, Printing, and Delivery of the final proposal to be invaluable. Bud Porter-Roth's generous inclusion of examples, charts, illustrations, and checklists will save you time and effort, clarifying the process and making possible a level of organization and professional delivery once reserved exclusively for large sales-response staffs.

Regardless of whether you're with a large team from IBM, a smaller vendor with limited marketing resources, or find yourself charged with creating the proposal yourself, I believe you'll find *Killer Sales Proposals* to be of tremendous value in creating and writing a proposal. I know my company will be relying on it heavily for our next important sales opportunity (and what sales opportunity isn't?).

—Greg Fuller
Fairlead Technology Group Inc.
Sausalito, CA

PREFACE

The purpose of this book is to provide you with a practical guide to writing and organizing winning sales proposals. Whether you are a novice or experienced proposal writer, you will find tips and techniques that will be beneficial to you. Instead of discussing salesmanship 101, sales theories, and proposal war stories, this book focuses on developing a process and on the mechanics of writing proposals.

A process may be defined as a method for achieving consistent results that involves a number of identifiable steps and operations. For a process to be successful, it must be repeatable; otherwise, it is not a process at all, and any results—good or bad—are only accidental. Being able to win proposals consistently is not accidental; it is the result of utilizing a well-planned process. (Having a good product helps, too!) This book defines the basic steps that are a part of that process.

These steps include but are not limited to

- having the discipline for a critical reading of the RFP, or a critical understanding of the sales opportunity.
- developing an outline for your proposal.
- writing a tightly focused proposal that responds to the major *identified* requirements.
- planning and scheduling your resources and facilities.
- preparing a competitive analysis and using it.
- reserving time for a final review of your proposal.

- ensuring that your pricing is in the ballpark.

Having an easily applied process reduces time wasted in the mechanical aspects of coordinating a variety of disparate materials, such as maintenance descriptions, product descriptions, and other areas that are typically lifted from standard corporate literature. Instead, you can devote time to better understanding the opportunity, developing a winning strategy, getting the right pricing, and working with the customer.

This book is a "soup to nuts" review of proposal writing and the proposal development process. It is written with a best-case scenario in mind, though you may not have access to all of the resources and facilities listed. This book is useful not only as a writing guide, but also as a resource to show management how professionally written proposals are resourced, managed, and written. If you are going to build a proposal development group, this book will help you.

This is the fourth edition of this book. While the basic principles of good proposal writing haven't changed, technology has given us new tools that allow us to work better, faster, and smarter. Current desktop technologies allow the average user to produce a proposal that will compete on any level. These technologies include

- high-quality laser printers.
- color printers.
- scanners.
- digital cameras.
- word processors.
- spreadsheet and statistical programs.
- illustration programs.
- desktop publishing software.
- groupware or collaborative software.
- Internet resources.
- company Intranet resources.

Today there is no reason a smaller company or individual sales representative cannot produce a professional-quality proposal—both in appearance and in content. With the help of this book, all it takes for you to write winning proposals are your own skills, knowledge, and initiative.

One increasingly important tool for RFP writers is the Internet. With the Internet, individuals and companies can easily share files; access boilerplate caches; collaborate in the development of a proposal; research potential customers; and create a virtual proposal center where such important items as proposal strategy, competitive information, and answers to questions can be posted. This allows the team to be geographically dispersed and yet able to work together, regardless of the place and the time zone. For the more technologically advanced, computer teleconferencing and online whiteboards add to the tool bag.

In the near future, and it has already started, companies will use Internet-based RFP software to write their RFPs, and you will respond using the designated online response software. This means that your shop will have to be in order, with all of the tools, files, documents, etc. to write an online proposal. This book will help you to get organized and to have the information you need at your fingertips.

These technologies and other new ideas are explored in this new edition. But the tried-and-true principles of writing a good proposal remain, regardless of technology. You, the proposal writer, still need to understand the opportunity and to propose the correct products at a reasonable price.

Who Should Read This Book?

Having been a company proposal manager and an independent proposal manager, I have worked with all kinds of people from all types of companies and departments. I've found that many companies do not have proposal-writing guidelines, procedures, or support, and rely on company history and previously written proposals for guidance and source materials. If there is no previous history of writing proposals, a company may turn to consultants for help, or ask customers for copies of previous proposals that can be used. I have been asked many times if I could send someone a "good" proposal as an example.

Neophytes who have been assigned to write their first proposal and, perhaps, have little history and support to draw on, will find this book invaluable. There is a suggested proposal outline; a wealth of examples; and good, solid advice that will guide you from starting the project to signing the contract.

People who are old hands at proposal writing will find that this book supplements and adds to their existing expertise, in addition to providing some fresh examples for developing technical and management sections.

This book is written for those who need proposal-writing guidance, procedures, and direction. People who should read this book include

- sales representatives.
- sales technical support.
- marketing personnel involved in proposal writing.
- information technology managers asked to write or manage a proposal effort.
- business owners and managers who may not have dedicated proposal support and find that they need to write a proposal.
- consultants who are responsible for writing proposals or helping their clients write them.
- training department personnel for companies wishing to start or improve their company proposal-writing program.

- university and college professors looking for primary or supplemental course material on proposal development and writing.

After reading this book, you will be able to

- organize the proposal project effort.
- outline each proposal section.
- write an executive summary that is geared toward business issues and understanding the business drivers.
- develop, write, and review proposal sections—technical, management, and pricing.
- qualify the sales opportunity before expending critical resources.
- understand the project's evaluation criteria for evaluating proposals and improve your opportunity to win.
- prepare for postproposal activities such as site visits, demonstrations, reference checks; plan and schedule implementation activities; and put in place realistic project management plans.

There is no prerequisite to reading this book—you do not need to be a senior IT manager, purchasing manager, or certified sales rep. The book provides a standard format for the recommended sections in proposals and includes examples for each section, as well as examples of how to respond to technical and nontechnical requirements for each section.

—Bud Porter-Roth
Porter-Roth Associates
Mill Valley, CA

ACKNOWLEDGMENTS

As in any endeavor of this magnitude, there are many people who have provided constructive criticism, positive encouragement, and support. I would like to thank all of the reviewers who took time from their busy workdays to review and comment on this book. *Writing Killer Sales Proposals* is much better due to their efforts.

Special thanks to Greg Fuller for reviewing this new edition and graciously agreeing to write the foreword. Greg is a small-business owner who is "in the trenches" when it comes to writing proposals, and I appreciate his comments.

Finally, my wife, Anne, and daughter, Lizzie, endured many early mornings, late nights, and missed weekends as I toiled away, writing and revising the manuscript. Their support helped make this book possible. Thanks!

INTRODUCTION
Build a Winning Proposal Process

More than ever business is becoming more competitive, more demanding of the vendor, and buyers have little patience with vendors who are not responsive to their needs. Competition among businesses is a driving force causing many businesses to adopt increasingly complex technological solutions to stay ahead of their rivals while still meeting the bottom-line need for profitability.

It is not only businesses that are becoming more efficient. Workers at all levels of government—federal, state, and local—are seeing that they can cut costs, trim budgets, and provide more value to the taxpayer by adopting new or more complex technologies and services.

Buyers' requirements, or Requests for Proposals (RFPs), have grown in sophistication as buyers become more knowledgeable about the technologies and products they are interested in buying. Buyers are doing their homework, writing specifications and RFPs that demonstrate in-depth understanding of not only the products, but all aspects of the intended project—testing, implementation planning, project management, training, and maintenance.

A new trend within the buyer community is to orient complex purchases and RFP projects toward what is termed performance-based purchasing, or performance-based contracting. Performance-based purchasing and contracting is an effort by the buyer to not describe in precise detail what system is needed, but to describe the job and the goals that the system will perform. Vendors are responsible for understanding the project performance goals, formalizing the project's requirements and developing a system or service that meets those goals. In other words, the buyer is making vendors responsible for the requirements analysis and the system description in their proposals. The winning vendor is then on the hook to meet the performance goals with the system they propose.

Performance-based contracting places more weight on your customer references, reviewing current and past projects, project presentations, and project demonstrations. Customers are no longer satisfied with reading proposals; they want to see the company, see the system or service, and talk with your customers as references. All of this information has to be included in your written proposal and postproposal work, which can keep proposal effort and work alive for an extended time.

So what does this mean to you, the proposal writer—the person who has to be the salesperson, write the proposal, do the pricing, make the presentation, and worry about references and site visits that you can't control? Well, it means that you are probably seeing more requests for proposals, that requirements are more detailed and demanding, and that the customer is no longer willing to sign a contract without a written proposal, firm pricing, and a statement of performance goals. You may be writing more reference account descriptions, writing presentations, and developing demonstrations scripts (No canned demos allowed!). In other words, you need all the help you can get.

On the other side of the fence, other vendors—your competition—are becoming more sophisticated with software-based proposal-writing tools, more corporate emphasis on proposal writing, better competitive analysis via consultant services, and better-planned and better-resourced demonstrations and presentations. Buyers are quick to notice the "presentation" differences among proposals—the outstanding qualities of those that are well laid out, make good use of graphics, and incorporate sophisticated selling themes backed by comprehensive selling tools, such as a total cost of ownership study, return on investment (ROI) analysis, "actual" implementation project plans reflecting real dates and people, and research whitepapers that show industry strategies and direction. While a more sophisticated proposal (better graphics, better look and feel) may not win the deal, it can provide extra weight when a decision is between two otherwise equal vendors.

Writing Killer Sales Proposals will help you to understand how to organize your basic proposal and how to incorporate graphics to more fully support the text. It will detail other essential areas that must be addressed, such as providing an ROI analysis of the project at hand (see Appendix J). We'll review important concepts such as the difference between features and benefits, and the value of solution selling instead of product selling. We emphasize getting a clear selling theme established early and revisiting that theme as often as possible. And finally, we help you to understand how to organize and structure a proposal process that allows you to work more quickly and efficiently on the proposal mechanics, with more time to develop better-selling scenarios, work on the all-important presentation, basic pricing, pricing options and alternatives, and pricing presentations.

The following is a brief overview of each chapter. While it is better to read the chapters in order, it is possible to skip ahead to, for example, Chapter 3 if you are interested in qualifying a current opportunity.

Chapter 1, Why Do We Write Proposals? reviews how the buyer begins to define a project, develop specifications, write requirements, and get the project into your hands. Understanding how and why the customer develops a project will help you to understand how to respond and why all project requirements are not good, valid, or even needed. By understanding a customer's business problem, you are better able to propose a "business solution" rather than selling products looking for problems. Selling to a "business problem" is key to winning more proposals.

Chapter 2, Develop a Winning Proposal Process details the complete proposal-writing process, from receiving the request to giving the final presentation. Throughout this chapter, we offer guidance and suggestions to either establish a process or fine-tune your existing process. If you are new to proposal writing, this overview will ground you for the rest of the book. Even if you are an old hand at proposal writing, this chapter may give you some new ideas.

Chapter 3, Qualify the Opportunity is featured as a separate chapter because it is so important to understand who the buyers are and what they are asking for—before you begin writing a proposal for a potentially questionable project. Many companies waste resources on proposals they can't win, at the expense of proposal opportunities they may have a greater chance of winning. The result of qualifying an opportunity is a formal Bid/No- Bid Process in which you work with management to determine whether an opportunity has merit or not. A plus to this process is that if management agrees to go forward, you have their buy-in.

Chapter 4, Evaluation Considerations and Strategies is an important part of any proposal process. By understanding how your proposal will be evaluated, you have a better chance of "weighting" certain areas in your favor. Understanding where the evaluation weights are going to be will help you to locate the "hot buttons" for the project and to effectively address those hot buttons in your executive summary. Some of the evaluation hot buttons will be the result of your customer qualification process, and you will be able to use this information to your advantage.

Chapter 5, Format the Proposal covers how to physically organize and format your proposal. By reviewing this chapter before beginning to write, you will save time and achieve a more consistent presentation in your proposal. This chapter will help you to develop an internal proposal-writing process by understanding the parts of a standard proposal. Remember that the presentation of your proposal can be the deciding factor between you and the competition.

Chapter 6, Develop and Write Your Proposal dives into the actual proposal development and writing process. It reviews each of the major sections of a typical proposal, explains who reads your proposal for that section, and offers examples for each section.

Chapter 7, Follow the Submission and Delivery Requirements is an essential part of any winning proposal process. Too often proposals that represent potentially winning solutions are disqualified because they didn't follow the submission criteria, missed an important date, or failed to include an annual report. Use this chapter to develop submission checklists for your proposal process that can become part of an established process.

Chapter 8, Organize the Postproposal Activities ties together all of the details that are needed to finish and win the proposal. Once your proposal is submitted, the next phase starts if you make it to the short list. We review how to get ready for the presentation and possible demonstration, how the customer is going to check references, what happens when the customer wants to review and change your proposal, and other concluding steps that will help ensure that you win the proposal.

Chapters 9, 10, and 11 address the mechanical aspects of printing and delivering your proposal, developing and using proposal boilerplate files, and establishing and using illustrations in your proposal. These chapters serve as infrastructure chapters to help you develop your internal resources and learn how to use (and not use) boilerplate files. Boilerplate files are both good and bad; they help you by saving time, but they can hurt you if not kept up-to-date.

Appendixes A through J cover a variety of topics, from checklists to a whitepaper on writing a return on investment (ROI) analysis. We encourage you to use these appendixes as models for checklists that you will develop and use to meet your own needs. For example, Appendix I, Proposal Status Sheet, provides a method for organizing and tracking each proposal that goes through your shop, and for formalizing the Bid/No-Bid Process. Adapting it to your own use, putting it on an intranet and ensuring that it is followed will help you to establish and maintain a company-wide awareness of the proposal process and its importance to your company.

Summary

One thing this book *can't* do for you is to write your proposal. You will still have to write the actual text, understand and address the business problem, and be timely and responsive to the customer's demands.

However, *Writing Killer Sales Proposals* is written as a "hands-on" book that you can immediately use to help you write winning proposals. The examples are real examples taken from past work, proposals, and RFPs; the checklists can be adapted for immediate use within your company; and the process outline for writing proposals is based on experience in the real world. Whether you use this book to develop a company-wide process or use it for help in writing your next proposal, the information will help you to win your next proposal.

WHY DO WE WRITE PROPOSALS?

Proposals are written in virtually every public and private business sector. A request for proposal (RFP), for example, is a document that outlines a need and solicits proposals that explain how that need can be solved. A proposal, then, is an answer to a question. It could be as simple as a letter response for pricing in which a price sheet is supplied, or as complex as a multivolume written response that takes months to complete and additional months to be evaluated. The most common types of proposals are sales proposals, which explain a product or service, and grant proposals, which request funding or resources for a project. This book will focus on sales proposals.

Sales proposals are generally written to provide a buyer (or customer) with information about your product or service and its pricing. Proposals are written in response to a meeting with the buyer ("That sounds good, Maryanne—write something up, price it, and get it back to me by Friday. ... "), or they can be unsolicited proposals. Unsolicited proposals are sent to a prospective buyer who may be interested in your product or service but has not requested a proposal from you. You may not have had any previous contact with the buyer or the company.

A third type of sales proposal is written in response to a request for proposals (RFP) in which the buyer has provided a written document that contains a list of specifications and requirements describing what the

> **Tip** A proposal is an answer to a question.

buyer is trying to purchase. Your proposal is a document that responds to those requirements and proposes a solution to them.

A buyer will release an RFP to a number of potential bidders with the intent of developing a competitive situation among vendors that will produce the highest quality products and services at a *competitive price* or the "best value."

However, competitive price does not necessarily mean the lowest price. Lowest pricing is rarely the determining factor in a complex system RFP, and many procurement manuals state that pricing is only considered after a proposal has been evaluated for technical merit. So, pricing is always compared in relation to the products and services being offered. This is often referred to as a "best value" procurement. One definition of best value is the "cost/benefit analysis [needed] to define the best combination of vendor performance capability, quality, services, time, and cost considerations over the useful life of the service."[1] The quote below is from an RFP and illustrates that price is not always the determining factor:

> *The evaluation criteria reflect a wide range of considerations. While the vendor's pricing is important, other factors are also significant. Consequently, a vendor may be selected that is not necessarily the lowest-cost solution. The objective is to choose a reliable and experienced vendor capable of providing effective products and services within a reasonable cost.*

For example, two companies may bid on a computer system, and the winning company's price is actually 10 percent higher than the second-place company's. However, the winning bid is justified because its overall cost of ownership is 25 percent lower over a five-year period, thus saving the company money in the long run.

---

[1] *Dictionary of Purchasing Terms*, Fifth Edition, National Institute of Government Purchasing.

I managed an RFP for a county government, and when we started to discuss the evaluation criteria one of the "old timers" held up his hand and said, "What are we discussing this for? Low price wins—that's the only evaluation criteria I go by...." Well, we did have to work him over a bit, and he did begrudgingly acknowledge that it was in the county's interest to get the right solution and not necessarily the cheapest solution.

We did not choose the vendor with the lowest price in this case: the final two vendors had relatively the same equipment, but the vendor we awarded the contract to had a significantly better work history and financial position, and we thought his company had a better project management capability. While this was a technology purchase, factors other than price and technology were key to deciding the winner.

This is only one simple example, but "best value" is always considered as the relationship between price and product. Maybe that old adage, "You get what you pay for." has finally got some traction in the procurement world. There are other procurement strategies being implemented in both the public and private sectors that we'll review later in this book.

Winning a competitive bid involves certain skills in developing, writing, and selling your proposal. Even with a superior product or price, it is possible to lose to a better-prepared proposal that offers more value to the buyer. Proposals that win are not "brochure-ware proposals"[2] but are proposals that show the buyer how a company will provide more functionality or service than the competition—in addition to providing the right solution. Winning proposals actually demonstrate an understanding of the buyer's business issues and problems and offer, as a team, to solve the problem. Brochure-ware proposals are simply selling hardware or

---

[2] Brochure-ware proposals are proposals that consist of a cover letter and a set of datasheets, glossy brochures, and maybe an annual report. These types of proposals are generally not acceptable.

As a consultant, I write RFPs and help my clients evaluate proposals. One RFP I managed was for a corporate intranet search engine. The RFP was short and the requirements were well defined. The administrative section cautioned vendors to keep it short and sweet. Generally speaking, the proposals we received followed the instructions. But one of the absolute worst proposals I have ever received came from a large Fortune 500 company. Their proposal did not follow the RFP instructions and it was almost impossible to follow their response. It was a total "brochure-ware proposal" that was also the largest (number of pages) proposal received.

While we (the RFP team) had looked forward to reading this particular proposal, it became the first one to be disqualified. In our first evaluation meeting, the team agreed that this proposal was DOA and tossed it out without further consideration.

software or services; they are simple product pitches with pricing and are not proposals that represent business solutions.

Writing proposals can be hard work for all involved. If we get behind in the writing, we tend to start adding more and more nonessential data in an effort to make our proposals "heavier," hoping that the customer will be impressed with the volume and not notice that we didn't do so well in responding to the requirements. The following quote from George Bernard Shaw is well stated for our purposes: *"I'm sorry this letter is so long. I didn't have time to write a short one."*

Most customers, however, are looking for a short, well-written proposal that clearly and simply tells them what they want to know. A typical RFP preparation instruction will caution that, "Proposals should be prepared simply and economically, providing a straightforward, concise description of the bidders' capabilities to satisfy the requirements of the RFP. Proposals that are overly elaborate and use extensive attachments are neither required nor necessary. *Emphasis should be on completeness and clarity of content."*

Tip Emphasis should be on completeness and clarity of content.

Think about the RFP team, or the person putting together the requirements, who has just spent 6 to 12 weeks, away from their *real work*, putting together the RFP. Just as they are getting caught up on their normal work (while vendors are writing proposals), 12 100-page proposals are delivered and the team has only 15 business days to evaluate the proposals and make a recommendation. Wouldn't you, as an evaluator, be more inclined to read and positively respond to a proposal that concisely responded just to the requirements without any excess verbiage, complex eye-chart diagrams, overly complicated graphs, or other information that really didn't add value to the basic message?

Whether you're responding to an RFP, sending an unsolicited proposal, or providing a postmeeting proposal, the same rules apply: You must understand the business proposition from the customer's point of view and your proposal must address the key issues in a direct and understandable manner. While this book addresses proposal writing in response to an RFP, the information about analyzing needs, structuring the proposal, and doing the postproposal follow-up still apply, and perhaps even more so. Why? Because with an RFP, you are provided a detailed list of instructions to follow—without an RFP, you may have little or nothing to follow except a brief conversation with the customer. This increases your chances of forgetting something, missing a step, or not being prepared for the follow-up steps.

A key point to successful proposal writing is understanding RFPs—why they are written, how they are written, and who writes them.

> *Tip* A technically correct RFP makes your job easier.

What Is an RFP and Why Do I Have to Respond to It?

The following discussion about RFPs will help you to better understand that although RFPs are not always the clearest documents and can be confusing, they ultimately cannot be avoided. RFPs, whether clearly written or not, offer you an excellent opportunity, if you understand how to respond to them.

One of the primary keys to winning a proposal effort is to understand the RFP from the position of the group that writes it. People who write RFPs are typically not dedicated to writing RFPs and purchasing products—they are office and department managers, supervisors, workers, and others who must produce this document while also doing their regular work. It is entirely possible that they have not written an RFP before and will ask you (and others) for examples of "good RFPs" that they can use and copy.

The typical RFP is written by an ad hoc group that has been assigned to study and define the problem, determine what solutions are available, develop an estimated budget, educate themselves on technologies and products, write the RFP, and then evaluate the vendor responses. These people may or may not have previous experience with the potential technologies and may or may not have a technical understanding of how the products work. In many cases, they must depend on going to conferences, talking to vendors, getting presentations and demonstrations, and perhaps talking to other companies that use the technology.

One of the most difficult issues that surfaces when reviewing an RFP is that many buyers believe that technology will solve all of their problems, or at least that the vendor can be blamed if it doesn't. Many times, I have had to explain that if you automate a mess, you get an automated mess. Always be on the lookout for false or inflated expectations on the buyer's part. Inflated expectations are usually the result of overselling by some vendors who are focused on getting the business first and letting the back office iron out the details.

In short, the people writing the RFP may have only a surface-level understanding of what they are trying to buy; therefore, the RFP may be incomplete or have confusing requirements and unrealistic goals and expectations. It is also possible that the RFP will demonstrate tremendous understanding of the technologies, products, and their capabilities, and will be very well written and detailed in scope. If you are lucky, you will get a good RFP from a team that has done its homework. This will make your job much easier.

It becomes your job to understand what an RFP is all about, why it is perhaps unclear in some areas, and what problem is to be solved. While writing a proposal may be more painful than striking a deal over lunch or the "Back 9," you understand that if you don't write the proposal you will not get the business.

What Is an RFI and RFP?

An RFP is a purchasing tool used by governments and businesses to buy equipment, products, and services by promoting *competitive* proposals among vendors. Through this competitive process, vendors offer a wide array of potential solutions and prices, competing with each other to win the business and produce the best value for the buyer. Buyers evaluate the many different solutions and pick the one that most closely fits their needs and budget.

To enable vendors to provide a proper response to the RFP, it must present a clear understanding of all the issues (Technical Section), provide a project plan for installing the equipment (Management Section), and provide the vendor with an acceptable price and method for doing business (Price and Contract Section).

Developing and writing an RFP serves numerous purposes for the buyer. First, the RFP process allows an organization or company to develop a detailed analysis

Tip An RFP helps set the expectations for both the customer and the vendor.

of the problem or issue they are trying to solve. Second, when the business issues driving the RFP are understood, those issues can be clearly communicated to potential vendors. Third, communication between all parties can be crisp, based on mutual understanding of the requirements. Fourth, a contract between customer and vendor is more likely to be successful because mutual expectations have been established and agreed upon.

Writing a good RFP necessitates a clear understanding of the forces that initiated and are driving the RFP. Properly organized and executed, an RFP is an excellent tool for selecting the best solution and developing straightforward relationships with vendors. Preparing the RFP depends on, but is not limited to, the following:

Tip RFI responses provide the customer with multiple approaches to the problem.

- Recognizing a deficiency in current operations that could be resolved through the purchase of equipment or services
- Developing a plan for understanding the problem
- Identifying appropriate potential solutions
- Developing and specifying the return on investment
- Gaining visibility and internal acceptance of the problem and potential solution—key stakeholder buy-in
- Determining the projected budget
- Building a project schedule
- Selecting the project leader and supporting personnel

Often the customer will send out a "pre-RFP" or RFI (request for information) to test the technological and budgetary waters. RFIs are described below, but their basic purpose is to help the customer determine whether there are products and solutions available that match the need. From both the customer and the vendor points of view, why waste the time and money sending out an RFP if there are no products to fill the need, or if the price is way higher than the budget? An RFI is *potentially* valuable because it helps a company set realistic goals and budgets for its project.

And it means that the RFP will be better because the buyers have already sorted through the technology issues or budget issues or implementation issues with the RFI. What appears in the RFP should be very possible and reasonable—and very fundable.

Request for Information (RFI)

An RFI offers a way for a company to determine what is available from vendors who are capable of solving their problem. It is also a way of determining whether the project requirements are reasonable, and finding out if technology is available that meets the needs of the RFP within the established budget. If there is little interest or negative responses to the RFI by vendors, the company either returns to a study phase or drops the project.

Typically, an RFI encompasses all of the known requirements and is structured just as the RFP would be. It is important not only to put forth the technical issues, but to list what is expected for project management, maintenance, training, and support. Thus, potential vendors are allowed to comment on all aspects of the procurement and to establish for the customer what is possible and what is not possible—from the vendor's point of view.

Part of a normal RFI instruction is to encourage vendors to critique the RFI requirements and possible solutions. Responding to an RFI, a vendor may say, for example, that it is not possible to combine an accounting software package with a records management software package and that there are reasons the two applications should be kept separate.

Based on this type of feedback, the requirements (and project) may be restructured, with the final RFP bearing

Tip   RFIs are used to gain information.

little resemblance to the original RFI. The changes may reflect your input to the RFI and may have, in some manner, allowed you to get a leg up on the competition. The interchange between you and the buyers brings additional recognition from the buyers, something that other companies may not enjoy because they chose to not respond to the RFI or did not interact with the buyer to the extent that you did.

The RFI team must separate the wheat from the chaff during proposal evaluations, so that the resulting RFP does not favor one vendor or certain technologies. But this is your opportunity—and it's why you should respond to an RFI— to influence the direction of the RFP and to make it more difficult for your competitors to respond to it. Of course, those competitors will be doing the same thing to you—*if they are on the ball.*

The following paragraphs were taken from a typical RFI.

One RFI that I participated in writing (despite my protests) was so vague on the issues and requirements that I felt the resulting proposals would be meaningless and equally vague. My protests were to no avail, though, and sure enough, several of the proposals contained only cover letters and a set of brochures, while others were composed of monosyllabic responses to the questions asked.

When I spoke privately with several of the vendors, they said they felt the RFI was so meaningless that the company must be trying to pull a fast one on them. They felt that the RFI was a ruse and that a vendor had already been selected. Therefore, while they didn't plan to not respond, they were not going to spend a lot of energy on the RFI, either.

When the "team" members realized that they would have to do more research, that I would have to stay on the project longer, and that they still could not go back to their key stakeholders with "good news," the stakeholders put the project on hold while other more pressing projects were reviewed. I, of course, was out of a job.

[Our company] is in the process of researching electronic document-imaging systems that support the document-imaging needs of the accounting department. The objective of this RFI is to obtain information about potential systems that are available from a selected set of vendors.

It must be clearly understood that this RFI is being used as a vehicle to obtain information about potential document-imaging systems and vendors. The RFI should in no way be interpreted as a contract (implicit, explicit, or implied), nor does it imply any form of an agreement to candidate vendors. In addition, no inference should be made that we will purchase and/or implement in the future, any of the optical-imaging systems proposed by the vendors responding to this RFI. Vendors who do not respond to this RFI may not participate in the RFP.

In this case, the customer is making it very clear that an RFI is being released solely to gain understanding of this type of technology (electronic document-management systems) and to establish who the vendors will be for the RFP.

Establishing contact with the customer, getting him or her to your company for a site visit and technology demonstration, and writing a great response to the RFI will help you gain the advantage over your competition when the RFP is released. *Sometimes* a customer is so impressed by a single company during the RFI stage, and so unimpressed by other companies, that the RFP is bypassed and a contract is awarded. (This is rare, but it has happened.)

Many companies only send the subsequent RFP to those vendors who responded to the RFI. Therefore, your response to the RFI becomes an important document and ensures your place on the bidders' list for the RFP. As a cautionary note, consider the possibility that an RFI may be a way of getting vendors to write a free study of multiple approaches to the customer's problem—i.e., the buyer may want you to do the homework. If an RFI is poorly put together, has little focus, and requires vendors not only to comment on requirements, but also to suggest

> *Tip* To get the RFP, you must respond to the RFI.

and document alternate technologies and solutions, you should try to determine if this opportunity will bear any fruit. Many RFIs and RFPs die on the vine and are never released because the customer has severely misjudged the technology, the implementation time, the vendor community, or the price. Thus, any time that you spend on this type of RFI—sometimes referred to as a "science project"—may be wasted.

On the other hand, an RFI is the best way for a vendor to try to influence the development of the customer's RFP and, therefore, be on the inside track when the RFP is released. An old proposal proverb goes something like this: "If you didn't write the RFI, don't bother with the RFP."

Request for Proposal (RFP)

An RFP is a more formal document that contains the final (one hopes) version of the requirements. An RFP may be written without benefit of an RFI if the RFP team feels strongly that they understand the internal issues they're trying to solve and the diverse technologies that can resolve those issues.

The RFP becomes a vehicle that allows both buyer and vendor to establish a dialogue and work from the same set of rules, requirements, schedules, and information. The winning proposal is expected to be "right on target," and there should be no surprises when implementation begins. The following is taken from the proposal preparation instructions of an RFP:

> [This company] reserves the right to award the contract according to the evaluation criteria.... The vendor chosen for award should be prepared to have his proposal incorporated, along with all other written correspondence concerning this RFP, into the contract. Any false or misleading statements found in the proposal will be grounds for disqualification and removal from the project.

Tip Your proposal becomes part of the contract.

Unlike an RFI, in which the customer is still fact-finding, the RFP represents a decision to buy technology or services. Proposals submitted in response to an RFP often are incorporated into the contract as an addendum or exhibit in order to contractually obligate the vendor to comply with statements made in the proposal, and to provide legal recourse if the vendor cannot meet the requirements as stated in the RFP and agreed to in the proposal.

An RFP represents a significant opportunity for vendors to sell their products, systems, or services. An RFP provides a stable set of specifications and requirements for vendors to work from as well as a platform for describing and promoting products; it gives vendors a rare insight into how a business is run, and it offers them a chance to interact with the company in a structured manner.

Proposals, by their very nature, are a vendor's interpretation of an RFP's requirements. RFPs, therefore, promote a diversity of thinking among vendors and encourage them to provide unique solutions based on their products and services. RFPs are used when:

- multiple solutions are available that will fit the need.
- multiple suppliers can provide the same solutions.
- buyers seek to determine the best value of suppliers' solutions.
- products for the project cannot be clearly specified.
- the project requires different skills, expertise, and technical capabilities from suppliers.
- the "problem" requires that suppliers combine and subcontract products and services.
- lowest price is not the determining criterion for award.
- final pricing is negotiated with the supplier.

An RFP is a difficult document to write—more difficult than a proposal in some respects, because it is the initial definition of a problem by people who often do not

Tip Like proposals, RFPs are written by committees.

fully understand the problem or the best way to solve it. The RFP will have to address not only the technical aspects of solving the problem, but also the political issues (internal advocates for IBM or HP) and territorial issues (which department owns the problem and pays for the technology) associated with implementing new technology within a closed company environment.

In summary, we can say that an RFP is a written document that represents a great amount of time, energy, and money spent by a buyer to communicate an understanding of his or her business needs. Interpreting and responding to the buyer's needs with a proposed solution, resulting proposals involve the expenditure by the vendor of a commensurate amount of time and resources.

Because of the time, effort, expense, and justification for getting new equipment, a proposal that is sloppy, has no business focus, and does not meet the primary requirements has very little chance of winning. On the other hand, aggressive, innovative solutions that push the limits of the requirements (but stay within them) are what evaluators are looking for, and what should be proposed.

Figure 1-1 illustrates the typical cycle that a customer goes through, from developing an RFP to awarding a contract.

Summary

Proposals are responses to a customer's need and are typically written in a competitive environment. Your proposal has to stand out against many other proposals that may be equally well-written and even have a certain edge over you and the competition.

Sometimes the requirements may not be as clear as they could be (or you may not have any written requirements!), and the direction of the customer may be somewhat confusing or wrong. But it is your responsibility, as an expert in your particular field, not only to analyze

FIGURE 1-1 RFP Project Cycle

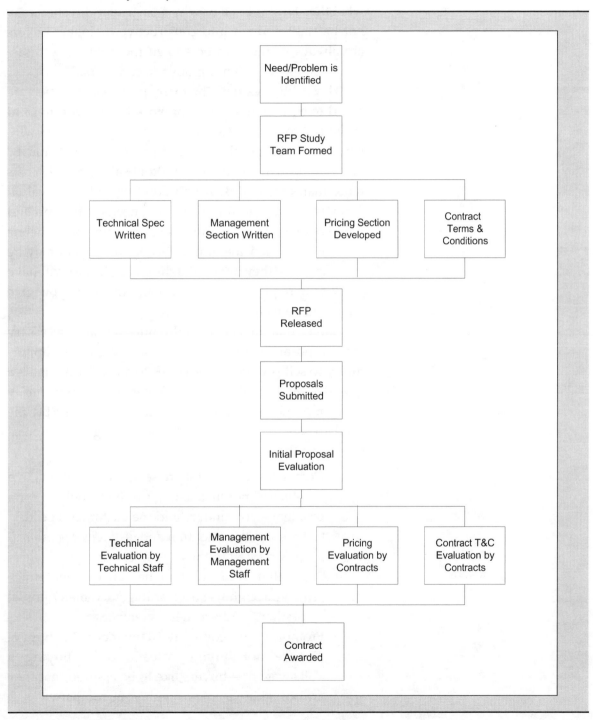

your customers' issues, but also to help them understand what they have missed or why a particular direction may not be right. Drawn into constructive dialogue, buyers are always thankful to be shown the potentially disastrous results of continuing down a certain path.

Those who evaluate the many proposals received are asked to do a huge amount of work in a short time, and they need to be able to justify your proposal as the winner. Why is Proposal C better than Proposals A and B? Why are you recommending Proposal C, which costs more than Proposal B? If you don't provide the evaluators with the ammunition he or she needs to recommend your solution, they will most likely recommend someone who *has* provided the ammo. While the buyers may be conscientious, they are on a tight schedule and will have work that requires their attention. Any help you give them will be reciprocated.

Rather than be considered a nuisance and necessary evil, proposal writing should be considered as an opportunity to sell products or services to a company that is a qualified buyer with a budget. Whether the opportunity is an unsolicited proposal or a response to an RFP, the need to sell with clarity is the same. A good proposal should do the following:

- Demonstrate that you are selling a "solution" to a "problem," not just selling products looking for a problem—you understand the customer's need.
- Get the buyer's attention and *distinguish your product or service* from those of other vendors.
- Show that your solution has an excellent track record through its successful history, many implementations, and excellent references.
- Promote your company. Remember the phrase, "You're not buying a car, you're buying a Volkswagen"—buyers like to be assured that they are not taking a chance with your company.

DEVELOP A WINNING PROPOSAL PROCESS

When preparing a proposal, you will need the help and expertise of many different people. This chapter explores how to prepare for proposal writing.

The Proposal Team

It is essential to immediately start identifying the resources that you will need to write your proposal. This will be different for each company as some companies have dedicated help and resources for proposal writing and other companies have no dedicated resources aside from the sales representative.

The best approach to this depends on the politics of your company, but one rule holds: Make a strong case for requesting your best people and physical resources, and make it clear that they will be dedicated to the proposal effort for its duration. If you have gone through a bid/no-bid process, the request for appropriate resources should have been part of your request.

The following are typical personnel resources needed to participate in a proposal effort:[1]

- Technical support staff
  - Systems analysts/systems engineers

---

[1] I recognize that for some companies a proposal team is the sales rep and a systems analyst, and sometimes it is just the sales rep. All corporate and noncorporate resources that can be drawn upon should be identified as early as possible for use within the proposal time frame.

  – Quality control analysts
  – System testing and user testing
  – Project management
  – Training and education
  – Service and maintenance
- Writing/editing resources
- Illustration/photography/graphics
- Reproduction services
- Administrative/clerical
- Marketing support
- Competitive analysis
- Legal resources
- Financial/costing
- Purchasing/contracts
- In-house reviewers and evaluation personnel
- Management approval and sign-off people

Tip Make a case for getting the best resources and people.

As you can see from the above list, a large proposal requires many people. The greater the number of people, the more administrative support will be needed. Figure 2-1 shows a basic core proposal team consisting of the section leaders (resource managers) who report to the proposal manager. The resource people listed below the leaders are on call, and will work only as needed and then return to their respective groups (a matrix management program).

Work Space, or the War Room

Physical resources are important to consider and often harder to acquire and hold than people. A typical proposal resource effort will initially concentrate on getting the people assigned and reading the RFP. Once the proposal is underway, someone will probably realize that there is not enough office space, that there are no PCs to write the proposal on for "imported" workers or consultants, or that other basic necessities are missing. This causes confusion, wastes valuable time, and may subtly suggest to the team that their proposal is not important enough to have the right equipment and supplies.

FIGURE 2-1 Basic Proposal Team

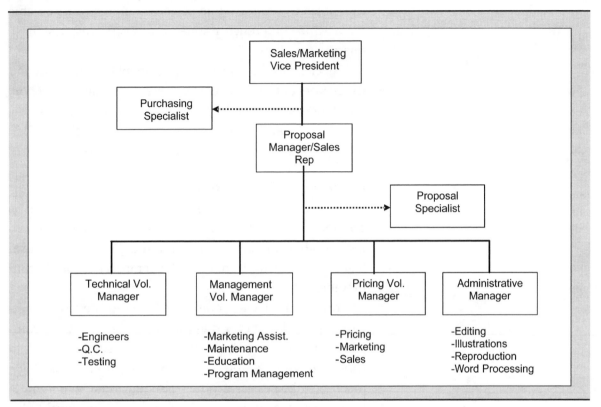

Designating a Work Area

To effectively support a proposal effort, it is important that the personnel resources have a designated place to work other than their own offices. If your personnel remain in their own environment, they will be subjected to the usual daily interruptions and will have difficulty working on your proposal in addition to their normal work. *If possible*, establish a large proposal war room as a meeting and working area. This room should have ample whiteboard space, chartpacks, wall space, and tables, and it should be lockable.

If part of the team is in a remote location, it is also advisable to have video conferencing available so that all team members may see the work being done and comment

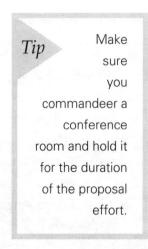

Tip

Make sure you commandeer a conference room and hold it for the duration of the proposal effort.

on it in real time. This type of meeting software allows associates to see the same projected images and be able to, with a conference phone connection, discuss those images.

As close to the war room as possible, locate a second room or set of rooms where team members can set up shop. This workroom should offer all the necessities such as PCs, whiteboards, and wall space, and should be lockable. Plan on owning this space for the duration of the proposal.

Designating a Virtual War Room

If the proposal team cannot gather in one place, it is possible to form a virtual war room. You may want to have both a physical space for the primary proposal team and a virtual area for the remotely located team members.

Your virtual war room would be located on a network-accessible server that can be reached via your company intranet or the Internet. The virtual war room should have available copies of the proposal strategy, meeting minutes, and other essential data that remote users will want to read and review. The site should also house all the anticipated proposal boilerplate text and

I was hired as a proposal specialist by a company that was working on a major proposal effort. They decided to install a proposal-writing software package in order to better manage the potentially large proposal. They had never used proposal-writing software before and did not, it seems, understand how it really worked. After about two weeks, the proposal was in such a mess that they unloaded the software and returned to a more manual system to manage the proposal. I would caution any company not to try new software on a "live" proposal. Load it first and test/play with it before using it on a real proposal. This type of software does offer many advantages and can be very helpful in administering the overall proposal effort, but it is a fairly complex database that must also be managed.

illustrations, and/or provide a reference link to the primary site.

The site can feature informational material, boilerplates, and the live proposal sections. Proposal sections, whether completed or in process, should be posted to the site.

Depending on your company's capabilities, the virtual war room could be open to your outside team members. People outside your company could access the war room via an Internet connection and post or ftp files to the site. They would be able to download current boilerplates or illustrations, as well as current schedules and the latest marketing updates.

In addition to a virtual war room, proposal writers could use collaborative software links that allow them to collaboratively write and review files online. The advantage of this is that concepts and new ideas can be discussed prior to being added to the proposal. Collaborative software can track additions and changes while also maintaining the original version of the section. The volume or section leader can have access to changes and be able to finalize the section.

Along the lines of the virtual war room, groups of remote writers can be connected to an electronic whiteboard, or the conference-meeting software, and be able to participate in real-time discussions. A host moderator can lead the discussion and be responsible for taking notes on the whiteboard. These notes are available to all participants and may be saved as files when the session is complete. Proposal team members who may have missed the session can access these "chalk-talk" sessions at a later date.

An example of a virtual conference is the proposal kickoff meeting described below. This meeting is traditionally held at headquarters, with primary personnel flown in over several days. To maximize time, the meeting should be tightly structured and result in definite

Tip Collaborative work over a network can help contain costs.

I consulted with a company that was writing a major proposal, and they had set up a tele-conference center to include an engineering office in another state. Each day at a desig-nated time (an hour before the remote-office quitting time) we would log on to the net-work with a laptop and a projector. The remote office had identical equipment. We would review and discuss current issues via an "issues list" that was developed each day, and then we would review certain parts of the proposal being written. Each office could see what was being projected and we con-versed over a conference telephone. At the end of each session, there was a "to-do" list and assignments were made. This worked very well and saved the company many thousands of dollars in travel expenses.

decisions and actions. If proper facilities are available, this meeting may also be held online, with great savings to the company.

The functionality of this type of virtual war room will continue to grow and should be enjoyed whenever pos-sible. The expense of bringing together a team can be eas-ily offset by the use of virtual war room technologies. Another great boon to efficiency is the ability of remote writers to download files, collaboratively discuss con-cepts online, and upload completed files. If a library management program is employed, potential adminis-trative chaos can be minimized.

Develop the Winning Strategy

Along with developing the mechanical aspects of the pro-posal effort, it is important to develop proposal "strategy" and "win themes." The strategy can be as simple as low-balling (or buying through low pricing) the opportunity or as complex as positioning your product as a 20-year solution based on life cycle modeling. The win themes are the big benefits or long-term value that customers realize when they buy your product or service.

Technical win themes may be your exclusive product features, your adherence to standards, your ability to

Tip Online meetings allow geographically dispersed people to meet.

customize without changing core technologies, or your ability to integrate diverse products while allowing the customer to maintain existing investments.

Management win themes may be your "ontime, on budget" track record, your vast experience and depth of resources, and your "exclusive" online computer-based user training. Here are some ideas for developing your win themes.

What is the "real" problem being solved? Customers don't need computers, they need spreadsheets, word processors, customer databases.

What's wrong with the current technology or service? Is it a problem of limitation, lack of features, lack of technology?

How will our approach/product/service improve the current situation? How do *we* know it will be successful? Do we have a history of successful projects?

How will our success be measured, and how will customers know the project is successful? How do they measure success? (Let's go a little deeper than "It works!") When will the customer know it is successful?

What, if any, are the return-on-investment opportunities? Will our approach/product/service pay for itself? When will this happen? (See Appendix J for a more detailed review of ROI strategies.)

These strategies and ideas are generally developed in brainstorming sessions with people who have read the RFP or know the customer's requirements, know your product, and know the competition. Ideas are presented during the proposal kickoff meeting and attendees are encouraged to add to, question, or come up with new ideas.

A list of strategies and win themes should be maintained, updated, and given to the proposal team to be used in writing their sections.

While the basic strategy and win themes are generally solid, you should be prepared to modify or add or reprioritize as new information is assimilated. I have found that once the actual writing begins, a whole new set of ideas begins to flow. Sometimes too, a whole new set of "issues" and "we can't do this" problems will emerge.

You should, however, concentrate on one central theme, if possible, and use the lesser themes to bolster your primary strategy. For example, in a competition between software operating systems, one may be a standard not owned by any corporation while the other may be proprietary software owned by a single corporation. If we were bidding the "open" standard product, our central theme might be that the software is open, which means that it is built using standards adopted by an international committee. This would prevent it from ever becoming proprietary, or supporting only proprietary applications, and would allow it to be continually updated with the latest features available.

Features, Benefits, and Needs

Many books have been written and will be written on selling products and establishing the customer's need. This book cannot do justice to this topic, as selling products is a book in itself. However, we need to acknowledge that a proposal is a selling document—it is a sales document—written with one purpose (well, two really): to sell your product and to crush the competition (for future bragging rights).

We would be remiss if we didn't discuss one of the primary duties of your proposal: to make your sales pitch clear, reasonable, and believable. Whether you are responding to an RFP or sending an unsolicited proposal, the key to selling is understanding exactly what the customer needs, and how your product or service can fulfill those needs. Matching your product or service against customer needs is where the selling begins.

Many proposal writers miss this key selling point, or don't quite understand the difference between features, benefits, and needs (requirements). They may not even know which one they are selling. Many people believe that by listing the features, the product will sell itself.

Features are product characteristics, such as 350 horsepower in a car, 200 page-per-minute print speed in a printer, or self-diagnostics and repair in a software package. A benefit is the value to the customer that is derived from a feature. A need is the problem that your customer is trying to solve. Features and benefits demonstrate how you can meet the customer's need.

Let's take a simple example: I need to nail some boards together **(my general need)**, but I broke my hammer. I go the hardware store and see at least ten different hammers on the rack. Not wanting to buy the wrong hammer again, I ask the clerk to describe the differences between all the hammers and to recommend one that's right for me.

Clerk: "Well, it really depends on what you're going to use it for **(general need)**,but let me go through these with you." He picks up one of the hammers. "This baby has a 22-ounce head **(feature)**, which means you can drive bigger nails with fewer strokes because of the added weight **(benefit)**. It has a fiberglass handle **(feature)** that is lighter than wood **(benefit = faster head speed and less tiring)** and more durable than wood" **(benefit = lower cost of ownership)**.

The first task, before starting to write your proposal, is to nail down your customer's needs and requirements. In my example of the hammer, the general need is to drive nails into wood, but a specific requirement is to drive *big* nails into *large* pieces of wood. Without establishing the need first, features and benefits are meaningless and may actually hinder the sales effort. In the above hammer example, had I not established a specific requirement (big nails in thick wood), any hammer might have looked attractive to my untrained eye. I even could have bought the wrong tool, such as a lightweight hammer that is not adequate for the job.

While it is part of selling to showcase features and benefits, it is also necessary to understand what the problem is and how the "tool" will be used to solve that problem. Far too often a proposal is just a long list of features with no corresponding relationship to the need or the benefits, and the customer is left to discern the feature/benefit relationship on his own.

The features-and-benefits discussion in your proposal should neither be held in a vacuum *nor presented as a simple data sheet*. The discussions should relate directly to the customer's requirements and the specific selling opportunity, as many customers may lack the skills and knowledge to translate features into benefits on their own.

Remember, your proposal is a selling document competing with other proposals that may offer better products, services, and references. If you believe your proposal can stand on its own, strictly on technical merits, chances are you will be outsold by a lesser product.

To hammer this point home, let's review some other basic feature benefit statements.

Need	Feature	Benefit
Access the Internet	Fastest Internet connection available (So what?)	Saves you time because downloads are faster, and people get more work done because they are not left waiting.
Lots of paper documents you can't find anymore	Scan documents (digitize them) and store them on your computer. (So what?)	Documents are more accessible, easy to locate, never lost, and can be worked on simultaneously.
You can't keep track of your customers.	Our customer relationship management system is a customer database. (So what?)	Allows you to quickly find all customers and automatically tracks the next action needed by the due date.

Outlining Your Proposal

While you are trying to jump-start the proposal effort, it is important to begin reviewing the RFP and making notes about what is important, what issues need to be addressed right away, and how to organize your proposal. It is also important to begin outlining what your proposal is going to look like because you will need this for the next activity, which is the proposal kickoff meeting.

The outline that follows in Figure 2-2 is a first cut at the proposal outline. Its purpose is to identify major areas of the proposal and could be taken directly from the proposal preparation instructions (PPI) found in

Tip A win strategy evolves from a close reading of the RFP.

FIGURE 2-2 Typical Proposal Outline

Section 1—Executive Summary
Introduction
Technical Summary
Management Summary
Pricing Summary
Company Overview

Section 2—Technical Proposal
Technical Approach
Product Description
Implementation Schedules
Quality Control and Testing

Section 3—Management Proposal
Program Management Summary
Project Personnel Resumes
Facilities and Capabilities
Service and Maintenance
Education and Training

Section 4—Pricing
Introduction to Pricing Methodology
Equipment Pricing
Project Management Pricing
Service Pricing
Totals

most RFPs. This outline will become the basis for the table of contents for your proposal.

Another reason to begin outlining the proposal is that it forces you to read the RFP. A careful reading will provide further insight into your strengths as well as yield a list of potential problems. These insights form the basis of your win strategy and will help you communicate the customer's requirements to the rest of the proposal team. An excerpt from an RFP reads:

This paragraph describes in detail the required format of the vendor's reply to this RFP. Any deviation from this format will be considered unresponsive. The remainder of this paragraph will provide additional descriptions of the desired content of each item in that outline.

Once your outline has been completed, the next step is to develop a spreadsheet that allows you to assign names and due dates to the various writing activities. Figure 2-3 is an example of the type of worksheet that needs to be used to assign writers and track progress. You may want to develop an overall proposal status sheet that tracks the various sections and activities. Figure 2-4 is an example Proposal Status and Tracking form.

By displaying these spreadsheets in a common area, local and remote team members can see their assignments and due dates. The proposal manager will be able to track progress and check the status of the effort.

FIGURE 2-3 Proposal Writing Schedule

ACME Proposal Writing Responsibility				
RFP No.	Proposal No.	Paragraph	Deadline	Writer
3.1	1.1	Executive Summary	7/20	John Smith
3.2	2.1	Technical Approach	7/10	Mary Adams

FIGURE 2-4 Proposal Status and Tracking

Section	Title	Leader	Draft 1	Review	Draft 2	Final	Print
1	Ex. Summary	Jones	2/9	2/10 finished	2/12	2/14	2/16
2	Technical Volume	Williams	2/5	2/6			2/15
3	Management Volume	Adams	2/4	2/5			2/15
4	Pricing	Anderson	2/10				2/17
5	References	Billings					
6	Demonstration	Hopper					
Appd. A	Data Sheets	Peters					
Appd. B	Annual Rpt	Peters					
Appd. C	Contract	Peters					

Proposal Kickoff Meeting

Once the decision has been made to bid on an RFP, a proposal kickoff meeting is in order. The kickoff meeting is a combination of a serious work session and pep rally. To prepare for the kickoff meeting, you will need, at the minimum, the items listed below. Give these materials to the team as early as possible to allow them sufficient time to prepare questions and to contribute intelligent comments during the meeting. If you distribute the materials the day of the meeting, team members will be reading instead of listening and will not be prepared to ask relevant questions.

- Copies of the RFP
- One- or two-page overview of the opportunity
- Detailed outline of the RFP by volume and chapter, with section leaders' names assigned
- The proposal timeline with milestone dates assigned
- Review and evaluation criteria

- A style sheet
- Competitor information
- Information on the customer such as annual reports, brochures, newspaper articles
- Information on subcontractors and their products

Depending on the size of the proposal, the kickoff meeting could last from a few hours to all day. Be prepared to finish the agenda because it may be your first and only time to assemble the whole team in one place at one time—at least until the end-of-the-proposal party.

The kickoff meeting acts as a pep rally to generate the enthusiasm and energy needed to sustain the proposal effort. Remember, this is not the day-to-day work of most people, and while it may be exciting to help in the design process, it requires a 110 percent effort.

The agenda that appears in Figure 2-5 is generic and may not fit your proposal or your purpose. However, the general breakdown of major points may be used for all proposals.

Morning Activities

The agenda is arranged so that the basic and, in some respects, less interesting items are presented in the morning. If you wait until after lunch, chances are you will have a limited audience and attention span.

If the proposal is large and you need to ensure visibility within your company, ask the marketing vice president, or even the company president, to open the meeting and demonstrate his or her commitment to the proposal. This is critical to the proposal effort and for generating the proper support that will be required to obtain the appropriate resources. This dynamic introduction will counter the normal reaction to doing proposals *("Not another fire drill!")* and demonstrate upper management's belief in and commitment to the proposal manager: "And we have given Sara full authority and resources to make this

FIGURE 2-5 Kickoff Meeting Agenda

KICKOFF MEETING AGENDA

PC Network Proposal

8:30–9:00	Coffee and Introduction
9:00–9:15	Management Support
9:15–10:00	General Introduction
	RFP Overview
	Major Deliverables
	Marketing Approach
	Technical Approach
	Management Approach
10:00–10:30	General Discussion—Questions
10:30–10:45	Break
10:45–11:15	Evaluation Criteria
11:-15–11:30	Proposal Schedule
11:30–12:00	Writing, Illustration, Style Sheet Review
12:00–12:30	Catered Lunch
12:30–1:30	Competitive Analysis
	Known Competition
	Review Competition
	Gather Information from Group
1:30–3:00	Assignments

a successful proposal. We feel sure that with Sara's experience and dedication, our proposal will be a winner!"

With a lead-in like that, the proposal manager now has to prove herself to the group. Her first agenda item is to make a detailed but brief review of the products and services being proposed. What will the marketing approach be, what is being proposed, who is the competition, and how is our proposal going to be superior? It is the general introduction by the proposal leader that will provide the needed spark of enthusiasm or sound a note of doom.

Plan a question-and-answer period. The Q&A session is essential to a kickoff meeting, for it not only helps you to keep on schedule, but also gives participants a definite time to raise objections and get answers to their questions. It is important to keep a tight schedule and not get off track. If someone is really confused, tell that person to wait for the question-and-answer time or agree to see him during lunch.

Lunch should be served in the meeting room, if possible, or in an area that can be reserved for the team. Lunch is an important time for the group members to talk things over, answer some questions, and informally get to know one another.

Afternoon Activities

The time after lunch is devoted to really getting started on the actual proposal assignments. However, putting the competitive analysis section first will get everyone's attention because it is interesting. Some or most of the people involved will not be familiar with a marketing analysis of the competition and will most likely pay attention.

If there is time in the schedule, consider having breakout groups for more detailed discussions of individual sections.

Work Assignments

Getting high-level visibility and approval will be crucial to the success of the proposal. Getting *anybody* to work on a proposal can be a tricky business—acquiring the right people can be difficult, if not impossible. If the proposal is important, start at the top. Once you have completed the bid/no-bid process, go to the senior vice president or head of your division and request authority to recruit the people you need.

Depending on the size of the proposal and how it has been divided and assigned, team members will work

Tip — The diverse styles of many writers can be standardized with the use of a style sheet.

either full or part time. This means that people working for you on the proposal will not be working at their regular jobs and not be controlled by their assigned manager.

Management Personnel

The proposal manager has to take overall responsibility for the success of the proposal. This person must be, above all else, the one who is the most excited and provides the most energy and direction. Without a strong proposal manager who has the respect of the proposal team, the outcome will be marginal at best.

Proposal Style Sheet

Pulling a team together to write a proposal means that you will have as many different writing styles as you do people. Keep in mind that writing skills and styles vary widely depending on each writer's background. Engineers lean toward a highly technical approach, while salespeople tend to use marketing buzz words and hard-sell adjectives. Ideally, if your company is large enough to afford it, you would have an editorial staff to meld the various styles so that the proposal has a consistent approach throughout. But many sales proposals are done in the field office, with little or no help offered by headquarters. Lacking editorial support, what is your alternative?

One viable solution is the development of a style guide, often called a style sheet. The main purpose of the style sheet is to make the proposal look like it comes from one company with one consistent message. It should not be so complicated that no one will use it. It should address the overall format of the proposal (such as treatment of section titles, level heads, headers, footers, figure references, etc.); the correct spelling (including use of capital letters) of other companies' names and products (as well as your own); often-used expressions (both English and Latin); and some general guidelines for style

> *Tip* The style sheet should not be overly complex.

in regard to compound words, hyphenation, treatment of numbers and dates, and the like.

Proposal Activities

Proposal Leader's Responsibilities

Once the team is formed and the kickoff meeting has taken place, what are the primary steps in keeping the proposal on schedule? Depending on the size of the effort, the proposal leader should at this time be concentrating on outlining the Executive Summary and cover letter, and developing the pricing material.

The Executive Summary is exactly what its name implies: a summary of the proposal, which will be read by a busy top-level executive who will often have time only to read this part of the proposal (and take a look at the pricing). It follows, then, that the proposal manager should devote a considerable amount of time to summarizing exactly what you can do, how you will do it, how many times you have already done it, and at what cost. This summary usually turns into a living document, reflecting changes as your proposal strategy evolves, and is often the last section completed, even though it was the first started. More detailed discussion on Executive Summaries is provided in Chapter 6.

In addition to doing some of the writing and managing the pricing section, the proposal leader will have to be available to answer questions, make critical decisions, settle disputes, and enforce schedule deadlines. Because of these managerial functions, his or her actual writing duties should be kept to a bare minimum.

Developing RFP Questions

Another ongoing activity will be developing and sending to the buyer questions that clarify the RFP. The question-and-answer activity is very important to the RFP/proposal

> *Tip* An Executive Summary is a short, concise, and self-contained document.

process. It opens the way to "official" interaction with the prospective buyer and gives you the potential to develop a relationship with the people associated with the RFP. Questions and answers should be viewed by both sides as a positive means of communication between customer and vendor. During the actual RFP period, communications are restricted and limited, sometimes forced or strained, and always suspect by the customer. Developing a good rapport throughout the Q&A period allows both parties to interact officially and to develop a good working relationship, if one was not established before the RFP was released.

There are strategies for asking questions. One is to let the first round of questions be submitted and answered, and hope that your questions will be asked by your competitors. This enables you to keep your bidding and position somewhat quiet while allowing your competition to expose their positions. Good question writing is a delicate balance of giving them enough information to understand the problem, but not enough for your competition to understand your strategy.

Generally, all questions submitted are gathered by the customer and answered as a group; all questions and responses are then returned to all bidders. Published questions usually do not include your company name, but it is often possible to identify companies because they give away too much information.

There will be some questions that have to be asked before your proposal effort can move forward. One of the first steps in organizing the proposal effort is to get the RFP to the key technical people for their review. If these critical questions are not discovered until near the end of the cycle, *it may be too late*. Questions can usually be submitted several days before the bidders' conference so that you can receive the answers quickly. The paragraph below is from an RFP administrative section concerning the bidders' conference:

> *Tip* Good questions can give you a strategic edge over your competition.

Written questions submitted prior to the bidders' conference will be answered first and a printed copy of the answers will be sent to all bidders. Oral questions will be answered as time permits except when a question is deemed too technical to be adequately answered during the conference. All oral and written questions will be responded to in writing.

RFPs are written to satisfy a general need and may have conflicting standards or products that do not actually exist in the marketplace. If you allow conflicts to remain unquestioned, or try to use these conflicts as a means of justifying a noncompliant bid, there is a reasonable chance that your proposal will be disqualified.

Developing questions to be submitted should be a carefully monitored activity. All federal and state RFPs carry this type of statement: "All questions and answers from all bidders will be published and returned to all bidders without identifying the submitters." Many commercial companies are now adding this line to their RFPs. This means that all questions should be carefully screened before being sent, in order not to compromise your solution. If you need to ask a question that could give your competitors an advantage, first contact the person listed in the RFP as being responsible for all contacts and determine whether your question will be published for all participants. If you are able to submit a question in confidence, pose that question apart from all others, submit it in a second envelope, and mark it *Confidential and Proprietary. Confidential and Proprietary* should be marked on the page with the question.

How to phrase and ask questions should be considered. There are generally four types of questions asked:

1. The first identifies a requirement or statement that is possibly incorrect in the RFP and you are seeking clarification. This could be from ignorance or a simple mistake on the part of the RFP writer. For

> *Tip* Try to be circumspect when writing questions that will be published.

example, a requirement may call for a 41-page-per-minute (PPM) printer when there are no printers on the market that are rated at exactly 41 PPM.

2. The second type of question asks if your interpretation of a requirement is correct. A question of this type might ask if supplying two 16-page-per-minute printers would satisfy a 32-page-per-minute requirement.

3. The third is to ask (and demonstrate) that a requirement be revised because it is too limiting, revised because it is not an industry standard, or deleted because technology is not presently available. For example, the requirement is for a UNIX operating system, and that eliminates other operating systems that could offer a competitive solution.

4. The fourth is a general question such as "We are requesting a two-week extension on the proposal due date."

Because all questions can be read and reviewed by all participants, questions can become a source of competitive information. If your company is the only one with an XYZ operating system and you identify it in the question, you have possibly given your competition an edge in understanding your position.

A copy of all questions and answers should be kept with other documents associated with the proposal. As questions are asked and answered, the RFP specifications and requirements may change. These changes may not always be included as an addendum to the RFP and, therefore, not incorporated into a subsequent contract. If you win the award and are asked to negotiate a contract, be sure that the contract acknowledges all questions and answers as part of the RFP, Proposal, and Questions and Answers.

Generally speaking, if a question causes a requirement to be changed, a formal addendum to the RFP will

> *Tip* Don't hesitate to question conflicting requirements and standards.

be published. Answers to questions are not, in the strictest sense, recognized as officially changing requirements unless accompanied by a change addendum.

Below are some sample questions culled from various RFP/proposal efforts. They are meant to give you a flavor of the detail of some questions and the responses by the customers. The fictional company ACME (the buyer) will be used in place of an actual company name.

Q. Will ACME be responsible for writing the host side of the system control software interface link?

A. Yes. ACME will provide the host side of the link; however, bidders must provide a specification for the link.

Q. Paragraph 6.4 requires printing of images that have been rotated. This is not possible given the printer specifications. Will you rescind this requirement or change the printer requirement?

A. We rescind the requirement for printing rotated images.

Q. Who performed the needs analysis for this RFP?

A. ACME performed the needs analysis with internal resources.

Q. This requirement calls for an effectiveness level of 90 percent, which appears to be in conflict with paragraph 5.2 that states a 95 percent effectiveness level is required. Please clarify.

A. You are correct. The requirement will be amended to require 95 percent effectiveness level.

Q. This vendor requests that the demonstration plan be due two weeks after the initial proposal submission.

A. The requirement remains as stated.

Q. The RFP training price table does not include travel costs. Are we to assume that travel costs for trainers are reimbursable?

> *Tip* ▸ Questions are generally available for all to see. Be cautious in your wording.

A. No. Travel costs will not be separately reimbursable but should be included in the fixed price for each class.

Q. Please delete the evaluation of performance tests and reviews. This gives an unfair advantage to certain products.

A. The evaluation will be conducted as stated.

It appears that some questions are meant to annoy the customer. It also appears that some questions have been asked because the vendor did not completely read the RFP. From these questions customers get a sense of which vendors are "for real" and which vendors are not serious. Being labeled as "not serious" will have a potentially negative impact on your efforts.

On the other hand, good questions, even aggressive questions, demonstrate to the customer that you are reading the RFP and have given it serious consideration.[2]

In-House Review

One of the more important jobs to be completed is an in-house review and sign-off of the proposal. The process of assembling and fine-tuning your proposal review team starts when you select the proposal team. As early as possible, reviewers should be selected and given copies of the RFP. Their job is to begin reading their section of the RFP to gain an understanding of what the customer is asking for, not necessarily what is going to be proposed. In most cases, it is better not to give the reviewers advance copies or high-level summaries of the proposal so that they may keep their *customer perspective*.

The selection of reviewers should be based on the subject of the proposal. For example, if the proposal is to

> *Tip* The review team must understand what the customer is asking for, not what is being proposed.

---

[2] Having been on the writing side of RFPs, I can say that there is much discussion among the RFP team as to which vendors are "with it" and which vendors are "clueless." Many vendors hurt their chances by demonstrating their lack of knowledge of the RFP and their industry by their questions.

Tip

> *Tip* The Red Team's review simulates the customer's evaluation of the proposal.

design and implement a large data communications network, you would need a specialist in network design on the team. However, don't get caught in the "technical-only" trap. This means that each major section of the proposal should be reviewed as closely as the technical section. A nontechnical section could deal with customer education or how service and maintenance will be provided.

This in-house evaluation, normally called a *Red Team Review*, is considered a formal process. The Red Team will use the evaluation criteria in the RFP as a basis for evaluating your proposal. This review is supposed to simulate as closely as possible how the customer will make his or her evaluation; while it may sometimes get bloody, and should, it is meant to be constructive. The Red Team Review should be a milestone on the proposal schedule, with adequate time to hold the review and integrate the corrections, comments, and notes that will be its results.

To be effective, the review team should use a copy of the proposal that is very close to being finalized. This copy should be assembled and printed with all illustrations, photographs, and other artwork, just as it would be for the final proposal.

The Red Team members should be isolated during the review and not allowed to work at their normal locations. This will prevent reviewers from being distracted and interrupted, which would lower the quality of the review. Make clerical assistance available when needed to minimize interruptions. If the proposal is short and can be reviewed in one or two days, accommodations such as lunch and dinner can be made in advance.

Hold a debriefing session with the review team and the proposal team when the reviews are completed. The purpose of the debriefing is not to nitpick, but to identify general trends and ideas that will make the proposal stronger. To prevent this from becoming a general bull session without purpose, the proposal leader and Red Team leader should formally direct the debriefing.

The Red Team can write its comments on the proposal itself, or use a specially made form that allows the reviewer to identify sections and paragraphs and has space for comments and suggestions for correcting the problems. In all cases, make sure that each reviewer signs and returns his or her copy of the review and the proposal.

Be prepared for a difficult time, if you are the proposal leader, from both the reviewers and your own team. It is natural for a certain amount of animosity to be generated during this process. One common complaint from the proposal writers is that "We've worked for weeks developing the XYZ network and some hotshot tears it apart in one day without even knowing what was behind the design." If the Red Team criticism is valid, the customer may have the same problem and ask the same questions. It is the proposal manager's job to maintain an objective attitude toward the criticisms and settle any disputes that might arise.

After the review, do you have to incorporate the Red Team's comments? Although some comments will not be valid or relevant to the proposal because of a misunderstanding on the reviewer's part, all comments should be noted with the understanding that if a reviewer from your company, ostensibly familiar with your equipment and services, had a problem, the real customer's reviewer may have the same problem. That is, parts of the proposal can be technically correct but worded so poorly as to cause confusion.

When the review is complete, those review items that will have impact on the proposal should be separated from the general lot. If you are working with a team, the section leaders will receive the comments that are appropriate to their sections. The proposal team is responsible for incorporating the changes.

If the changes are so sweeping as to impact the proposal schedule, the appropriate Red Team member(s) can

Tip ▷ Keep inevitable conflicts that arise from a Red Team evaluation in proper perspective.

be drafted to help make the changes (it is part of their charter). For example, a major design change may need extensive work and may depend on the originator of that change to formalize the new specifications.

Virtual Red Team

If you are using technology to develop a virtual war room, you may also want to develop a virtual Red Team concept. The Red Team members would not have to be collocated and would be able to provide their reviews as part of an online video conference. Comments on proposals could be uploaded to the Internet site and distributed to members of the proposal team. If Red Team members had electronic copies of the proposal, their comments would become red-line comments using the red-line feature of the word processor. This way, comments could be incorporated directly into the proposal, if appropriate.

The concept is to have the general comments and reviews made as part of the video conference, and supporting documentation available through the Internet war room site.

Schedule

Most proposals prepared in the field office are not adequately reviewed before being sent out because the review is treated as a "We'll do it if there's time" situation. Allotting time to a proposal is more important than anything but is often the most neglected consideration.

The most common mistake in proposal writing is poor scheduling and, consequently, not realizing how many actual working days are available. For example, let's take an RFP that is received on the first of the month and is due in 30 days. The first step is to work backward from the due date. A more formal schedule should be created that reflects all the tasks associated with the proposal.

> *Tip* Reverse scheduling gives a true indication of the time required.

If a project management software package is utilized, the software will track much more detail, allowing you to drill down to the lowest-level task. However, these programs require a fair degree of updating and maintenance, which may begin to impact other time required for writing and reviewing. If the proposal is large enough to warrant the use of this type of program, and you have adequate resources, it will be very helpful.

First, if the proposal is due at 2:00 P.M. and the customer's receiving point is not in your state, you basically have two choices: finish in enough time to mail the proposal or work up to the day before, forcing you to use an overnight service. Or fly it there yourself. Either way, two days are lost in transport and delivery. That means you now have 28 days.

Second, if you are having a print shop copy your proposal on a professional machine, they will want at least one full day to do the job. Actually, depending on the size and quality required, printers will not schedule your job if you can't give them two full working days. Two more days are now lost to printing and packaging the proposal. The 28 days now become 26 actual working days. Companies that have their own in-house print shops can probably print and package all but the largest of the proposals in one day.

Don't forget that many RFPs now require an electronic copy of the proposal on CD. Arrangements must be made for this, and the proposal can't be uploaded until there are no more changes/corrections to be made.

Third, if the proposal is large enough to warrant visibility at the higher levels, those higher-level viewers will want to review and sign off before you release it to a customer. Plan on one day for the review and sign-off, and one day to make the corrections. This now leaves 24 working days. However, one full day is usually consumed in getting ready for the review, so only 23 days are actually available.

Tip ▶ Anticipate problems and develop solutions.

Fourth, if the RFP was not addressed to you, you did not receive or start working on the proposal the day it arrived. It is possible that the RFP was sent to the division headquarters vice president because the customer thought it would get more visibility, or the VP may have been at a trade show and talked with the prospect. The secretary who received the RFP probably put it in the VP's "must-read basket" because he didn't know what to do with it. Also, RFPs are often sent to corporate purchasing because the company's purchasing department name is on the qualified bidders' list. In any event, the RFP took two full days to get to you or your boss, who said at 5:00, "Got a minute?"

Finally, we're down to 21 actual working days without any work whatsoever having been done on the proposal. Take one more day to thoroughly read the RFP and we have reduced the working time by 33 percent. And this does not take into account other normal holdups that occur during the proposal-writing period, such as getting the RFP printed so that copies can be distributed or waiting for the customer to respond to questions that have stopped the effort until answered.

Don't forget that someone on the team may not be able to work every weekend and that people may have other appointments that need to be attended to.

If a schedule is not developed and followed, it will be almost impossible to complete and submit a reasonable proposal. As with most projects, time spent in planning will more than pay for itself. When developing your proposal schedule, try to plan time as realistically as possible.

On the other hand, suppose you are printing your proposal on your office copy machine Thursday night and it breaks down. It's already past closing time, so getting repairs is out of the question. Look for and plan for problems, anticipate bottlenecks, and develop potential solutions.

If all else fails, ask for an extension to the due date by writing a letter to the customer explaining why you need the extension. This request should be made as soon in the proposal cycle as possible. Figure 2-6 is an example of a request for extension letter. A request sent the day before the proposal is due indicates poor planning on your part

FIGURE 2-6 Sample Request for an Extension

SoftCom Industries
1000 East Industrial Park
Some Town, CA 94000

September 6, 200_

Mr. R. B. Walker
Vice President
Strategic Planning
State Bank Group
Mill Valley, CA 94000

Dear Mr. Walker:

We have received your addendum to your request for proposal, RFP-12B-3, and have reviewed the changes to the original requirements. After a careful review of your addendum, we are confident that we could fulfill your maintenance needs and submit a responsive proposal.

However, we feel that in view of the scope of the changes we cannot prepare an adequate response in the time allocated. Therefore, SoftCom is requesting a ten-day extension to your requested completion date of January 30.

With this extension, SoftCom will have the needed time to more fully evaluate the changes and redesign our solution to meet the new requirements. Only after the redesign effort can we begin to develop new pricing. If the extension is not granted, SoftCom will not have had the appropriate amount of time to develop and write a satisfactory proposal. Without the additional time, we would have to submit a no-bid to your request.

Thank you for your consideration.

Sincerely,

Bud Porter-Roth

Bud Porter-Roth
President

and the request may not be granted. In the letter try to be as factual as possible and point out that you will complete the proposal.

Postproposal Activities

When the proposal is finished and turned in, there are still many tasks to be accomplished. After a long proposal-writing period, it is natural to leave the cleanup to administrative personnel, and for the primary participants to move on to the next sales opportunity while proposals are being evaluated. Not completing and attending to the postproposal work is one way to lose control of postproposal activities. (See Appendix G, Postproposal Checklist.)

First, all associated documentation for the RFP and proposal should be filed in chronological order. This will establish an audit trail for you when you begin negotiations and the customer wants a detailed explanation and justification for your proposal. Establishing the audit trail is most important for nonstandard products and pricing, and will allow you to recreate the circumstances and understand why a product was chosen, how it was priced, and what trade-offs were made at that time. Having the audit trail for pricing decisions will be invaluable when you are trying to determine the basis for a greater-than-normal discount.

Second, when the proposal has been awarded to your company, there will be several requests by internal departments in your company for a complete copy of the proposal. For example, if a project manager has been assigned, he will want a copy of everything to start his project notebook. This will include why product decisions were made and the corresponding documentation that supports those decisions. It is probable that both legal (or contracts) and accounting will require copies of the proposal once the final negotiations are started. Don't forget the maintenance and training department, if they will be involved.

Tip Having an audit trail will be invaluable at the completion of the proposal.

Third, after your proposal has been turned in, there are other activities that will generate questions from the customer and responses from you and the proposal team. These documents should be filed with the proposal documents and include any appropriate annotations for future analysis.

Customer-generated questions are a good sign and mean that they are giving your proposal a close reading. Any response that is less than 100 percent will hurt your effort. Getting a proper answer may mean going back to a team member (who has already returned to his regular work) and working with him to understand why something was decided or positioned a certain way.

Fourth, if your proposal makes the *short list* or you become a finalist in the competition, there will be several more steps required of you and your company before the contract is awarded. Typically, customers will weed out proposals that are not compliant in an effort to get down to two or three vendors—the short list. For those who have made the short list, there will be an oral presentation of the proposal followed by a demonstration of the equipment proposed. The customer will visit at least one of your reference sites and may request a headquarters visit and tour of your company (and its books). Finally, there will be a negotiation period once the customer feels that you have the winning proposal.

Negotiations will usually be in writing and may cause you to change your proposal and pricing to match the agreement. For example, a customer may decide to have training on-site instead of at your facility (or vice versa), and that changes the price and other contractual incidentals.

Proposal Disposition Activities

When the customer has made a decision and the contract is awarded, a win/loss review should be held. The purpose of this review is to help you discover why you won

> *Tip*
> If you make the short list, additional postproposal activities will be required.

or lost, and how this information may be used by you and your company in the next proposal. See Appendix I, Proposal Status Sheet, for an example of a proposal-debriefing questionnaire.

Tip   The customer will also send you questions to clarify your proposal.

If you win the proposal, it is good to understand how you won, and apply that knowledge to your next proposal. You'll also want to incorporate that knowledge into the corporate proposal database. Being a winner makes it easier because your enthusiastic new customer will be happy to tell you why you won and the others lost. Documenting why the other companies lost will enhance your understanding of how you won. This is part of developing your own internal "Best Practices," which are written to guide others in your company.

If you lose the proposal, you should be keenly interested in why your efforts (time, money, resources, and reputation) were not rewarded and how you can improve your next proposal process. The information received from the customer should be reviewed with your managers, and if correctable problems can be identified, a plan should be launched to make the necessary adjustments.

In either case, you should formally contact the customer and request a debriefing. This should be in person, or at least as a teleconference, with at least one-half hour allocated to it. The person you meet with should be someone on the RFP team, not a contracts or procurement person. Be prepared to be diligent in asking your questions and getting to some real issues. Most customers are hesitant, if you lose, to get into too much detail, and may cite the standard "Your pricing was too high." Of course, this may be the reason, but high-bidders often win proposals, so I would not let that be the end of the session.

The real reasons for losing a proposal can be varied and mixed.

- Your proposal didn't really address the requirements, and instead sold what you make, not what was asked for.

- Your proposal may have been total boilerplate with little or no substance to document your effort.
- Your demonstration/site visit may have been ill-coordinated, leaving the customer with a negative impression of your company and management skills.
- Perhaps your proposal was poorly written, with many grammatical and spelling errors, and this reflected poorly on your company.

Responses like these should be brought to management's attention. They are correctable and reflect a company's values, especially in areas of tactical and strategic thinking.

Listing the reasons for your win will reinforce the value of setting up a proposal development program. The cost of the program, compared to that of previously losing proposals, can be justified as the win rate increases and more resources become available.

Alternate Proposals

Alternate proposals are usually a headache for both you and the potential customer. Most RFPs include a statement that alternate proposals will be accepted and reviewed subject to the time available. The RFP will say that in the event of an alternate proposal submission (most federal and state governments are firm on this point), a fully responsive proposal to the original requirements also must be submitted.

> *Vendors may submit more than one proposal, each of which must satisfy the mandatory requirements of the solicitation in order to be considered. All vendors wishing to submit an alternate proposal must submit a baseline proposal that is fully compliant to all requirements. No alternate proposals are accepted as stand-alone proposals.*

From your point of view, since the RFP was written without specifying your technology, the customer either

> *Tip* The solution you bid may meet the requirements but not be considered responsive.

did not do his homework and was unaware of the technology you could provide, or does not believe that your technology can solve the problem. You may believe that by taking an alternate approach to the problem—using technology not asked for in the RFP—you could more than satisfy the RFP requirements.

It is almost impossible for any customer to keep ahead of today's rapidly changing technologies. Other difficulties, including the high cost of writing RFIs/RFPs, and decreasing time due to intense competition, may result in RFPs that are not as well researched as they might be. And because of personal prejudice and ignorance, some technologies are not even considered when an RFP is written. For these reasons, the technology you bid may in fact meet the requirements but not be considered responsive.

For example, an RFP asks for a personal computer system that will do desktop publishing using a certain type of software specified by name. This requirement effectively eliminates the software that you would normally propose to satisfy the requirements. If you were to present your solution only, your proposal would be eliminated. But if you were to propose the requested software, and in an alternate proposal offer your software, your proposal would be evaluated.

The hitch in this course of action is that your company may not represent the "other" technology and therefore you could not actually propose it. See the sections above about writing a no-bid letter and about writing questions.

Evaluators will put alternate proposals on the shelf until all baseline proposals have been evaluated. If there is time and the alternates have potential, they will be reviewed.

Most companies have enough trouble submitting a single responsive proposal, let alone a complete alternate proposal. There is no simple answer to the alternate-proposal trap except to talk to the RFP director before writing the alternate proposal. If your technology is not present in

Tip Alternate proposals are risky and time consuming.

the RFP and you have to submit an alternate proposal in order to bid your product, you should carefully consider what your chance of winning is and whether you should spend time writing a proposal.

Writing Levels

There are basically three levels of writing in a proposal:

1. *Technical detail.* The first level of writing explains how your product works and describes how it meets the requirements. This is straightforward, cut-and-dried writing that may use existing boilerplates to provide the technical details.

2. *Marketing detail.* The second level of writing covers marketing themes based on the benefits of using your products: saves space, increases productivity, reduces manpower, etc. This is the "features/benefits" pitch and is a combination of existing standard themes that are tailored to the RFP requirements.

3. *Business detail.* The third level of writing develops a business case for purchasing your equipment by specifically relating the technical and marketing detail to a particular situation. The object of this last type of writing is to develop specific and tangible examples of why and how your equipment will enhance the customer's business. This is fresh writing geared directly to the RFP.

An example will illustrate how these three levels of writing are applied, and the consequences of omitting any of them.

Electronic document management is a technology that enables a company to electronically scan all its paper records and store those records on optical disks. This requires a customer to buy new computers, optical disk drives, storage machines called *jukeboxes* to house the optical platters, and other associated equipment that may not connect to any other device or computer currently installed.

Because this is a very competitive industry, many companies are selling technology: faster computers, more memory, bigger disk drives, faster communications, etc. They may concentrate only on the first level because they believe *bigger, better, and faster* is all they need to sell the product. However, unless you proceed to the next level, the benefits, the *customer* will have to determine why your bigger, better, faster is more advantageous than your competition's bigger, better, faster, and the customer's assessment may not be correct.

The second level of writing found in document management proposals typically describes such benefits as reduced storage space, reclamation of floor space, fewer workers, faster access to documents, and increased productivity. One proposal highlighted the following as a prime benefit of its system:

> *The workflow facility within our system is aimed at automating the flow of work through the procedural office. No longer is paper-based information "in the mail" or sitting in an in-box. No clerical staff is required to manage the movement of important files and documents through an organization. This reduces expenses associated with the processing, storage, and retrieval of paper-based information.*

In this case, no contract was awarded to any of the competing vendors, even though the above benefits seemed substantial at first reading, i.e., reduced staff, reduced storage, etc.

Two separate but related reasons conspired to stop the sale.

1. The customer recognized that his company was experiencing increasing costs and diminishing returns due to an increase in paper-based work, but he did not understand how to solve the problem, what he needed to buy, or how to deal with the way his business would be affected by the purchase of new equipment. The customer determined

that he could gain more than half the benefits proposed by all vendors by simply hiring more people and renovating his filing system, thus saving substantial money by upgrading existing equipment and work routines, rather than automating. He concluded that computerization would be confusing, add nothing new, and not be worth the money.

2. The vendors failed to recognize the customer's fundamental requirements by offering automation and listing the gains without providing an overall financial analysis of how the system would affect his business. In this case, no cost justifications were completed to substantiate the benefits.

The last sentence of this proposal begins, but does not complete, the transition to the third level: "This reduces expenses associated with...." The customer was been left to interpret what those reduced "expenses" might actually mean. Not being an expert in this area, and not able to justify the system, the customer made the safe decision: Don't buy.

What this customer really wanted, and all the vendors failed to provide, was a system that would show a return on his investment. In any technology purchase, the safe decision to not buy must be overcome. Many customers who really want to buy *don't* buy—simply because vendors did not do their job.

The third level provides the customer with a detailed financial analysis of the proposed benefits. Third-level writing is illustrated in the following excerpt:

Purchasing an optical-based storage system has many advantages in addition to simply adding efficiencies to your operation. Many of our customers have not taken into account the hidden costs associated with paper-based systems. These hidden costs include repair and replacement of filing cabinets and hardware; costs for reproduction, including buying and/or replacing reproduction machines; maintenance and service on reproduction machines; paper costs; time and motion inefficiencies due to physical paper handling; replacement costs for documents that are lost, misplaced, mutilated, or simply worn out from use; and customer-service delays caused by documents that are not available. While some costs are tangible (such as annual repair and replacement of filing cabinets), others, although somewhat less tangible (such as the amount of time it takes to access a paper document in a file as opposed to accessing it electronically), can be analyzed and a value placed on them. The following table is an industry survey that represents approximate costs and savings by adopting imaging technology. The second table represents a suggested return on investment analysis based on our understanding of your current situation. We suggest that [our company] be allowed to do a similar study for your specific application in order to determine the actual return on investment period that will serve as a baseline for future evaluation of the project.

The last example demonstrates a number of important concepts:

- An in-depth understanding of what is being sold
- An understanding of the customer's requirements
- An awareness of the needs of the customer
- A willingness to help the customer make the right decision
- A demonstrated knowledge of the cost benefits

Although the above examples were taken from one type of business, computerized document storage and retrieval, the basic principles hold for other industries and services. That is, capital expenditures need to be justified against other projects being considered. A financial analysis of the various projects under consideration will determine which projects are going to produce the best return on investment.

Reviewing the three levels:

1. The first is technical detail that provides the customer with a good foundation.
2. The second begins to weave the features and benefits, and positions your product against the competition.
3. The third provides a financial and business basis for making the decision.

Summary

A proposal is unique in that it combines an individual's and a team's strengths, weaknesses, and product knowledge, under circumstances not quite controllable, into a document that cannot be duplicated given a similar set of people and requirements. Understanding and duplicating the "winning" proposal process is difficult. Trying to institutionalize and codify the process is an almost, if not outright, impossible task—as if we could understand and re-create at will what is basically a creative and synergistic process. However, as a process, a proposal does have definable and repeatable steps that will help you get closer to winning. That's what this book is about.

Winning and losing is not based on the proposal or document itself but on a set of almost controllable variables such as customer knowledge of the technology, pricing, personal contact, sales skills, and a number of intangibles. One often-heard quote from proposal writers is, "I'll take luck over hard work any day." But this is not to say that winning a proposal is sheer luck or that you have no control over the process.

It may be easier to understand how proposals are won by examining why they are lost. An analysis of the following excerpt from an RFP debriefing will demonstrate this principle:

> *[Many] bid responses were received; however, none of the bidders met the specifications for the computer system. Listed below are some of the requirements that were missed:*

Tip Every proposal is a unique project requiring a creative, synergistic process.

- *File server was not included as specified.*
- *Specifications called for a landscape-type monitor and bid was for a portrait-type monitor.*
- *Data transmission rate was only 2.5 Mbps and specifications called for 10 Mbps.*
- *Specifications stipulated enough RAM to store 10 documents at the workstation. System bid does not store documents at the workstation.*
- *Printer stations did not include a controller as specified.*
- *Bid price did not include cost of training as specified.*
- *Delivery prices were not included as specified.*
- *Installation prices were not included as specified.*

Therefore, it is recommended that all bids be rejected, that specifications be modified, and the item be re-bid at a later date.

> **Tip** Examining why a proposal was lost can give you valuable insight for the next proposal.

Some proposals are lost simply because someone didn't follow the rules. A bidder believes his product or service to be superior to that being sought in the RFP but neglects to meet the requirements as stated, believing his superior proposal will win anyway. Some proposals are lost because of negligence, such as not providing all pricing data required. Some bidders do not follow the proposal preparation instructions to the letter, thinking that their technical solution is enough to win.

It is a mistake to think that a proposal will win on its own merits, whether those merits include the best technical solution, the lowest price, or overall compliance to the requirements. Every vendor will have a technically superior solution, stand ready to offer the lowest price, be the most compliant, or have excellent reasons why they do not need to be compliant. Everyone is selling.

A proposal may be compared in some respects to a person using a resume to get a job. The job seeker will not be hired based solely on resume, but will be interviewed once or several times before a decision is made. However, it was the superior resume that got the interview, and without the interview there would be no job offer.

A proposal is similar to a resume in that few, if any, contracts are based solely on the evaluation of the proposal. If the proposal is good, meets all or most of the requirements, and has a reasonable pricing structure, it will get you through the door and on to the short list. The short-listed proposals are then given a very thorough evaluation, and detailed questions are usually asked by the customer. The technical level of questions and what area of the proposal is being questioned will give you an indication of what to expect when you are making an oral presentation. Vendors who are on the short list have a chance to demonstrate their solution, sell that solution at the oral presentation, readjust their strategy, and negotiate pricing, if asked. Also, the short-listed vendors have the face-to-face contact with the customer that is critical to winning the proposal.

There are certain fundamental steps that can be institutionalized in the proposal *development process:*

- *Read the RFP.* This is the most important step, the easiest to remember, and yet the one usually not given enough attention. Many RFPs are so poorly written that a casual reading of their ill-defined requirements will simply not suffice.
- *Qualify the customer.* Understanding the background reasons for the RFP, including who is involved and at what level, and determining if the project is funded are key points in qualifying the RFP. A well-written, no-bid letter could save you and your company time and money. Knowing the business reasons behind an RFP will give you additional customer insight and help you write a better proposal.
- *Prepare a competitive analysis.* Bidding without doing competitive analysis will cause one of two things to happen: you may overprice in an effort

Tip ▷ A proposal is similar to a resume for your company. First impressions count.

Tip Although each proposal is unique, there are steps that can be institutionalized.

not to leave money on the table, or you will under-price and leave money on the table. Competitive analysis shows you where your product stands vis-à-vis the competition. It also lets you emphasize your strong points, minimize your weak points, and expose possible flaws in your competition.

- *Organize your resources.* Only when you understand the magnitude of the effort (by reading the RFP) can you determine what resources are required. Most inexperienced proposal writers wait too long to get started. When they finally do get going, it may be too late to solve some internal problems, ask questions, and do a competitive analysis.

- *Develop a proposal plan.* The success of the proposal will depend entirely on the execution of the proposal plan. The most common error is planning only through the end of the proposal and not including postproposal activities such as questions and answers, oral presentations, demonstrations, site visits, and final contract and price negotiations.

- *Get the proposal plan approval.* Organization, resource allocation, and scheduling will fall short unless the "resource owners" make the resources available. Selling your proposal effort to management is required. (In some cases this will be tougher than selling to the customer.)

- *Hold a bid/no-bid meeting.* A bid/no-bid meeting is a formal method of identifying risks, assessing them, addressing them, and getting group consensus about continuing or halting the proposal process. It allows you to formally identify potential resources needed to "cover the bases."

- *Have management review the completed proposal.* Similar to the bid/no-bid agreement, you are now getting management approval for how you handled the risks identified in the bid/no-bid meeting, and general concurrence with the final proposal.

- *Read the RFP.* Once your proposal is complete, a careful rereading of the RFP will reveal any missing elements in addition to allowing you to check your selling strategies.

I have worked with some people who nearly missed the deadline because of their fanatical effort to make the proposal perfect. It is essential to strike a balance between getting the job done as well as you can and the time given to do it. A perfect but late proposal will accomplish nothing for you or your company.

Your company will reap many benefits from an organized, well-planned, and carefully written proposal, in addition to attracting more business. Once you become proficient and begin developing and preparing more and more successful proposals, you will discover that winning can become a definable and repeatable process.

Your company will benefit from an organized and efficient proposal development process. Setting down procedures for bidding/not bidding, organizing company information, training people involved in proposal writing, and following up on why you win or lose proposals will increase your win rate.

QUALIFY
THE OPPORTUNITY

Now that we have reviewed how proposal-writing opportunities arise, let's walk through and discuss the steps involved in initiating and qualifying those opportunities. Winning proposals are rarely a fluke, nor are they just lucky breaks. Winning proposals are the result of a well-organized and well-planned process. Complex documents to write, they must incorporate information from many different areas of your company—product development, training programs, maintenance programs, corporate communications, and pricing information, to name a few. It's not easy to assemble and mold all this information into a proposal that has a good selling message, appears to be consistently written, and is believable. Writing proposals can be time- and resource-intensive projects, and therefore, before you start, you should ascertain that the opportunity is not only valid, but a good fit for your product or service.

Consider first whether the opportunity has merit. It could be an RFP that you received or a verbal request to write one, but in either case, how do you know whether the opportunity is a fishing expedition, or just some tire-kicking?

A typical RFP scenario may go something like this:

Worst-Case Scenario
The person who will be responsible for responding to an RFP is not always the first person to receive it. At least several working days are usually

Tip Valuable
time may
be lost
inside your
company.

spent, after receipt of an RFP, determining what product line this RFP is addressing and what department should receive it. So a short fuse is made shorter, and the adage "Time is of the essence" acquires new meaning.

It often begins something like this: Late in the afternoon, just as you are getting ready to leave for the day, your manager appears at your door and says, "Got a minute?" She hands you an RFP that was sent to the Marketing VP who gave it to the Sales VP who gave it to your manager who is now giving it to you. Your manager actually got it yesterday, but didn't get around to looking at it until this afternoon. "Is this the ACME RFP you put on the forecast?" So even though you knew about it, and may have registered your name with ACME, the RFP still went to the corporate address and was shuffled around before getting to you.

Best-Case Scenario

You have been in contact with the customer, know the RFP is going to be released, and your name is on the mailing list. You contact the customer and confirm that the RFP was sent to you. The RFP is routed directly to you instead of sitting in the receiving department while folks try to figure out what this document is and who to send it to.

As we've seen, companies are not always on top of the vendor and product situation. If you are told that an RFI or RFP is coming out soon, ensure that your name and contact information are readily available to the company and its contact person. I can't tell you how many times an RFI/RFP is sent to an address picked off the Internet because the sales rep neglected to ensure that his/her contact information was available.

You may also send the responsible buyer a letter and e-mail with your address and a polite note saying that you are anticipating the RFP and have made time in your schedule for it.

Getting Started

Now that you have the RFP, how do you get started? Figure 3-1 depicts various activities involved in generating a proposal. Keep in mind that for a medium to large proposal, many of the initial activities shown will have to be worked on simultaneously if a reasonable response is to be created in the time allowed. Appendixes A through H contain a series of checklists that lead you through the process, from receipt of the RFP to submission of the proposal. Appendix I comprises four proposal status sheets that walk you through "signing in" the RFP to determining why you won or lost the proposal. All these checklists and status sheets should be used and modified to suit your own company and the type of proposals that you write.

The person responsible for the proposal is generally called the proposal manager. This could be the salesperson who asks for and receives the RFP, the VP who takes the project under his/her wing because of its size, or a proposal specialist whose department has responsibility for managing all proposal activities. Bottom line, however, is that the proposal manager is responsible for moving the proposal effort forward, ensuring that all dates are met for such items as BID response form and RFP questions submittal, and getting your proposal to the right address at the right time. One RFP admonished, "Proposals must be physically present at 4:00 P.M. Proposals that are dated, stamped, or otherwise still in transit will be considered noncompliant."

Qualifying Both the Buyer and the RFP

Perhaps the most important first step in proposal development is qualifying the customer and the opportunity. If you receive an RFP without previous account work or knowledge, or if you receive one from a customer you have had no contact with, then you should qualify both

FIGURE 3-1 Typical Proposal Flow Chart

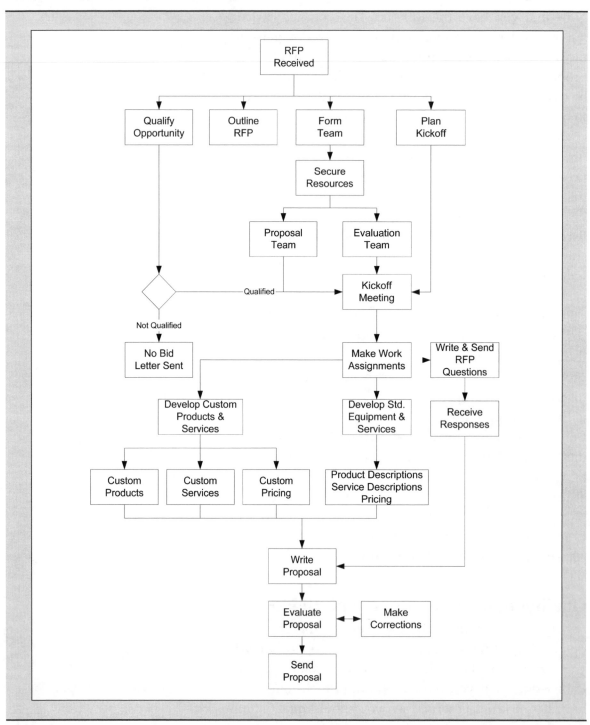

the customer and the RFP. Qualifying the customer means that you determine if it is a solid company that has strong credentials—both financially and within the industry. Many companies are "tire kickers," with no plans to purchase anything—they're mainly interested for "future needs" or are doing homework via an RFP that should really be an RFI. You may consider doing a financial background check to determine if the company has any cashflow problems or is engaged in "catastrophic" litigation wherein they will be forced into a poor financial position if they lose (the legal bill alone may cause significant cashflow problems). This information enters into the bid/no-bid decision that will be discussed later in this chapter.

In order to qualify the opportunity itself (aside from the company), the first step is a careful reading of the RFP. Is the RFP complete and well written? Does it demonstrate an understanding of the technology, and appear knowledgeable about all aspects of what they are trying to purchase? If the answer to these questions is yes, then the RFP would appear to be an honest effort. But you are not done yet.

Another important area to consider is whether the RFP requirements are a good technical fit for your product or if you will have to customize your product to fit the requirements. If the requirements require product

> *Tip* Qualify the opportunity first.

Many companies use the RFP process to see what is available and how much it costs. They may or may not have a "real" project on the boards and most likely have not established a budget yet. While it is possible that they could buy something, chances are they will not, or they will try to reduce the requirements and hence the scope of the project to a much smaller one. This is a "nickels and dimes" project, more likely to be an individual's personal pet project than an officially funded request. Beware of these "customers," as they will try to get you involved with the promise of a much larger and expanded project to come.

The following exchange took place at a bidders' conference:

Vendor: Is there a specified budget for this particular project?

Buyer: Yes, there is a budget.

Vendor: I wasn't sure.

Buyer: That question has actually been asked in the written questions, but I will just address it the same way that we do at every vendors' conference when it is asked. The appropriate response, and the responses that you'll always get from us, is that we are seeking the best value for the procurement. We feel confident that we have provided you with enough information for your company to determine a price. We will compare your price to all of the others and to our budget. We will not provide you with the budget, however.

Vendor: If we have a target, you know, not a specific number, but within a specific range,

we would know whether or not we could provide some of the functionality you are asking for within your budget. So I was just curious. That is why I asked the question.

Buyer: Are there any more contract questions?

Author: Well, that was fun wasn't it? While the chances of getting a budget figure are pretty slim, it doesn't hurt to ask, but perhaps a bit more intelligently. In another bid conference I was attending, the buyer did provide the budget numbers. The reason: he knew it was too low for the work requested and he was giving us vendors a heads-up. Many vendors just shook their heads. However, final pricing was within 10 percent of that number given at the conference. I can tell you, though, that the final pricing reflected less functionality and work. Maybe it was a smart move on the buyer's part?

customization, you should raise this issue immediately and get additional insight from your technical team. This issue should be put on the list of issues that are discussed at the bid/no-bid strategy meeting.

Also, don't forget management-related issues that may be in the RFP, such as having tech support during hours when your company does not support, or having an office located near the company that wrote the RFP. The contracts section may require performance bonds or have a liquated-damages clause that your legal department finds unacceptable. All this information should be "discovered" as early as possible to minimize any effort if you decide not to bid on the project.

If there is a vendor conference, go to it to meet the RFP team. Ask questions and try to get a tour of the area that will be affected, or where the work will be done. Make a point of asking about the budget. Is there a budget? Is it contingent on anything? How was the budget arrived at, and were there other companies or consultants that helped establish the budget and write the RFP?

If this appears to be a "good" opportunity, then you will want to study the RFP in greater detail and begin the proposal development process.

Whether intentionally or not, many customers use the RFP process incorrectly, which results in

- requests for products and services that do not exist.
- estimated budgets that are far below expectation.
- implementation expectations that are overestimated.
- oversimplification of the work itself.
- poorly defined requirements.

At some point, you may consider whether you want to spend time educating potential customers and if the RFI/RFP process affords you the greatest return on investment. Sometimes, RFPs are simply a means for a customer to justify a decision that has already been made. They have selected a winner but need to go through the formal RFP process because it is law, or company policy requires an RFP. Other times, the RFP writers are ill prepared, have not done their homework, and expect to be "educated" by the resulting proposals. When this happens, it usually means they don't have enough in their budget, they don't have enough time, or they think they can cut corners by doing the implementation in-house.

Remember that when a project goes south on a customer, it is the vendor's fault, no matter what the real reason is. Therefore, is it imperative that you qualify the project and know whether the customer has the budget and the related supporting personnel and facilities to make the project a success.

When such a customer receives proposals, and reality hits, the project is usually "taken off the street" and rethought. If the budget is underestimated, the project may be dropped and the money reallocated to a more viable project.

If you sense that the RFP is basically a fishing expedition, raise this concern during the bid/no-bid meeting and suggest that there are better opportunities on which to spend your time and resources.

One of the best ways for a customer to determine what new technology is available in today's market is to release an RFP asking for everything in the world, but reserving the right to purchase pieces, parts, and separate components. This customer will reserve the right not to award any contract and is probably not ready, for whatever reasons, to make a major purchase.

The purpose of this type of RFP is fact-finding and obtaining pricing information. This type of opportunity should be considered a high risk, and other more qualified RFPs in your queue should be brought forward. This type of RFP is usually a waste of time for vendors. Continued effort on this type of RFP should be constantly reevaluated as new information is gathered and the situation is better understood.

Wiring the RFP

Many companies slant or *wire* an RFP to favor one vendor or technology. This may be a conscious effort to keep an incumbent's equipment or services. It may also be the work of your competitors, who have convinced the customer to favor their requirements. Or it may simply result from the RFP team's lack of in-depth education to understand the different solutions available.

There are many, many reasons RFPs are written and used incorrectly. Your job is to sift through the evidence and make sure you are not wasting your time and the company's money. I recently spoke at a meeting hosted by a state government to determine why vendors were not responding to their RFPs. In my presentation, I asked the vendors in the room if they thought that most RFPs were already wired for a vendor, and the majority of them raised their hands. This was shocking to state officials, who believed all of their RFPs represented fair and open competitions.

So why would a company or government agency go to the trouble (and expense) of writing an RFP if they had already decided on a vendor? The reason is that many companies have a policy that requires competitive bids for anything over a certain dollar amount. It stands to reason that if the requesting department is basically happy with the incumbent's equipment or services, they will try to write the RFP in a way that will specify this equipment or service. When an RFP is wired, the competitive bidding process is used to validate a decision that has already been made.

Even if an RFP is wired, careful analysis and qualification may indicate that a competitive proposal may win.

- Incumbents frequently have older technology; their response to the RFP would normally be to upgrade existing technology, which may not be a long-range solution.

- Incumbents may write a sloppy proposal, assuming they have already won.

- Incumbents may overprice new equipment and services, thinking they can't lose.

- Incumbents may be forced to respond to requirements for features and services that they don't have "yet"—but your product is already built with those features and services.

- If you do your homework and can understand the differences between your product and an incumbent's product, you may be able to identify large holes and deficiencies that you can fill.

Your proposal will have to demonstrate that new technology has many features and benefits that cannot be gained simply by "upgrading." Your selling point may be that it is actually less costly to start with a clean slate (your product) than to upgrade, rebuild, and carry the previous product's shortcomings into the new system. This is the type of "win strategy" that is developed during the proposal kickoff meeting and carried through your proposal.

Determining the Project's Budget

Determining whether a project has a budget may be more difficult because the amount of money reserved for the project is usually not released—for obvious reasons (review the discussion earlier in this chapter). However, most customers will respond if asked directly whether or not a project has a budget. ("Yes, we have a budget but no, I'm not telling you how much.") If you can determine that the project *does not have a budget*, you may want to carefully consider whether to spend any further time and resources. Many proposals have been written, only to have the procurement placed on hold because of "unanticipated expenses associated with acquiring this technology" or having initial requirements revised "due to changing technology" in the marketplace or, "Due to internal realignments, we have selected other technology projects at this time."

For a successful project, the customer must understand the technology involved, in addition to the financial aspects of acquiring that technology. Part of your job when qualifying the account is to determine whether the customer has

- sufficient technical expertise to understand what is being procured.
- sufficiently researched the cost and financial impact that the procurement will have.

> *Tip* One choice the customer always has is to not buy.

Perhaps the most important qualifier is "how much pain" is the customer in? This is an apt metaphor because you need to find out why the customer is putting out the RFP. If you can determine that they are losing money, losing clients, or that there has been a definitely negative impact on their business for not implementing a technology, then you can be sure that they will be buying and not tire-kicking.

This pain, which represents the business reason for the RFP, should become one of your central selling themes if you can clarify it with the buyer or glean the information from the RFP. For example, a company that has not implemented a point-of-sale Internet site may be losing business to competitors who are selling through Internet sites. Until they acquire this technology, they

Tip Does the customer understand the technology?

The quote below is from a bank RFP. This is a good introductory statement that shows us why they are writing this RFP and what business reasons are driving the RFP. We can take this information and use it to develop our response themes.

> ACME Bank is releasing this request for proposal (RFP) for the implementation of an electronic document management system for loan servicing and processing. ACME is seeking to implement a global solution with a potential user base of approximately 20,000 users worldwide and would expect a solution of an appropriate scale.
>
> Currently, loan documents and portfolios are managed in their paper document form, kept in secure vaults, and copies are faxed or couriered nationally and internationally when needed for review or signature. Electronic document management technologies will eliminate the need for faxing and courier services while providing secure storage, faster access to documents, and disaster recovery capabilities.

If we dissect the second paragraph, it is clear what their problems are.

1. Paper documents plus no backup plus no disaster recovery equals potential catastrophe.

2. Faxing originals is not good enough for signature documents.

3. International courier costs can be expensive; see also #1 above.

---

will lose sales, lose market share, and suffer the ignominy of being perceived as not having a "high-tech" operation.

Their "pain" is losing product sales to the competition in larger than normal numbers. Finding out that dollar figure may play an important role in doing a rough cost justification to show a positive return on investment for this opportunity.

You might ask if the customer has performed a return on investment (ROI) analysis for the project. If an ROI analysis has been performed, and they are continuing with the project, this means several things:

- The ROI was positive, and they expect to get a payback within (most likely) two years.
- To do the ROI, they had to develop a budget. So there is money in the pot.
- To develop the budget, they must have done their homework with the vendor community, which means the budget may be fairly accurate.
- The buyer must feel confident that this is a solid project.

Bid/No-Bid Decision

One key element in the proposal development process is to include a basic bid/no-bid step. The bid/no-bid decision is made when you have enough information to make an intelligent decision about this RFP opportunity. A bid/no-bid decision process will help you to qualify an RFP and determine whether it is 1) a good fit for your products and services and 2) an opportunity that is worth pursuing—relative to other more qualified possibilities.

Some basic criteria should be established when making a bid/no-bid decision, such as compatibility with existing products/services, amount of custom work required to make a good fit (too often we try to make our products fit where there really is not a good match), existing/nonexisting account relationships, and potential customer's internal customer politics. (Their IT shop is IBM Blue through and through!) Review Appendix H, Bid/No-bid Checklist, for additional detailed ideas on account qualification and bid/no-bid procedures.

The bid/no-bid process may also include an estimation of the type of resources needed to write the proposal and how much time those people and other resources are needed. This is an important area to cover as there may be other proposals being written, people on vacation, or resources generally not available.

The following points may appear obvious, but very often companies fail to make a thorough assessment of a potential opportunity in terms of what the implications will be if the contract is won. More than once I have heard the phrase, "The worst thing we could do is win that contract." A variation on this theme is, "The good news is we won the contract; the bad news is we won the contract."

A simple bid/no-bid qualification list might include some of the following:

- Does your company have the products/services? Or is this an attempt to fit a round peg into a square hole? (Don't laugh—as an RFP manager, I often see vendors bidding a product that does not fit the requirements.)
- Do you have the capacity to meet (manufacture) the order, or will it mean adding new people, facilities, and equipment? How much will that cost? What will the impact be on existing contracts?
- Can your company afford to win the business? Will your company be spending $10 to win an $8 contract? (See above.)
- Is this request in line with your future direction? Or will it take your company off-course?
- Will winning be at the expense of other product lines and services? Can this be justified?

- If a new product is developed (or existing product customized) to win this business, can the new product be produced and the development costs amortized?
- Is this a new account? Has the sales representative developed an account relationship?
- Is there an incumbent? If so, how entrenched is the incumbent and how does the customer perceive the relationship?
- Who is your primary competition?
- How has the sales rep qualified the account? What if the "request" is totally unqualified—you have not had prior contact with this customer?
- Which department within the customer's company is responsible for the RFP? Is it the end user, the MIS department, or a special independent study group? Knowing this, how will you change your proposal?
- Is this a request for a fishing expedition? How do you know?
- Who are the competition and what are they going to do? Often we bid, hopelessly overpriced, knowing the competition has the edge.
- Will winning be at the expense of losing or hurting other potential accounts? Can you afford to do this?
- If you were to lose this bid, what would be the primary reason? Can this be corrected?

When to Bid

Perhaps the most important factor in deciding to bid on a project is having the product, service, or technology being requested by the customer. Once you have determined that your product meets or even exceeds the requirements, other considerations such as price can be dealt with and resolved.

If you do not have the product fit, it becomes a product development exercise. Some types of companies specialize

Who is on the bid/no-bid committee? It can be different for every company, but generally speaking, the committee is composed of the following people:

- *Sales Manager/VP.* This is the person who has to commit the resources and be comfortable that this is a winnable job. This person is your champion, and will stand up for the opportunity in the face of adverse opinion. If this person is not on board, you may as well forget it.
- *CFO.* The CFO will look at the numbers and help determine if the job is worth the investment in time and money. The CFO may need some explanation and detail if the job involves custom work that takes internal resources.
- *Technical Manager/VP.* The tech department will look at the RFP requirements and help you to determine whether they are doable and if your company is comfortable with the technical aspects of the RFP.
- *Services Manager/VP.* If the RFP requires service, maintenance, training, and consulting, the services manager will help decide how to approach the requirements and if she is comfortable with the requirements.
- *Marketing Manager/VP.* Marketing plays a key role in gaining market share and company credibility for your company and products. I've found marketing managers to be very effective when helping to determine whether an RFP is a good project or not, and they may have additional information about the RFP company.

Together, in a meeting, these people will review the bid/no-bid criteria and your sales pitch to move forward with the RFP and proposal. Their decision will be to go ahead with the proposal or to stop it in its tracks.

The scope of the committee will ensure a fair and reasonable hearing.

in developing new products specifically for new markets, and some companies specialize in putting together "systems" to meet a need (systems integration). But if your company does not do this as an existing line of business, you may find that time and resources are against you.

So, when do you bid? If you (who are in charge of this opportunity) have done your homework, prepared the bid/no-bid criteria, and set up the appropriate resources, then it is the bid/no-bid committee's decision—but you are providing the ammunition they need to make the right choice.

Even if you haven't established a bid/no-bid committee, it's still beneficial to step through the bid/no-bid criteria to see whether you have a reasonable chance of winning the RFP.

When Not to Bid

Knowing when *not* to bid is a harder decision. The basic decision comes down again to product, price, and capability. If you don't have the product, or your price is above the known price range, it may be better to not bid the opportunity. Perhaps you have the product and a good price, but the RFP requires that the product be installed in locations you don't have service offices for, and the installation schedule is more aggressive than you can handle. (The CFO will have something to say about this.) Often companies force a product to fit, win the job, and then realize they are going to lose money overall in making the many changes needed to satisfy the customer. A well-written no-bid letter can be better than a hastily prepared proposal that will not win.

A no-bid letter should be written when you actually cannot comply with the required specifications, and even if they were relaxed or changed you still could not provide the equipment or service. This letter is a courtesy to the person and company that released the RFP and explains why you are not bidding. See Figure 3-2 for an example of a no-bid letter.

A well-written no-bid letter will accomplish as much as—if not more than—a poorly written or hastily prepared proposal, and it will save time and money. A no-bid letter could have several purposes, depending on the situation and your understanding of the account.

A no-bid letter is sometimes written as a last-ditch effort to get the specifications changed so that you could bid on the RFP. The letter might state that you would not

FIGURE 3-2 Sample No-Bid Letter

SoftCom Industries
1000 East Industrial Park
Some Town, CA 94000

September 6, 20xx

Mr. R. B. Walker
Vice President
Strategic Planning
State Bank Group
Mill Valley, CA 94000

Dear Mr. Walker:

We have received your request for proposal, RFP-12B-3, inviting potential bidders to prepare a proposal for providing contract maintenance services to your facilities. After a careful review of your request, we are confident that we could fulfill your maintenance needs.

However, we feel at this time that our solution would not be cost-effective for your facilities or our company. A thorough review of your RFP requirements indicates that your basic requirements can be met by companies that specialize in limited contract maintenance. We feel that while SoftCom Industries has the capabilities to provide the functions requested, our full potential would not be realized. Therefore, we are asking you to accept our no-bid to your request. However, we request that we be kept on your list of qualified bidders for future solicitations.

Because we feel that our programs could be effectively used in your industry, we would like to invite your company to a meeting concerning our capabilities in this field. We would be willing to review your RFP and submit a proposal pending changes that would allow us to fully utilize our resources. In addition, we would be pleased to present an overview of our company and where we, as a company, are strategically heading. SoftCom Industries is making a strong commitment in this direction and would appreciate the opportunity to explore common interest with you.

Sincerely yours,

Bud Porter-Roth

Bud Porter-Roth
SoftCom Industries

bid if the specifications remain as they are, but that if changed sufficiently to allow your solution, you would be able to bid. This type of letter can work, as the RFP committee may not have realized that the specifications were too tight, and they would really like to see you in the competition. Also the receipt of one no-bid or several no-bids would lessen the competitive nature of the bid. (Typically, companies like to see a large number of bidders so that the procurement will be more competitive. It also allows them to select a "short list" of vendors and play those vendors against each other.)

However, if you are the only vendor protesting the requirements, it is not likely that the RFP will be changed. Generally speaking, it is the combined weight of several vendors that forces the RFP committee to make changes. Therefore, don't be shy—your letter could be the one that makes them change the RFP.

Even if the requirements are not changed, there are several reasons you might want to bid on a job you are unlikely to win.

First, you want to remain on the bidders' list. It is possible that by not bidding on a job, your name will be

---

I received an e-mail from a company with an RFP attached to it. The next e-mail was from the same company with a list of questions and answers. I had no previous knowledge of this company. I opened the RFP and saw that it was due a week from the day I received it, but the date on the RFP was two weeks prior to my receiving it. I talked to the procurement manager and he said they were continuing to "find" potential bidders and send them the RFP in an effort to get as many vendors as possible to submit proposals. When I asked for an extension, he said it would not be allowed, and that if he gave me an extension he would have to give everyone an extension. Needless to say, either this company felt no obligation to the vendor for providing a proposal or they really didn't understand the RFP process. Either way, this company and its RFP were not worth any further time.

taken off the bidders' list and your company will have to requalify for future opportunities.

Bidding on a first opportunity may give you a chance to bid on a second job that might be more beneficial. Not bidding on the first eliminates you from bidding on the second opportunity.

Bidding gives you the opportunity to establish a relationship with the potential customer, allowing you to begin the education process about your company and products.

Summary

Qualifying the opportunity and going through the bid/no-bid process is not simply an important step in moving forward with your proposal effort; it can be a very complex task with long-range goals and objectives. By presenting to the bid/no-bid committee and getting their approval to move forward, you are committing them, the bid committee, to helping you get the resources and people you need to produce a credible and winning proposal.

If the bid committee is established at your company, it most likely is not a rubber-stamp committee and the decision is taken seriously. This means that in order to receive their approval, you have to sell them on your relationship with the buyer, the good fit between your products and the buyer's needs, and the potential to make a profit.

Your selling strategy may involve more than just a good opportunity and a good product fit. You may be selling this as a strategic opportunity for your company—breaking into a Fortune 100 company, a chance to open a new market territory such as a federal or state government or a new geographic area, and the possibility of creating new sales opportunities because of a teaming arrangement. The bid/no-bid meeting is a chance to get your company excited about your opportunity.

The bid/no-bid meeting is the right forum to present any technical issues or stumbling blocks, project implementation issues, and pricing issues. If the opportunity is deemed a "strategic opportunity," many of the hurdles you would normally face may be replaced with offers to help.

You'll need your champion to help you get through the bid/no-bid meeting by anticipating problems and suggesting solutions. If the deal is going to be price-dependent, for example, and you need to discount your pricing, your champion needs to carry the message and get the others on board.

EVALUATION CONSIDERATIONS AND STRATEGIES

A CME Bank will select the successful bidder through a formal evaluation process. Consideration will be given to products and advantages that are clearly described in bidders' proposals, confirmed through presentations and demonstrations, and verified by information from reference sources.

All proposals will be initially reviewed to ensure compliance with the RFP. The initial review will encompass administrative and mandatory requirements, and if proposals are not administratively compliant, they may be dropped from further consideration. If proposals do not meet the mandatory requirements, they will be dropped from further consideration. All other remaining proposals will be given a thorough review.

The evaluation of your proposal is an assessment of its conformity to the requirements contained in the RFP. Typically, the RFP team will maintain a list of the requirements in the RFP, along with other concerns and issues that suppliers should have addressed in their proposals. The evaluation, in essence, is the comparison of the requested items to the response.

Typical steps in an evaluation may include

- a first reading of proposals and disqualification of any that are noncompliant. This is a "quick read," usually by the RFP manager, to eliminate obviously flawed proposals. Some of the red flags are: not on time, did not follow administrative requirements, missing requested information, not bidding specific requirements, etc. These proposals are disqualified before the real evaluation begins, so even if your product is a great fit, your proposal won't be read.

- a second, more detailed reading by the RFP team, and the "scoring" of the proposals. This step produces the "short list"—usually two or three proposals that are the finalists. This is a good in-depth read of your proposal. Some proposals will be disqualified for noncompliance if several reviewers notice missing requirements and exceptions. Others will be disqualified due to a low evaluation score. The purpose of this reading is to reduce the number of proposals to the short list.

- reviewing the short-list references, calling them, going on site visits, reviewing presentations and demonstrations, visiting the vendor's HQ, and comparing pricing. This last step in the evaluation process determines which vendor offers the best all-around value—best product, price, performance, etc.

- awarding of the contract.

The evaluation process is a critical step in the proposal development effort. By evaluating your proposal with the customer's point of view in mind, you can gain valuable insights into the customer's real requirements and how best to meet them. In order to do this, however, you must be able to answer such questions as these: How will proposals be evaluated? Who will evaluate them? What criteria will be used? How can I be sure which area (such as pricing, for instance) is most important? What else may be done to help the evaluation? What are our potential strong/weak points vs. the competition?

Questions like these should be asked the day you receive the RFP. Plan for the evaluation as you would all other phases and parts of the proposal, and make this activity a regular item on your proposal checklist. You may greatly enhance your chance of winning by asking and then determining the answers to such questions. Review Appendix E, Evaluation Checklist, for a list of evaluation activities.

As an overview, let's take a brief look at each question posed above:

How Will the Proposal Be Evaluated?

Probably the first thing that the evaluators will do is check for the obvious.

- Were you on time?
- Did you provide the requested number of copies?
- Did you follow the suggested format?
- Did you provide a complete set of data sheets?
- Did you provide the requested annual report?
- Is the cost volume separate?
- Is your price in the ballpark?
- Did you take exception to any important item requested?

Tip — Taking an exception is a risk. You may be noncompliant.

An exception means you are not complying with a requirement in the RFP or that you want to substitute an alternative solution. For example, suppose that the RFP required black-and-white laser printers for a certain workstation configuration. You may make an exception, proposing a color laser printer, and demonstrate that the color printer is of the same quality as the black- and-white, and the same price. (It's actually cheaper because you are getting added value for the same price.)

These initial checks are to eliminate any proposals that didn't adequately respond to the RFP or took so many exceptions that what was left wasn't worth considering. After these initial evaluations are made, the proposals that merit an in-depth study are commonly referred to as having made the short list.

Confessions of a Proposal Reviewer

Part of my business is to write RFPs and review proposals with my customers. Each time it is different, but one thing is common to almost all of my experiences—sloppy, noncompliant proposals. There is almost always one proposal if not two, that is sloppy—not organized according to the RFP requirements, poorly written, containing no direct answers—just plenty of boilerplates, and a basic kind of disorganization. As we all sit around the table and discuss the proposals, we invariably wonder: Why did someone waste his or her time on a proposal so obviously doomed for immediate disqualification?

Who Reads the Proposals?

The proposals on the short list are usually divided among evaluators who are experts in certain areas. For example, terms and conditions probably will go to the contracts specialist, the management section will go to the project leader, and the technical section could be divided up between many people. A large proposal will not be read by just one person. The evaluation is a group effort, and usually the winner is chosen by several people.

What Criteria Will Be Used?

Naturally, the criteria will vary with each proposal depending on what the customer needs and requires. The evaluation criteria may be categorized into two general types: that which is formally stated under headings such as Evaluation Criteria, and those you learn through account contacts and by reading "between the lines" of the RFP.

Generally, the formal evaluation criteria can be very broad and not very informative:

> General evaluation criteria will include the completeness of the response to this RFP and the ability of the bidder to meet the objectives and requirements.

This tells us nothing that we would not surmise on our own. On the other hand, the following quote from another RFP tells us something very different and important. It is the last item under *Evaluation Factors*.

The professionalism of the proposal and marketing/ technical staff involved will provide valuable insight into each organization's ability and willingness to satisfy our complex and changing needs.

The following evaluation criteria are more specific as to where the major points are to be found, but still do not provide specific information:

The criteria to be used by ACME's evaluating team shall include the following areas:
30 percent: Ability to meet the RFP's functional and technical requirements
30 percent: Installed and long-term pricing
20 percent: Installation, support, and commitment
10 percent: Experience with projects of similar configurations and applications
5 percent: Viability and stability of vendor
5 percent: Contract conditions and performance guarantees

The above criteria tell us that pricing and technical requirements are equally weighted and that the installation, support, and commitment to the work is almost as important as other areas.

> **Tip** There may be unwritten evaluation criteria.

How Can You Be Sure One Area Is Most Important?

In the example above, the evaluation is heavily weighted toward the "project" aspects of the RFP—35 percent is given to project-related functions. Reading between the lines, this means that the customer is very concerned about vendor experience and ability to execute the project. Strong emphasis should be placed on this area.

Again, read between the lines. When the customer emphasizes a certain requirement, you can be sure this requirement is foremost in his mind. If he emphasizes compatibility with his current equipment, don't try to sell him something at a bargain price that is not compatible. Price is obviously not the major concern, as shown in the evaluation instructions below:

> *The evaluation criteria reflect a wide range of considerations. While the vendor's pricing is important, other factors are also significant. Consequently, a vendor may be selected who does not necessarily offer the lowest-cost solution. The objective is to choose a reliable and experienced vendor capable of providing effective products and services at a reasonable cost.*

What Can Be Done to Help the Evaluation?

The most important way you can help the evaluation is to enlist the best available people to work on the project, from the proposal team manager to the experts in your company who will review the RFP. Then questioning the customer as much as possible and reading the RFP thoroughly (with the customer's point of view constantly in mind) are the next best measures you can take to help the evaluation.

What Are Your Potential Strong/Weak Points vs. the Competition?

A careful reading of the RFP (or "opportunity") will show you that this is not a "product" purchase. Rather, the customer is more concerned with implementation and project management. If you have done your homework on the competition, you may know that, for example, they have a better implementation record and program than your company. This will be a weakness that you must counter in your proposal. If you don't counter this, the competition will gain some points and you may lose some—a double whammy. Try to write your proposal, if possible, with an awareness of critical evaluation criteria and how these criteria can be a positive or a negative for your proposal.

In-House Proposal Evaluation

The place to start finding out about the evaluation is in the RFP itself. If there is a section on evaluation, read it and make sure the proposal team reads it. During the proposal kickoff meeting, go over the criteria and ask for questions. Write the questions down and submit them to the customer. Ask that the customer's review of evaluation criteria be part of the agenda for the bidders' conference.

Tip Don't be shy about asking questions.

The bidders' conference is hosted by the customer, and all vendors who have received the RFP are expected to attend. (Although not always mandatory, it is recommended that you attend a bidders' conference, if offered.) At this conference, the customer explains the ground rules, goes over the RFP, and accepts procedural questions. This is the time to ask any questions regarding the evaluation criteria. Technical questions usually have to be written and submitted to the customer. Responses by the customer will also be written.

Rating the Proposal

For purposes of evaluation, RFPs are broken into sections and each section is given a value or weight. For example, a typical RFP has a Management Section, a Technical Section, and a Cost Section. The customer may assign a total value of 100 points that break down as follows:

Management Section = 40 points

Subject Area	Points
Project leadership	10
Implementation schedule	15
Quality control	15

Technical Section = 40 points

Subject Area	Points
Technical approach	5
Design	5
Performance	10
Compatibility	20

Price Section = 20 points

Subject Area	Points
Hardware price	5
Software price	5
Service price	5
Training	5

Tip Understanding evaluation criteria will help direct your efforts and prevent lost time.

Not all RFPs will go into this much detail, but for purposes of illustration, let's assume that you have this information. Looking through the management section, the point spread is fairly close so you would want to pay equal attention to all areas, perhaps spending a little more time on the 15-point areas. For example, you may want to propose a very tight and aggressive implementation schedule as the customer appears to be looking for a fast implementation. You can verify this by looking elsewhere in the proposal to find hints that the customer wants a quick install.

In the Technical Section, however, we can see clearly where the most time should be spent. Obviously, this customer doesn't care how you do it; she is interested only in whether you can be compatible with existing equipment and configurations. The most time and effort in this section should be spent convincing the customer that your product is completely, totally, and unquestionably compatible with his existing equipment.

In the Price Section, the customer may not be greatly concerned about the initial purchase investment. What he is really looking for is how much your service and maintenance is going to be. Therefore, in the Cost Section, you may give standard prices for equipment and not offer a discount. No discount on the equipment price would then enable you to lower the service cost.

It is essential to determine this kind of information as early as possible to avoid spending valuable time directing your attention to the wrong issue. If, in the example above, the proposal team failed to study the evaluation criteria, the assumption might be that the customer would be attracted to the proposal with the least expensive equipment, which in this case, was not the issue at all.

Understanding the Evaluation Criteria

Whether a proposal is being prepared by one person or a large team effort is involved, the proposal leader is responsible for developing the proposal evaluation criteria (PEC). There are several good ways to start this development.

- Read the evaluation criteria given in the RFP.
- Ask the customer for additional details.
- Read between the lines of the RFP.
- Find out if you have an existing account history with the customer, and if so, identify past "hot buttons."

From this type of research, you should be able to begin a PEC list of what is important and what is not important to the customer, and direct your proposal accordingly.

Reading Between the Lines
An example of reading between the lines would be repeated questions and statements about service and maintenance. If the RFP section on service is very

Tip Develop a list of evaluation criteria as soon as possible and pass it on to the proposal team.

detailed, and reference to long-term service contracts is included, you may assume that the customer is placing great weight on service issues. You may then direct a question to the customer to test your assumption during the bidders' conference. (But be careful not to tip your hand to other vendors.) Through research, you may find that this company is in a high-growth state or that a bad experience with another vendor has inspired their emphasis on implementation and project management.

Evaluation criteria are often spread throughout the RFP and sometimes can be confusing, offering what amounts to conflicting information. For example, in the general preparation instructions of one RFP, it states: *"While pricing will be considered competitively, we are not obligated to consider the lowest-priced proposal."* Further into the RFP, in the technical overview, pricing is given a little different value: *"Evaluation will be on the basis of two criteria: First is overall price performance of the technical approach and second is the ability of the system to sustain continued growth."* And finally, in the proposal evaluation section, pricing is placed last in a list of three criteria: *"The following attributes will form the basis for the overall selection: 1) Technical approach, 2) Demonstrable history of project management, and 3) Price performance tables."*

Reading further into another evaluation section, a recurring theme of simplicity seems to carry weight: *"A simple and straightforward design. . . ."* And on the next page: *"Attention will be given to the simplicity of the project management plan and its ability. . . ."* And last, these two statements that reflect the need for simplicity: *"The ease with which the overall project can be implemented. . . . We expect to undergo significant internal change and the ease with which these changes can be accommodated will be a very important criterion for evaluation."*

In this particular RFP, the idea of simplicity and ability to upgrade seems to be a common thread running through both the technical and management sections. An

> **Tip** Sometimes the evaluation criteria offer conflicting information.

alert reader would home in on this and try to develop themes that address this need. At the proposal kickoff meeting, these themes would be given to the proposal team with the request that "simplicity of design" and "standards-based technology" be stressed whenever possible.

While this was fairly easy to spot, other needs in the RFP were buried. One hidden need, touched on above, concerns the company's expectation to "undergo significant internal change" in a short amount of time. This type of statement should be researched carefully because a drastic change may result in the postponement and eventual cancellation of the project. Such was the case in this situation in which the RFP was cancelled.

Figure 4-1 is an example of evaluation guidelines from a larger RFP.

Tip Look for a common thread that runs through the RFP. Think of it as the counterpart to your sales themes.

FIGURE 4-1 Evaluation Guidelines

I. PROPOSAL EVALUATION

A. *Introduction.* Proposals will be formally evaluated to determine responsiveness to the administrative and technical requirements set forth in this Request. The final selection will be made on the basis of the highest composite score for those proposals that meet all the requirements.

B. *Receipt.* Proposals will be dated and time-stamped as they are received and verified that they are properly sealed. All proposals will remain sealed until the designated date for opening.

C. *Initial Evaluation.* At the designated time of opening, all proposals will undergo an initial evaluation for the following four items:

1. *Proposal opening.* Proposals received by the specified date will be opened and checked for conformance to the requirements set forth in Volume 1, Section 2, Proposal Preparation Instructions. Proposals not in conformance with the required information will be marked nonresponsive and may be rejected.

2. *RFP Requirements.* Proposals that are responsive to the above will be checked for compliance to the mandatory requirements outlined in Volume 2, Section 3, Mandatory Requirements. For proposals not meeting these requirements, the deviation will be defined as approved or not approved. If approved, the proposal will be processed and the deviation noted. If not approved, the proposal will be deemed nonresponsive and returned to vendor.

FIGURE 4-1 Evaluation Guidelines, continued

3. *References.* All references on the Customer Reference List will be contacted and interviewed for the following: a. Equipment satisfaction b. Satisfaction with vendor's support c. Ease of installation d. Quality of training and instruction e. Quality of vendor's documentation.

   Overall customer satisfaction must be displayed to remain responsive to this Request. Negative responses may be cause for rejection.

4. *Cost analysis.* Proposal costing information will be checked against required format. Cost schedules will be checked for mathematical accuracy, and any resulting inconsistencies will be handled according to Volume 1, Section 2, Proposal Preparation Instructions.

D. *Evaluation Methodology.* Proposals will be evaluated using a weighted score system and must achieve a minimum number of points to be considered responsive to this Request. Proposals meeting or exceeding the minimum acceptable level will be deemed responsive.

A technical score sheet will be completed for each proposal and points awarded for mandatory, desirable, and variable items as follows:

1. *Mandatory.* All requirements described in this Request as being mandatory will be simply scored as approved or not approved. These mandatory requirements must be fully satisfied or the proposal will be rejected and returned to the vendor.

2. *Desirable.* All requirements described in this Request as being desirable will be assigned a numeric value reflecting the benefit of that requirement. Desirable requirements can only have a positive effect on the overall score. Absence of desirable requirements will not incur a negative score.

3. *Variable.* All requirements described in this Request as being variable will be initially scored as approved/not approved. Variable requirements scored as approved will have a proportionate value according to the weight and benefit assigned to each requirement.

E. *Final Selection.* A summary score sheet will be completed for each vendor and a composite score for each proposal will be calculated. Selection of vendors for negotiation will be based on the highest composite scores achieved. Final award of contract will be based on satisfactory contract negotiation and a successful demonstration.

Tip Separate and objective reviews can only help your proposal.

Forming an In-House Evaluation Team

If your proposal is going to be a winner, you must take the time to have it reviewed and evaluated by a third party. This third party could be your manager, or his manager, or a group of people that duplicates the customer's evaluation team. The evaluators need to be identified early and given a copy of the RFP so they can become familiar with the specifications and requirements.

Identify a date for the in-house evaluation and begin work on a rough draft of your proposal for the evaluation team, also known as the *Red Team* (see below). An evaluation checklist, such as the one shown in Figure 4-2 is a useful tool for the leader of the evaluation team. Explain to the evaluators that on that date, you will expect them to have read the RFP or their assigned section, and to be prepared to read your proposal and evaluate it. The evaluation should be from the customer's point of view.

FIGURE 4-2 Evaluation Checklist

	Activity	Notes
	Evaluation team formed	
	Technical team	
	Management team	
	Pricing team	
	Date and time established	
	RFP distributed to team	
	Space for team established	
	In-room lunch and coffee ordered	
	Team assembled for evaluation	
	Proposals distributed	
	Evaluation form distributed	
	Proposals and forms signed	
	Debriefing held	
	Proposals and forms collected	
	Results determined	
	Corrective action determined	
	Proposals revised	

Performed by in-house people who tend to know the products, the evaluation may turn out to be less objective than it should be. Your manager, who knows the products and who is also evaluating your proposal, might agree with a decision to offer something other than what was asked for rather than questioning your decision. For this reason, be sure to stress that the proposal is to be evaluated from the customer's point of view.

The Red Team

The in-house evaluation team is known as the Red Team. A Red Team is typically formed at the same time as the regular proposal team and is assigned a team leader. The Red Team's job is to constructively tear your proposal apart and offer advice on how to put it back together. The Red Team is recruited from inside and outside of your company and may include a recognized expert hired as a consultant. To be as objective as possible, Red Team members should not have had any working position on the proposal.

The Red Team is established as an equal to the proposal team. It must have the same clout and its recommendations must be taken seriously if it is to serve any useful purpose. The Red Team leader is usually assigned by the same person who assigned the proposal leader. Adequate time must be given for the Red Team to review, correct, and implement all recommendations.

Although the results of a Red Team evaluation can be absolutely devastating, it's likely the customer would approach the proposal in the very same way, finding the same problems and offering the same objections.

Customer Evaluation

Your proposal is not read by one person but by many. The customer's evaluation team is composed of people similar in makeup to the proposal team. It usually consists of specialists in the technical fields, a specialist in

> *Tip*
>
> Stress that the proposal is to be evaluated from the customer's point of view.

project management, someone knowledgeable in the competitive market, and a finance person.

Often, these people are unfamiliar with your product or service and, before looking at your proposal, may not even have known that your company existed. Nevertheless, their job is to weed out all proposals that are not serious contenders.

One major problem your proposal may encounter is the likelihood that no one person on the customer's evaluation team will read the entire proposal; therefore, no one sees the overall picture. Each evaluator is assigned a section and usually does not have an opportunity to read other sections. Therefore, if you made an exception that was clearly identified and justified in the Executive Summary, and the evaluator who was given the technical section did not see it, he or she will reduce your score for not complying with all the equipment requirements.

Below is a list of typical evaluation criteria that will help you evaluate your proposal from the customer's point of view. Not all of these will always apply.

Tip For a large proposal, no single person may read the complete proposal.

- Are the basic criteria in the RFP followed? Did you follow the basic instructions for formatting?
- Is the proposal well organized and responsive to the basic specifications?
- Does the proposal demonstrate a grasp of the overall problem, or does it focus on individual parts that are not connected?
- Does the proposal address the major issues of the RFP with equal weight?
- Is the proposal's solution spelled out clearly?
- Is the proposal's solution believable?
- Is the proposal's delivery schedule believable?
- Is the proposal responsive to terms and conditions?
- Does the proposal demonstrate the capability to perform?
- Does the proposal demonstrate technical capability?

- Is this capability believable?
- Are the vendor's facilities adequate?
- Are the vendor's personnel resources adequate?
- Does the vendor have related experience?
- Is there demonstrable past performance?
- Can the vendor supply non-product-related deliverables such as documentation, manuals, and training?
- Is the vendor's company financially stable?
- Is the costing reasonable and believable?
- Is the cost broken down, or is it a lump sum?

There are also criteria that will never appear in writing. These criteria reflect personal biases, personal dislikes and likes, past performance problems, job-related fears, threats from above, and so on. In other words, they are intangible.

Following are some examples of intangible criteria:

- An RFP might be written using the incumbent's terminology in an attempt to lock in the incumbent and lock out everyone else.
- The incumbent's proposal guarantees additional jobs in the customer's city and the competing proposal doesn't add any jobs.
- A small company in California bidding on a service contract in Florida makes the evaluators feel uncomfortable with the company's presumed inability to respond to day-to-day problems. (Local presence!)
- If a proposal wins, it will jeopardize the jobs of a manager and his department (reengineering the workplace).
- A proposal may be a threat to one of the prospective customer's departments that has used a certain product for many years and is completely satisfied with the product. (The incumbent has the upper hand.)

- A company wants an extensive "pilot" system test, meaning they are not convinced this technology will work.

Although it's possible for the customer's upper management to go against the RFP team's recommendation, giving you the contract instead of the company that had the most points in the evaluation, don't count on it. When this happens, most likely the decision to award the contract to a certain vendor was made long before the RFP was written.

The Evaluation Team

Figure 4-3 is a simple diagram of a typical customer proposal evaluation team. The actual evaluation takes place with the people below the RFP director, who is responsible for the proposed project and may become the project leader after selection is made.

The evaluators read sections relating to their expertise and make recommendations to the RFP director. These, in

FIGURE 4-3 Typical Customer Proposal Evaluation Team

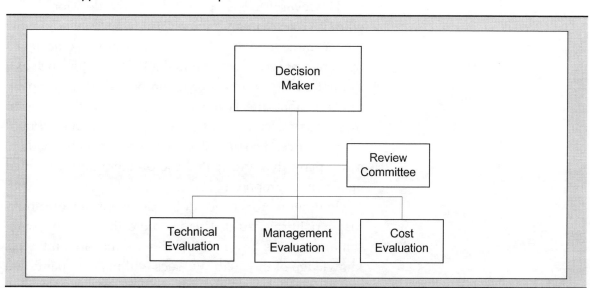

turn, are organized, and the points or comments compiled into a recommendation that is passed up to the decision makers. These people may have formed a review committee that would look at the recommendation, possibly alter it, and submit a recommendation of its own. The decision maker may accept the committee's recommendation or choose to go along with the initial recommendation made by the evaluation team, thus, in a sense, rubber-stamping the RFP director's decision (which is the most likely scenario).

In either case, it is important to remember that the RFP director usually cannot make the final decision. This adds another dimension to the proposal process. If it is the president or senior vice president who will make the decision, how can you reach this person in order to sell your proposal?

You may not need to. The decision maker of a company that has gone to the trouble of writing an RFP and setting up a committee to evaluate the responses will most likely follow the recommendation made by the evaluation team. The decision maker is someone who has the interest of the company as a whole in mind, not just this particular project.

However, it is also possible that the decision maker who has the company's interests at heart may not follow the recommendation. If he becomes aware of some development that was unknown to the RFP director, such as a dramatic cost reduction program or a shift in company direction that affects the whole company, the decision maker may decide to put the procurement on hold until the matter can be studied; or the award may be made to a company that anticipated the problem and presented an alternate proposal.

In other words, major dollar decisions are, or can be, major political issues. This is where the account representative earns her dollar. Without the account rep's knowledge of the political issues within a company, you should carefully consider whether to continue.

Tip

The final decision is generally a team decision.

Summary

Of the many factors and variables that go into making a proposal, paying attention to the evaluation process can contribute as much to winning as a competitive price, a brilliant technical approach, or a masterful Management Section. The in-house evaluation should be given as much attention as the writing of the Technical Section. Finding out how the customer is going to evaluate your proposal and what the political climate is, is as important as driving the cost down to its absolute minimum.

Proper evaluation practices will enhance your proposal's chances of winning. This two-step process begins with selecting an in-house evaluation team. Selection of the team or person should be done with the same care that you put in to selecting your proposal manager. It is essential to give the in-house evaluation proper acknowledgment and support; otherwise, everyone's time will be wasted. In fact, you must be ready and willing to stand behind the Red Team and its verdict, even if you do not agree with its decision.

The second phase in the evaluation process is to begin questioning the customer and getting as much information as possible about evaluation criteria. Most customers will respond to direct questions. They may not tell you everything, and sometimes what they don't tell you is just as important as what they do. Remember, the customer has spent a great deal of time, money, and effort writing the RFP. It is to his advantage to let you know as much as possible about what he wants to see and what he doesn't.

In other words, sell the customer what he wants to buy, not what you think he *should* buy. This means read the RFP with a critical eye, pay close attention to the evaluation criteria, question the customer, and read between the lines. Your rewards in new business will be well worth the effort.

Tip In-house evaluation will increase your chances of winning.

FORMAT
THE PROPOSAL

Although every proposal is unique in content and layout, there are basic sections that are standard to all of them. In this chapter we will consider cover requirements, the material that makes up the front matter, such as a title page or compliance matrix, and how the proposal should be formatted. The formatting suggestions are guidelines only. If the RFP that you are responding to provides you with a required format, you must follow that format.

Proposal Cover

Many salespeople who develop small proposals in field offices use no formal cover and submit the proposal in a binder or use a report-style cover. However, most of these proposals can be easily upgraded using simple graphics and a word processor. It adds a touch of professionalism to the proposal when the customer is identified along with the RFP project name.

A standard cover could be developed that reflects your company's product. If your company produces a significant number of proposals, you may wish to invest some time and money to have custom artwork designed that can be used for proposal covers as well as for special reports submitted to customers. A master copy of the artwork may be left with a printer who then can print the customer's name, project title, and other information on the cover as needed. The cost of printing covers with existing artwork is small and the turnaround time is relatively short.

If you are writing a major proposal for an important account, you may consider having a special cover designed with your company name printed or embossed on the front and spine. A unique or custom cover gives your proposal a professional look and makes it easy to identify.

Think of what best represents your company visually. Care should be taken not to clutter or make the cover too heavy and dense with text and illustrations. It should be simple, clean, and have impact. The following are some ideas for the types of illustrations that can be used on the front cover:

- If your company sells computer equipment, use a line drawing or a photograph of your equipment or a person operating it.
- If your company provides a software product such as a spreadsheet, a lightly overprinted copy of the output would be interesting.
- If your product is service, use a line drawing or photograph of people performing or receiving the service.

The information that is printed on the cover must include, at a minimum, all of the following (see Figures 5-1 and 5-2):

- Your company's name (use your logo, if you have one)
- The name of the customer
- The name of the project
- Volume information (optional but may be required in the RFP)
- The date

Always date the proposal cover with the due date that is stated in the RFP or Letter of Extension. Even if you think you will be submitting it early, you may have a delay and the cover must be printed well in advance.

FIGURE 5-1 Sample Cover

SoftCom Group

Assessment of Digital Technology
Proposal for Digital Communication Technologies

by
ACME Networks, Inc.
20xx
Due date January 14, 20xx

FIGURE 5-2 Sample Cover with Text Only

SoftCom Group

Assessment of Digital Technology

Proposal for Digital Communication Technology

June 30, 20xx

Prepared by:
ACME Networks, Inc.

In summary, a professional-looking cover and approach will do much to enhance your image with the customer. When it gets down to being very close in competition, perceptions of your company may tip the balance.

Various types of bindings are detailed in Chapter 9, "Print and Deliver Your Proposal." However, three-ring view binders are especially recommended for ease of use.

Physical Organization of a Proposal

A proposal is organized around two types of information: that which is constant for all proposals, *front matter,* and material that varies, *body sections,* and *appendixes.*

Constants

The constants, or front matter, include everything from the cover letter to (but not including) the Executive Summary.

- *Cover letter.* Also called a letter of transmittal, it provides basic information about your proposal such as your proposal number and how long your proposal will be valid, and references the RFP number.
- *Title page.* This is usually a copy of the front cover with additional information and without the graphics.
- *Proprietary notice.* The proprietary notice cautions the customer about unauthorized disclosure of your proposal.
- *Table of contents*
- *List of abbreviations*

Variables

- Section 1 Executive Summary
- Section 2 Technical
- Section 3 Management

- Section 4 Pricing
- Appendixes

The first four sections listed above constitute the body of the proposal. In very large proposals, these sections may be separately bound and assigned a volume number dictated by the proposal preparation instructions in the RFP. For multiple volumes, the cover letter need not be placed in all volumes. It is possible to make one volume the master copy and place all front matter in that copy. If there are appendixes, they are treated as a separate section at the end.

Front Matter

A careful reading of the RFP is required to determine the order of this front material. If there are no proposal preparation instructions or other guidelines in the RFP, follow the order listed above. There is no *standard for additional material other than that discussed here.* Included below are the basic materials that make up the front matter.

Cover Letter or Letter of Transmittal

The cover letter contains vital information about your company and your proposal. It makes this information readily accessible to the buyer. Consider the cover letter as a letter of commitment from your president to the customer's president (see Figure 5-3). *Note:* Some RFPs *require* that an "Officer of the Company" sign the cover letter and commit to the pricing contained in the proposal. If this is the case for your proposal, be sure to get the proper signature—and typically, a sales rep is not an officer of the company.

Some, but not necessarily all, of the key ideas that should be covered are

- an opening statement or summary sentence that concisely presents your marketing strategy. The opening sentence should be stronger than a

Sample Cover Letter

SoftCom Industries
1000 East Industrial Park
Some Town, CA 94000

September 24, 20xx

Dear Mr. Walker:

SoftCom Industries is proposing a complete solution for the your Records Management and Storage (RMS) project. SoftCom has the combined resources to ensure the RMS program requirements can be fully realized with mature software that meets and exceeds all technical requirements set forth in your RMS RFP.

SoftCom is proposing our Electronic Records Management System (ERMS) as the basis for your RMS project. The ERMS product is currently installed in more than 100 client sites and has been available for five years. We believe that ERMS provides all the core functions required in the RMS system and database customization will be provided for by using standard tools.

Because our ERMS meets all the requirements in your RFP, we believe that your 18-month schedule is not only possible but can be met ahead of schedule. See our project schedule in the Management Section.

As requested in your RFP 13-B, our proposal is valid for a 60-day period. Mr. Porter-Roth is an officer of the company who is authorized to make all commitments in this proposal. Future communications should be directed to your account representative, Ms. Anne Smith. Please refer to our proposal number 192-W in all communications.

We are looking forward to working with you and your team on the RMS project.

Sincerely,

Bud Porter-Roth

Bud Porter-Roth
President

"thank-you" for the chance to bid; it must be a positive statement about your product or service. This statement is your selling theme and the reason the customer will award you the contract.

- any special or unique ideas that the customer did not expect or ask for presented in your proposal that save money and time and that guarantee a risk-free implementation.

- special efforts you have undertaken to identify and resolve critical requirements indicated in the RFP. For example, if the customer constantly stresses speed in complying with his requirements and prompt delivery, make a clear statement that you understand his need and have made extraordinary efforts to guarantee shipment on or ahead of schedule.
- the closing statement. The closing statement should include the following: references to the RFP number (if there is one) and project name, how long the proposal will be valid (60 days, 90 days), a statement indicating that the person signing the proposal is authorized by your company, and the name and address of the person responsible for the proposal.

To summarize, use the cover letter to help sell your proposal by getting the attention of the evaluators and directing them to compelling reasons for buying.

You may want to ensure that all your vital information is available to the buyer in one easily accessible place. The following is an example of the cover letter instructions from an RFP:

- *Itemization of all materials and enclosures being forwarded collectively in response to the RFP*
- *Reference to all RFP amendments received by the vendor (by amendment issue date) to ensure that vendor is aware of all such amendments in the event there are any; if none have been received by the vendor, a statement to that effect should be included*
- *Certification that all information in the proposal is correct*
- *A statement that acknowledges and agrees to all the rights of the RFP, including the procurement rules and procedures, terms and conditions, and all other rights and terms specified in this RFP*

- *Assurance of the vendor's willingness to enter into an agreement with the COMPANY, which includes the terms and conditions of this RFP, the vendor's proposal, the contract included in Exhibit C of this RFP, and the complete RFP document including any amendments.*

  The cover letter shall include the following vendor information:

- *Business name, address, e-mail address, principal place of business, telephone number, and fax number of legal entity or individual with whom the contract would be written*
- *Names, addresses, and telephone and fax numbers of principal officers (president, vice president, treasurer)*
- *Legal status of the vendor (sole proprietorship, partnership, corporation, etc.) and the year the entity was organized to do business as the entity now substantially exists*
- *The federal Employer Tax Identification number or Social Security number*
- *The location of the facility from which the vendor would operate.*

  The cover letter must be written on the vendor's official business letterhead.

The above information acknowledges receipt of various items from the RFP in addition to providing information about your company. If you can imagine receiving 10–15 proposals and having to search through each one for a company's corporate information . . . having it in the cover letter makes it much easier to find and use.

Title Page

The title page contains all the information on the front cover in addition to the following (see Figure 5-4):

FIGURE 5-4 Sample Title Page

SoftCom Group

Assessment of Digital Technology
Proposal for Digital Communication
Technologies

Submitted to:

SoftCom Group
Mike Roth-Porter
Vice President, Engineering

SoftCom Group RFP 98-7

June 30, 20xx

Submitted by:

ACME Digital Industries
Proposal Number 98-7-03

- Response to requirements placed ahead of the project name
- The "submitted to" line. This line should have the name of the person who signed the RFP. Check the RFP for possible instructions that will tell you to whom, where, and how to submit the proposal.
- The "submitted by" line. In addition to your company name and logo, you should include your full address.
- Sequential company proposal number. If you number your proposals, and you should, the number goes here. It is professional to number your

proposal and refer to the number in the cover letter. Also request that the customer refer to the proposal number in any correspondence with you.

- Date. This should be the date the proposal is due, not the date you are submitting it.

If you are submitting several copies of your proposal, you may be required to designate one of the copies as the master. The master copy should be the one that contains the original cover letter and signature in ink. It is advisable to have a master copy even if it is not required. The words *MASTER COPY* should be printed on the proposal cover and title page.

Proprietary Notice

This is a statement to the customer that tells him the information you have provided in your proposal is not to be released to anyone other than the people who need it for evaluation purposes and contract information. The proprietary notice contains basically three ideas:

1. Although proposal information is proprietary, if parts of the information were public domain before submittal, the customer is under no obligation to withhold such information from the general public.
2. If the customer had access to information before the proposal, whether public or not, he is under no obligation to hold that information in confidence unless by prior agreement.
3. If the customer receives information from a third party and is not asked to hold that information as proprietary, he is under no obligation to hold such information in confidence.

If the proposal is being submitted to the government, read the RFP instructions very carefully about how to mark your proposal. You should know that because of the Freedom of Information Act, your competitors can

FIGURE 5-5   Sample Proprietary Notice

PROPRIETARY NOTICE

This proposal contains confidential information of YOUR COM-
PANY NAME HERE, which is provided for the sole purpose of
permitting the recipient to evaluate the proposal submitted
herewith. In consideration of receipt of this proposal, the recipient agrees to maintain such information in confidence and to
not reproduce or otherwise disclose this information to any person outside the group directly responsible for evaluation of its
contents. There is no obligation to maintain the confidentiality
of any information which was known to the recipient prior to
receipt of such information from YOUR COMPANY, or becomes
publicly known through no fault of recipient, or is received without obligation of confidentiality from a third party owing no
obligation of confidentiality to YOUR COMPANY.

ask for and receive copies of your proposal if it is not pro-
tected by the proprietary notice. Contact your legal staff
and local government contracting office to make sure
you are following the instructions correctly. If you arbi-
trarily mark every page *Confidential* or *Proprietary*, even
though there is nothing confidential on the page, the government will disregard all confidential markings.

When writing your proprietary notice, get help from
your legal department. The example given in Figure 5-5
may not be suitable for your proposal or your company.

Table of Contents (TOC)

The word processor program that you are using normally
generates the table of contents. Typically, you can specify
how many levels deep the indexing will go, and other variables such as a dotted line from the heading to the number.

It is recommended that you provide a table of contents with your proposal. It may be as simple as the

major headings or as deep as three levels down. Three levels down is generally far enough, unless your proposal is unusually long and complex.

The table of contents should be cleanly presented and easy to read. If section numbers are used in the proposal, the table of contents should also have section numbers.

When you have more than one physically separated volume in your proposal, you should include in the first volume the combined TOCs from all the volumes. Subsequent volumes usually contain only the TOC for that individual volume. However, there is nothing wrong with duplicating the complete TOC for each volume.

The list of illustrations (LOI) follows the TOC and should start on a separate page from the TOC. Tables follow on another page, as shown in Figures 5-6 and 5-7. However, if it is possible to combine both illustrations and tables on one page, it is acceptable to do so.

Abbreviations List

An abbreviations list should be part of your boilerplate library; it is not the same as a glossary. The abbreviations

FIGURE 5-6 Sample List of Illustrations

	List of Illustrations	
Figure A-1.	Project Management Structure	A-7
Figure B-1.	Proposed Software Solution	B-5
Figure B-2.	System Configuration Diagram	B-9
Figure B-3.	Proposed System Conceptual Process Flow	B-15
Figure C-1.	Project Schedule	C-2
Figure C-2.	Cost Summary Sheet	C-7
Figure C-3.	Bill of Materials	C-8
Figure D-1.	Executive Staff Organization	D-3

FIGURE 5-7 Sample List of Tables

List of Tables

Table B-1.	Compliance Matrix	B-4
Table C-1.	System Configuration Specifications	C-6
Table C-2.	Proposed Maintenance Schedule	C-9
Table D-1.	Printing from Non-Image Capable Devices	D-17

list is a key to the acronyms and buzzwords that are unique to your company or industry (see Figure 5-8). It should be placed in the front of *all* the volumes of your proposal, not just the first one. Placement is usually after the list of illustrations and/or tables.

FIGURE 5-8 Sample Abbreviations List

Abbreviation/ Acronym	Definition
AWM	Advanced Workstation Management. An Ajax-designed software management program
AIP	Applications Implementation Program. Ajax's collection of developers' tools used to build software applications
ASCII	American Standard Code for Information Interchange. The computer codes used to store general computer data (not images)
LAN	Local Area Network
MSA	Maintenance and Support Agreement
PPM	Principal Period of Maintenance
SSRC	Ajax's Software Support Response Center
TSC	Ajax's Technical Support Center

Additional Front Matter

There are occasions when other documents in addition to the regular front matter will be placed in the front of the proposal, before the text proper. The following are examples and explanations of some of these documents.

Compliance Matrix

This form is sometimes seen in state or government RFPs and requests that you state whether you are compliant with major requirements and specifications in the RFP (see Figure 5-9). As some people try to skirt the issue if they are not compliant, this is an effort to determine what specifications are not being met.

Even if not required, this is something that should be provided as a visible demonstration to the customer that you have met all requirements in addition to giving a cross reference of the RFP paragraphs to your proposal paragraphs.

FIGURE 5-9 Compliance Matrix

Compliance Matrix

The following compliance matrix serves as a cross reference to major paragraphs in your RFP and demonstrates our adherence to the requirements and specifications. Exceptions will be noted as noncompliant and will be fully discussed in Exceptions to the RFP.

RFP Number	Proposal Number	Compliant (Y/N)	Comments
2.1	3.1	Y	See Appd. B for additional ref.
2.2	3.2	Y	
2.3	3.3	N	External modem not required
2.4	3.4	Y	
2.5	4.1	N	Extended memory not optional

Exceptions List

If you do provide a compliance matrix and cannot be compliant in all areas, it is advisable to provide an explanation for each exception. As is sometimes the case, your product may already be capable of doing something that negates the necessity for doing something else required by the customer (see Figure 5-10). In addition, the list is highly visible and most likely will be read, providing you with a sales forum few competitors will have.

FIGURE 5-10 Exceptions List

This section lists all exceptions to the Johnson Corporation Request for Proposal, RFP No. ADH-583-1, dated December 20xx.

1. *Paragraph 1.21.3 Contractual Obligation.* The contents of the response of the successful Vendor and the provisions stated in this RFP shall be considered as contractual obligations.

Exception: This proposal has been prepared in accordance with accepted techniques for system design and our understanding of your requirements as stated in the RFP. However, it is to be understood that actual results in your operating environment may vary due to variations in volume, environment, personnel, and other factors that we cannot control. Therefore, while the greatest care has been taken to be accurate, we cannot warrant specifications given in this proposal.

2. *Paragraph 3.7.12 Compatibility.* The proposed software shall remain compatible with the existing applications software, peripherals, computer interfaces and terminal equipment as defined in the Technical Section 2 paragraphs 2.1–2.21 of this RFP.

Exception: Our software will not be compatible with the existing software and cannot be converted. We propose to use the software described in the Software Section of this response. Full specifications and costs are given with a description of the software and why it cannot remain compatible with existing software.

Bonds

Some RFPs require that a bond be established at the time of proposal submission. The bond request will be in the RFP and will be explained in the instructions. Be careful not to include the cost of the bond in with the pricing section since some RFPs specifically state that they are not responsible for the cost of the bond.

Buy USA Statement

This is a form that you are required to sign. Basically, it says that a certain percentage of the equipment you buy will be manufactured in the United States. Careful reading will explain its full intent.

Minority Business Enterprise Requirements

Many government RFPs require bidders to fill in a Minority, Small, Women-owned, and Veteran Business Enterprise (MSWVBE) form. The form applies to two basic conditions.

The first is if your company is an MSWVBE. If so, you may have to provide official status or registration from the state. If you are an MSWVBE, you will be eligible for additional point consideration on the evaluation. This means that you may be given, for example, a five percent add-on to your final point value in the evaluation. The percentage and method will vary from state to state. It is important that you correctly list your business and fill in the forms completely and accurately. If you want to apply for MSWVBE status, don't wait until the proposal is due.

An MSWVBE form would also be required if your business were employing an MSWVBE, as a subcontractor, for a percentage of your work. As above, if you qualify, you will receive additional consideration.

If employing an MSWVBE subcontractor, the requirements may be complex and require that you competitively procure the services of an MSWVBE. This means that your company is responsible for writing an RFP for the services and sending it to at least three MSWVBE companies, as well as advertising the RFP in an MSWVBE or public newspaper. This takes time, effort, and makes for additional work in preparing the proposal.

Be prepared, and review this section ASAP!

Proposal Road Map

A Proposal Road Map is sometimes required or desirable when a proposal is so complex that the logic of your response is not easily followed. The road map can be similar to a preface in a book, or it may be graphically illustrated as shown in Figure 5-11. This is somewhat similar to the compliance matrix and should easily be generated by your proposal-writing outline.

FIGURE 5-11 Proposal Road Map

Proposal Road Map

The following road map serves as a cross reference to major paragraphs in your RFP and our proposal.

RFP Number	Proposal Number	Comments
2.1	1.1	Executive Summary
3.1	2.1	Technical Section
3.2	2.2	
3.3	2.3	
4.1	4.1	Management Section

Proposal Organization

Some of the larger RFPs will require that a specified proposal format be followed for ease of evaluation. However, if the RFP does not specify a proposal format, it is up to you to provide one. Therefore, it is your responsibility to ensure that your proposal is organized and formatted to best demonstrate your product's features and benefits within the guidelines presented in the RFP.

Figure 5-12 gives an example of typical proposal layout instructions.

FIGURE 5-12 Proposal Layout Instructions

Vendor Proposal Format

A total of five (5) exact copies of your proposal must be submitted. One copy must be marked ORIGINAL MASTER and others marked COPY on the title page. Use a three-ring binder for each copy. The proposal must be divided into sections and tabbed as follows:

Section 1	RFP Response Requirements (refer to Section 2 of this RFP)
Section 2	Insurance (refer to Section 3 of this RFP)
Section 3	References (refer to Section 4 of this RFP)
Section 4	Qualification of Respondents (refer to Section 5 of this RFP)
Section 5	General Contract Requirements (refer to Section 6 of this RFP)
Section 6	Executive Summary
Section 7	Proposed System Operations (refer to Section 8 of this RFP)
Section 8	Proposed System Configuration (refer to Section 9 of this RFP)
Section 9	Project Plan and Maintenance (refer to Section 10 of this RFP)
Section 10	Pricing (refer to Section 12 of this RFP)
Appendix A	Terms and Conditions of Purchase (Refer to RFP Appendix A)
Appendix B	Business Information Form (Form XYZ01, Refer to RFP Appendix B)
Appendix C	Respondents Certification Sheet (Refer to RFP Appendix C)
Appendix D	Optional for Vendor's Attachments

Proposal Format

Style Sheet

If no proposal format is specified by the RFP (paragraph-numbering guidelines), developing and using a style sheet will save you considerable time and work, especially if you are working out of a small office with only a few people developing and working on the proposal. Otherwise you will see inconsistencies in such things as paragraph indentation and spacing, treatment of headings, margins, and illustration styles. If you have word processing operators or typists, you will save hours of time, effort, and frustration by providing them with a style sheet for the draft preparation.

The following are some items that can be standardized:

- Indentation of paragraphs (if any), and by how much
- Headings/subheadings
- Bullets
- Pagination (placement, spacing, section number, etc.)
- Margins
- Trademark names and logos
- Abbreviations
- Buzzwords
- Basic spelling (e.g., disc/disk)
- Dates
- Illustration formats and call-outs
- Footnotes

The key to a successful style sheet is to be realistic. You cannot expect a large heterogeneous group to read a 20-page style manual before they begin writing. If, however, during the kickoff meeting some discussion is spent on the style sheet, explaining why and how it will save time, most writers will make an effort to follow it. The best style sheet is a simple one that can be given to your writers and typists to follow when preparing the manuscript. There are several ways style sheets can be prepared. One may be simply a list of instructions with examples (see Figure 5-13).

Since word processors are commonly available, it is most efficient to provide the writers with a template style sheet developed with the word processing program to be used. The template can be an existing one that comes with the word processor, or it can be custom-built for proposals. This can be passed out on a disk or made available over the network. Each writer must be advised to install the template and **NOT TO CHANGE IT**.

FIGURE 5-13 Sample Style Sheet

Style Sheet

1. *Heads and Subheads*
   Level 1 major heads are typed with five spaces from text above and two spaces to text below.
   Level 1 heads: all caps, bold, no indent
   Level 2 heads: upper and lower case, bold, indent five spaces
   Level 3 heads: cap first word only, bold, indent ten spaces
   Level 4 heads: cap first word only, normal, indent 15 spaces

Example:
   LEVEL 1 MAJOR HEAD
       Level 2 Subhead
           Level 3 subhead
               Level 4 subhead

2. *Bullets*
Bullets are indicated with a small "•" and are indented five spaces in from the head or subhead under which they fall. Allow two spaces between the bullet and the text following it.

Example:
   MAJOR HEAD
   • Bullet item 1
   • Bullet item 2

3. *Dates*
   a. A full date is set off by commas.
   The meeting was held September 1, 1988, at the corporate headquarters.

During the kickoff meeting, the writers should be instructed on the basics of using the template. Some formatting does not support the use of templates, such as the placement of graphics. Written guidelines should be established for these.

If a graphics program is to be used for illustrations, standards for graphics should also be established. This usually requires that all writers use the same graphics program so that the prebuilt illustrations are consistent with each other. For example, a "computer workstation" illustration is different from program to program, and even within programs they may have variations on a server graphic. As a worst-case example, one writer refers to a workstation that is positioned on the floor as a "tower" case. Within the same section, another writer illustrates the same workstation as a "desktop" case with the monitor sitting on top of the case.

Abbreviations and acronyms call for a list of their meanings, as well as style (see Figure 5-14).

FIGURE 5-14 Sample Style Guide for Abbreviations and Acronyms

Abbreviations and Acronyms

Abbreviation/ Acronym	Definition	Style
AWM	Advanced Workstation Management. An Ajax-designed software management program	
AIP	Applications Implementation Program	Ajax's collection of developers' tools used to build software applications
dpi	Dots per inch	All lower case; one space after the numeric value Example: 300 dpi
GB	One billion (1024 x 106) characters gigabyte	No space between the numeric value and the abbreviation. Example: 2GB
LAN	Local Area Network	
MSA	Maintenance and Support Agreement	
NCSC	Ajax's National Customer Support Center	
OCR	Optical Character Recognition. A technique used to convert text contained in images to ASCII data that is suitable for use by word processing programs	
PPM	Principal Period of Maintenance	

DEVELOP AND
WRITE YOUR PROPOSAL

Although each proposal will be unique, there are basic primary sections that are standard to all proposals, such as the Executive Summary, Technical Section, Management Section, Pricing Section, and the Appendix.

These sections, in turn, have elements common to all proposals. For example, an Executive Summary generally contains an introduction, a statement of the problem, a review of the major sections of the proposal, and information about the company that is presenting the proposal. The Technical Section provides a description of the product or service proposed, and the Management Section explains how the product or service will be installed or implemented. The Pricing Section provides a breakdown of the prices of products/services, maintenance, training, and other items being proposed. Appendixes are generally reserved for information too detailed for inclusion in the main proposal, or information that may assist the evaluator that is not specifically asked for in the RFP.

These basic proposal elements may be thought of as modules, some of which can be prewritten as standard boilerplate files, such as a description of the hardware or a list of training classes. Some modules, however, *must be written fresh each time*, such as a discussion of how your product will meet the customer's requirements.

This chapter will cover the purpose of each primary section, who reads them, how to develop each section, what material can be standardized for use in all proposals, and what material must be custom-written for each proposal. These section reviews also contain examples of effective responses to RFPs and guidelines for formatting standardized material.

The Executive Summary

The Executive Summary is an abstract of your proposal. It presents a summarized view of each major section, reviews any unusual features and benefits contained in your proposal, delivers the major selling points, and supplies any pertinent information not requested in the RFP.

The Executive Summary is a real workhorse for your proposal. It not only summarizes the proposal, but also educates people not familiar with your products and company, inspiring a positive first impression. It translates complex technical concepts into understandable benefits, and it sells those benefits to the reader. To be effective, the Executive Summary must achieve the following:

- Tell the reader what he is buying—in simple, understandable terminology
- Explain complex technical concepts in terms that will be grasped by nontechnical readers
- Translate complex technical concepts and features into understandable benefits
- Sell the reader on the benefits of the proposed solution
- Show your solution to be superior to the competition's solution, features, and (perceived) benefits

One RFP provided the following guideline for writing an Executive Summary:

The Executive Summary is to be a short, concise, and self-contained document that focuses on the key issues of the RFP.

Tip Allthough each proposal will be unique, there are basic sections that are standard to all proposals.

Who Reads the Executive Summary?

Although read by a variety of people, the primary audience for the Executive Summary is the high-level decision maker. The executive reads the Executive Summary to gain a working knowledge of all proposals submitted in order to understand the primary differences among the proposed solutions and to determine relative values of products vs. price. This person is interested in *what* results will be achieved by your product, not so much in *how* they will be achieved.

Before diving into the detailed technical sections, the evaluation staff reads the Executive Summary. This summary provides them with an overall view of the solution that will later help them to grasp technical details in the body of the proposal. Providing the evaluation staff with the Executive Summary exposes them to the features and benefits of your proposal from a business point of view, rather than a strictly technical one.

Remember that evaluators are going to be reading three to six (or more) proposals that will be variations on the same topic. The Executive Summary shows the evaluation team what makes your proposal (solution) different from the pack. If the Executive Summary is done correctly, your Technical Section will be more easily understood and grasped by those who make decisions.

Tip — The primary reader is the high-level decision maker.

Development of the Executive Summary

As important as it is to your proposal, few RFPs provide specific guidelines for the development and content of an Executive Summary. If the RFP does not specifically request an Executive Summary, it is still advisable to try to fit one in. It could even be the opening section to your technical response. The following examples taken from recent RFPs demonstrate how ambiguous the guidelines can be:

The Executive Summary should consist of a concise description of how the proposed system will address the needs spelled out in this RFP. Excessive technical detail should be avoided in this section. After reading this section, the reader should have a clear conceptual understanding of the approach recommended by the bidder.

This section should be limited to a brief narrative that outlines the bidder's proposal. The summary should contain little technical jargon and be oriented to the non-technical executive. Pricing information should not appear in this section.

This section provides an overview and summary of the proposed system and its major components. It should contain a general system description, major functions or capabilities as they apply to future requirements, and any areas of concern that need to be addressed. It should be written at an appropriate technical level for senior management review.

The management summary section must provide an overview of the vendor's overall approach and include at least the following information:

- *A discussion of the proposed approach for meeting the requirements of this RFP*
- *An overview of the proposed technical solution*
- *A discussion of the vendor's organization and relevant experience*
- *A discussion of the costs required by this RFP*
- *A summary discussion of anticipated problems and proposed solutions*
- *A discussion of assumptions made by the vendor for the proposed solution*

As can be seen from the above examples, there does not seem to be any consistent or well-defined approach to writing an Executive Summary. In the first three examples, basically the same request is made—summarize the proposal—but the writer is left to interpret what *summarize* and *outline* mean.

The third example contains a reference that most proposal writers do not notice, or would like to avoid—

> *Tip* Few RFPs provide guidance as to how the Executive Summary should be prepared.

". . . any areas of concern that need to be addressed." These words are vague, but in general, the company issuing the RFP is asking you, the company writing the proposal, to list problem areas, how they will be addressed, and the risks associated with those problems. Many writers hesitate to list areas of concern, problems, and exceptions to requirements for fear the competition will not have the same problems. However, this type of statement in an RFP serves three purposes:

1. It asks potential bidders to think through their solution and list weaknesses and remedies.
2. It demonstrates to the executive and evaluator reading the proposals which companies understand the problems and are willing to address them.
3. The "weakness" may be in the RFP requirements, and you are pointing out to the reader areas in which the requirements were not fully thought through.

Being able to address potential areas of concern will allow you to position yourself against your competition, and perhaps make the reader question the competition. For example, an "area of concern" may be that existing software legacy systems will eventually need to be incorporated into the system being purchased. You know that the competition has trouble in this area and that you have the better solution, so you address this issue in detail, explaining how your software is able to link to legacy systems via the XYZ application. Therefore, you have cast a shadow on the competition while highlighting one of your features. That is good selling, especially at the executive level.

The fourth example provides the most information but is vague when it says the summary must include "at least the following information." The last statement suggests that the information requested is not enough, and the author may include almost anything else that may be of interest.

Tip Bidders often are required to list potential problems as well as solutions.

At a minimum, an Executive Summary should contain an introduction to the proposed solution, offer the solution, and identify who is providing that solution. Below is a possible outline for an Executive Summary. This outline is generic but does mirror the basic sections of a complete proposal. It is possible that some proposals would not include items 2, 4, 5, and 6, for example, as they may not apply to your company, service, or product.

1. Introduction
2. Design concept
3. Technical approach
4. Project management
5. Maintenance
6. Education
7. Pricing structure
8. Corporate profile
9. Future products
10. Areas of concern

> *Tip* The Executive Summary should introduce the proposed solution.

1. Introduction

The first paragraph of your proposal should begin selling your solution. Many proposal introductions begin by thanking the company for the chance to bid on this project ("ACME would like to thank XYZ for allowing us to submit a bid for this most important project. . . .") and then proceed to go into great detail about their own company, how great their products are, and their extensive qualifications. It may be several pages before the RFP, its requirements, and the Executive Summary of the proposed solution are first mentioned. Often, in this style of Executive Summary writing, stress is placed on company image or strength, and the product's strengths become of secondary importance. This results in a confusing message to the customer because the "solution" being sold is not clearly stated, and the reader is left to answer the question: Which is really more important—the company or the product?

Very few "trust me" proposals make it to the top of the short list. As an example, in the old days, the saying was, "You can't get fired by buying IBM!" This is a "trust me" proposal statement and large companies (not necessarily IBM) traded on their name. Today's buyers are more sophisticated and technically astute, and would not respond well to a poorly written trust-me proposal from a big-name company.

This is not to say that a company's name does not have value; it still does. Buyers respond to equally good technical solutions, whether they are from a big-name company or a start-up. If you were the startup, how would you position yourself? The final decision may be based on the safety of a large, established company if the alternative is a start-up with no track record.

Your proposal strategy may not necessarily focus on the product, but on the company's reputation and strengths. For example, if you are the small company and know your product is equal to or better than the competition's, you must focus on how buying from a smaller company will benefit the customer. For example, because you are smaller, your development team can react faster to on-the-spot changes instead of going through some monolithic development team that may take weeks to process the change. If you know your product is strong, focus your attention on your strengths, but don't ignore your weaknesses.

Generally, the larger the procurement (in dollars and business importance), the more important it is to sell the company itself—reputation, depth of resources, knowledge of the market, number of years in the business—than to sell the product itself. At a certain level, which will differ from industry to industry, it is assumed that the product will work properly; therefore, the issue becomes the ability of the company to execute the project—i.e., implement, install, maintain, and educate. Big established companies know this and exploit it whenever possible. Small

Tip The first paragraph of your proposal should begin selling your solution.

companies bidding on a large project must effectively counter the "big company" sales strategy (e.g., "If you buy from two guys in a garage, you'll get what you pay for").

Below are examples of introductions taken from actual proposals. The first is an excerpt from a winning proposal.

> *[This customer's] stated goal of growth by acquisition or expansion requires a computer system that can grow with it. The RFP states that the computer system should allow growth by expansion, not replacement of hardware, software, application packages, and personnel.*
>
> *Our solution will provide you with that incremental growth.*
>
> *It is our intention to prove this statement through our proposal and by demonstrating our corporate commitment to a broad compatible product line. A product line that allows you to grow incrementally, adding only as much capacity as needed to the existing platform.*

This is a very strong opener that in a few short lines restates the customer's primary goal and establishes these points:

- We understand your requirements and we are going to work with you to meet those requirements.
- We promise to meet your goal.

The third paragraph establishes the proposal theme: system growth through compatible product lines. This topic becomes a selling theme that is reinforced throughout the proposal. For example, in the section on training, the proposal states that overall training time and costs will be reduced over the life of the project because the hardware and software upgrades are incremental, and do not require new training because they use the same equipment and software.

This theme also weakens the competition by suggesting that the competition can't grow incrementally and therefore the customer may be forced to buy more capacity than is needed. In addition, if the customer has to move up to the next level of computer, there may be additional training required. Thus, expenses will be incurred each time the customer outgrows current capacity.

The second example comes from the opening paragraph of a losing proposal:

[This company's] systems meet the needs for highly reliable, general-purpose computer systems for users with heavy-volume processing. For such customers, computer system failures, damage to the database, or interruptions of computer service can result in serious financial loss. Our hardware and software minimize the risk of system failures and protect the information stored in the database. [Company] has the long-term stability and industry knowledge to provide superior products and services.

This opening paragraph has several problems:

- It is so general that almost any computer manufacturer today would fit that description. It is similar to a car manufacturer saying "Our cars feature four strong tires and an engine, and are suitable for transportation on roads."
- The second sentence is negative. Instead of explaining the advantages of a highly reliable system, it points out what could happen if a system were to fail. A negative, "what to avoid" approach is never as successful or as powerful as selling positive features. Also, this statement has negligible impact because it is true of any company using computers for day-to-day business operations.
- The third sentence continues the negative sales pitch by implying that this manufacturer is the only one who can protect you from system failures.

Your opening statement must be powerful, draw the reader in, and promise a solution that other vendors will

Tip > A losing introduction is too general, is weak, and uses negative selling.

have difficulty matching. The introduction will set the tone for the entire proposal. The most effective Executive Summary leaves the reader with a clear concept of what is being proposed, why your solution is better than other solutions, what is different about your solution, and most important, why she should make a decision to buy your solution.

Of course, we realize that these statements must be backed up by strong and believable Technical and Management Sections. And the executive will depend on technical staff to verify the claims made in the Executive Summary.

2. Design Concept

The second section of the Executive Summary describes how and why you arrived at your particular solution. In this section, the discussion should center on relating the design to the solution, and what factors influenced your decision. For example, an RFP may require personal computers to provide a number of functions, including word processing, accounting, desktop publishing, and office productivity tools, in addition to being on an intranet with e-mail.

In this particular case there could be many solutions; specifically, the solution could be based on Intel/Microsoft architecture, Apple architecture, or a UNIX or UNIX variation. The job for the design section is to explain why one hardware/software platform was chosen and how the customer will benefit from that choice.

The best approach is to rephrase the customer's requirements, which demonstrates you understand not only what is being requested, but also the problems that could be associated with proposing different solutions. This involves understanding the customer's requirements and then matching those requirements to your products.

Tip | The design concept section states how and why you arrived at your proposed solution.

If time, knowledge, and resources permit, this is an excellent place to include what are termed "trade-off studies." If, for example, you were selling UNIX-based workstations, you would list three solutions: PCs, Apples, and UNIX machines. Each competing solution would be briefly explored, with reasons given for their rejection. For example, a UNIX workstation may be better at multitasking or running several programs at the same time than the other two, but, there are not as many software business applications available. Although Apple equipment may have a better graphical interface than the other machines, it's not the primary computer in many companies and therefore a company would have to support two operating systems. That means buying application software twice, in addition to training and service redundancies.

This type of object trade-off analysis allows you to speak to the differences in solutions without being overtly negative. It may also cause the reader to compare your analysis to the competitor's proposals to substantiate your reasoning.

3. Technical Approach

Once you have explained why a particular approach was taken, the next section should provide details of that approach. The following example is taken from a winning proposal and is the lead-in paragraph to the Technical Section:

> *The purpose to be served by the [customer's system] is to provide an integrated information system that is acceptable and usable for a wide range of applications within the municipality. These applications will enable city employees to access comprehensive databases maintained on the server in addition to using local PCs and applications for data manipulation.*
>
> *Based on these considerations, [this company] recommends a system composed of a central processing complex located in the computer center linked to facilities located*

Tip Try to rephrase requirements as it helps when evaluating complex technical proposals.

in other metropolitan areas by means of a high-speed data communications network. Remote office site equipment is to consist solely of remote PCs, and printers connected via the communications network to the central processing site.

The first paragraph restates the requirements in general terms and introduces the reader to the key concept of centralized databases accessed by remote terminals. The second paragraph provides more detail and begins to draw the reader into a nontechnical description of the solution. More detail follows about the communications network, the database and data server, and the types of software programs that are available for the remote PCs. This sets up the reader for a key argument in the proposal, centralized vs. decentralized databases, because this company knows the competition is proposing a decentralized database.

After reading this portion of the Executive Summary, the reader should have a reasonably good grasp of the solution and be able to intelligently determine if it meets the general requirements in the RFP.

4. Project Management

Project management is becoming more important as equipment, systems, and projects become progressively more complex. Although many RFPs do not require a Project Management Section, a thorough and detailed project plan provides a clear understanding of responsibilities, milestone dates, and relationships between you and the customer. The following paragraph taken from an Executive Summary shows the level of detail needed in this section:

ACME stated nontechnical requirements are essential to a successful implementation of the system. Our approach provides a detailed project plan for implementation, applications development, system training, and system maintenance, and considers that ACME will be

> **Tip** The Technical Section provides details of the chosen approach to the solution.

required to take an active role in the overall project. Figure 1-3 is our first cut at a complete project plan with dates, activities, and assignments.

This section continues with a brief outline of the proposed project team, proposed schedule, and how the two companies will interface once the project is started.

Sometimes there is not enough data to accurately project dates on a project timeline. In this case, it is best to let the reader know that these dates are an estimate, subject to negotiation and the final contract. But the point is, you have taken the initiative and have laid out the key milestones for the project, which gives the reader insight into how the project will unfold. Compare this type of schedule to your competition's lack of a schedule, or a proposal that reads, "Project scheduling will be developed as part of the detailed design."

5. Maintenance

If your proposal is for a product that requires maintenance and support, it will be important to convince and sell the executive on your company's ability to meet those maintenance requirements. As equipment becomes more complex and an integral part of doing business—in some cases the basis for profitability in a business—the executive begins to understand, for example, that a computer system that is not operational may be costing his company thousands of dollars in lost revenue for each hour or day that it is not functioning. Many companies are beginning to include penalty clauses that require cash penalties for each hour a system is down beyond an agreed-to limit. This example was taken from an RFP to purchase approximately $1.5 million of hardware and software:

> *Contracts resulting from proposals will contain a penalty provision for excessive system downtime, equipment failure, or failure by the bidder to meet response times for repair requests.*

Tip

As systems become more complex, implementation plans become more important.

A written demand for quality maintenance programs, and the assurance of getting one, are becoming more prevalent for a number of reasons:

- The number of vendors and projects is increasing so rapidly that vendors cannot adequately train service personnel.
- Vendors may bid and win a job in an area where they do not currently have maintenance personnel.
- Vendors are subject to mergers and acquisitions, often leaving the customer without maintenance support.
- Vendors bid products that have not been fully tested, resulting in customers unknowingly becoming "beta" test sites.

An important factor in determining the return on investment is the overall cost of maintenance for the life of the project. In a growing number of cases, the cost of maintenance for a major computer system over a seven-year projected life cycle will equal or exceed the purchase price. For budgeting purposes, maintenance costs become a significant number, and potential customers are beginning to give the maintenance section a higher evaluation factor.

6. Education

Just as it is important for the executive to feel confident that your company can provide adequate maintenance, it is also important for him to know that you are able to provide high-quality training. Companies that bid products that are not ready for release are often behind in their development of training classes and materials.

To be effective, this section of the Executive Summary should contain a brief overview of your education plan and explain how your education department is especially well equipped to handle this project.

A well-written paragraph on training can convey to the executive reader that your solution takes into account

Tip | Education can provide long-term benefits by reducing the costs.

all aspects of a successful project. A well-written overview of your education department may convince an executive evaluator that your company is well established and fully able to support a large contract.

7. Pricing Structure

The pricing section of the Executive Summary often does double duty. First, it is the proper place for your price (unless you are specifically told not to include pricing in the Executive Summary). Second, it is often the place where contract terms and conditions are reviewed. Including pricing and contract information in the Executive Summary is optional if the RFP instructions are not specific.

The reason for its inclusion is to provide the customer an overview and summary of your total price and any noteworthy additions, exceptions, or special conditions that relate to your overall pricing. Before including any pricing information, read the proposal preparation instructions, as some RFPs specifically state that pricing information is to be provided only in the separate Pricing Section.

Including pricing information in the Executive Summary enables you to:

- demonstrate your price/performance advantages.
- justify pricing for an optional product not requested.
- clarify why you took an exception to a requirement.

Tip Pricing information in the Executive Summary provides the customer with an overview of how you arrived at your total price.

As a proposal evaluator and reader, I often find that smaller or less-established companies have little to offer in the education department. The classes are not well defined, the descriptions are a little sketchy, and the schedule is not convenient. As a proposal writer, try to avoid this mistake and the perception that your company has not given adequate attention to education.

- explain the basis for a discount.
- acknowledge special terms and conditions in the RFP.

Often, there is no other place in a proposal to explain how you arrived at your price, what special terms and conditions are being offered the customer, or why you have elected not to bid on a portion of the RFP. For example, if you were offering the customer what is sometimes called a showcase discount, you would need to explain why this is mutually beneficial. (A showcase discount is an offer to discount your price in return for your company being able to use that site and installation as a customer reference site and allowing you to use the installation for tours, as needed.) A second example would be to explain additional pricing for products or services not requested in the RFP, such as a project manager and related staff. A third example would be to justify additional money to meet an aggressive installation schedule. Customers will sometimes provide optional installation schedules, and additional evaluation points will be awarded to those companies offering the shortest installation time.

The price summary section may be a difficult section to write because:

- pricing cannot be completed until the technical solution is finalized.
- pricing is usually one section that requires management review, which means additional decision-making time.
- discounts cannot be fixed until total price is determined.
- discounts normally require management approval.
- how much discount to be offered is often subject to debate.
- additional time is required to write this section after all discussions are complete.

Tip No matter where it appears, pricing will be the first section looked at.

The price summary section may be one of the most powerful and influential sections that the executive will read. Pricing will always be a consideration when a customer is making a decision to purchase. Prices higher than those quoted by the competition will not eliminate your proposal necessarily; however, higher prices that cannot be justified may be cause for elimination from the competition.

Pricing that is uncommon, whether too high or too low, will draw the attention of a reader. If, for example, four proposals are priced at $850,000 and one is priced at $400,000, there is probably something wrong with the low-priced proposal. Pricing is where strong competitive analysis will certainly pay off. Also, proposal evaluators like to see prices grouped within 10 to 20 percent of each other because it indicates that they have done their homework in getting comparatively equal vendors to bid on the project with roughly equal pricing.

If prices range beyond 25 percent for more than one company, the buyer may want to delay the procurement to determine if RFP requirements were stated correctly, and what may have caused vendors to offer such diverse pricing. Pricing that is scattered and inconsistent means that the RFP has problems and may be pulled back instead of being awarded.

8. Corporate Profile

Providing a corporate profile enables you to promote your corporation and any special qualities that would differentiate it from other companies. It also allows you to provide some pertinent facts about your company that may not be commonly known or recognized. For example, many companies are growing at such a rapid rate that it is possible an evaluator may remember a company as being much smaller and less capable, unless told otherwise. A corporate profile should include at least the following:

> *Tip* A corporate profile enables you to sell your company and possibly provide some little-known facts about it.

- Date company was founded and primary objective/mission
- Types of equipment and/or services provided
- Special characteristics of the company or management style
- Basic company organization
- Number of people employed
- Primary locations or locations of major divisions
- Features and benefits of corporate organization

It is also helpful to include an organization chart of management—company president, vice presidents, and directors. This enables the executive to determine how your company is organized and where his or her project will be placed.

9. Future Products

This is an optional section for your Executive Summary that can provide the reader with a sense of your company's direction and show that your company is staying abreast of, or ahead of, current technology. Insight into future technology may convince a prospective customer that your solution will enable the company to grow and change with technology, rather than having to request bids every time technology makes an advance. Providing the customer with insight into your future products suggests that your company has technological and financial strengths that may not otherwise be obvious in your proposal.

Here is your chance to show the customer that you'll have future products that your competition may not have planned. This not only makes your products more attractive, but also makes the competition less attractive—without negative selling.

Summary

As one of the most important parts of your proposal, the Executive Summary should be clear, concise, and relevant

Tip Describing future products tells the customer your company is concerned about staying on the leading edge of technology.

to the issues at hand. If there are Executive Summary writing directions in the RFP, follow them. If not, use the above examples to guide your writing.

The Executive Summary should make use of strong illustrations and graphics whenever possible. Diagrams, photos, and spreadsheets will break up the text and help you to convey your message graphically. It will make your page visually appealing, encouraging your readers to spend more time reviewing and considering your sales points. Whenever possible, a feature should be linked to a benefit. Features and benefits go well together, but are often overused, overstated, or not correctly combined. A feature without a benefit is little more than a chest-thumping generality that will quickly try the reader's patience.

Above all, the Executive Summary is meant to sell by capturing interest with good writing and strong selling themes.

Technical Section

The Technical Section serves as the cornerstone for all other parts of the proposal. In one sense, the Technical Section represents the product that is being sold. The Executive Summary has explained why something should be purchased; the Technical Section explains what is being purchased and provides sufficient evidence that its claims can be verified. It provides the basis for the management volume that usually follows, and explains how the product will be installed, tested, serviced, and managed.

The primary purpose of the Technical Section is to define the product using the requirements in the RFP. A thorough understanding of the requirements must be demonstrated first in order to convince the customer that your solution is based on his needs. This understanding of requirements and needs expressed in the RFP becomes the basis for the Technical Section.

Tip

The Technical Section is the product that is being sold.

In addition to providing a detailed description of the solution and the products that make up that solution, the Technical Section must demonstrate your knowledge and understanding of the business issues that are driving the RFP.

Who Reads the Technical Section?

The Technical Section is read by the people who developed the RFP and who will be responsible for the project. This group is composed primarily of technical people, and although they may read other sections, they will approach this section from a technical point of view rather than from a marketing and sales or pricing perspective. This is not to say they will not understand marketing-generated benefits or a five-year pricing model.

Although evaluators of the Technical Section are generally competent in their individual areas of expertise, they may not be familiar with your technology and industry. Therefore, your Technical Section should make no assumptions concerning their knowledge or readiness to embrace your technology. It should be written on a level that is consistent with the audience's level of technological sophistication, but care should be taken to explain industry-specific concepts and, especially, concepts that are unique to your technology and company.

Development of the Technical Section

The RFP may provide specific instructions for the Technical Section or it may be very unstructured, offering little or no guidance. Whether the RFP instructions are specific or very loose, they are written as generalized guidelines that may reflect several authors' opinions, biases, and ignorance. This means that unless you completely wire the RFP to favor one vendor or technology, the Technical Section guidelines probably will not be

Tip ▷ The Technical Section should make no assumptions concerning the evaluators' knowledge and acceptance of your technology.

completely suitable for your company and its product. It is your responsibility to ensure that your story is properly presented, that you establish the forum needed to tell your story, and that this is done in a manner consistent with the spirit of the RFP. It will not be beneficial for you or the customer to ignore the RFP instructions and guidelines because you think you have a better idea and method for presenting your material.

The basic technical volume should contain the following:

- *Section overview.* The overview provides a short explanation of how the section is organized and may provide some additional information.
- *Introduction.* The introduction contains a technical discussion of the problem. This is a statement of your interpretation of the issues driving the RFP.
- *Technical solution.* The technical solution is how you propose to solve the problem.
- *Product(s) descriptions.* The description shows how your individual products are addressing each of the needs in the RFP.
- *Assumptions.* Some of the RFP's requirements may not be clear, and you have to make an assumption in order to explain why you are proposing a product.

Some of the items above may not be applicable—e.g., you may not be proposing computer equipment, or any equipment for that matter. However, whether you are bidding software products, engineering services, or maintenance services, the basic rules apply for a Technical Section just as they do for the Executive Summary and Management Section.

The following discussion of the section topics mentioned above is intended to supplement any proposal instructions you might have and provide you with examples. These examples will help you get started if the RFP contains little or no guidance.

> *Tip* Introduce the section by demonstrating you understand the problem and how to deal with it.

Section Overview

The section overview is a one- or two-paragraph introduction containing a brief statement concerning any issues that have been discussed outside of the RFP, and a statement addressing any issues concerning the RFP requirements. The overview may be used even if there are proposal instructions that outline the technical sections. It is possible to include a paragraph head, such as *Overview,* at the beginning of the section. This overview may report that several paragraphs have been added to the format to clarify your proposal. The following is a brief example of a section overview:

> *Section 2 of our proposal follows the proposal instructions. In addition, we have repeated verbatim, in italics, the requirement from the RFP that is being responded to before the response. Our response is based upon your requirements, information that was released during the bidders' conference, and two subsequent site visits and discussions.*
>
> *This section is fully compliant with all requirements. We have made a general assumption concerning the difference between the normal input rates and peak input rates. This assumption is documented in paragraph 3.5. We have also, based on this assumption, provided an alternate solution to the peak load requirements by proposing a split work shift.*

Notice how the introduction brought forward the assumption that is going to be made later in the section. This brief mention will help the reader to remember that the writer is proposing something that may differ from the RFP because, in the writer's opinion, not enough information was provided.

Introduction

This paragraph should be as concise as possible in restating the key issues driving the RFP. If the RFP is for

> *Tip* The overview section briefly discusses any previously addressed outside issues and RFP requirements.

a computer office-automation system, the key issues will revolve around worker productivity, greater office efficiencies, lower expenses, better customer service, and how these improvements will increase the customer's profit margin—whether it be by reducing expenses or increasing volume without increasing expenses.

The introduction reveals your *insight* into the issues and provides you the initial forum to establish your solution, or (as discussed in Chapter 1), the third level of writing in which you develop a business case for your solution.

Finally, after you have demonstrated your understanding of the requirements and shown how meeting those requirements will increase profitability, you should provide a technical summary of the solution. For example, one proposal for office automation equipment summarized its solution this way:

> *The technical solution is based on an open and adaptable architecture with a demonstrated commitment to industry standards. Workstations are PC-compatible, running standard software and connected together using your existing Ethernet. Scanners and printers are standard industry models and may be dedicated to individual personal computers or become multi-use. This configuration is easily adaptable to a changing environment.*

Technical Solution

In this section of your proposal, you will be required to explain in detail your solution and how it meets all requirements that are in the RFP. Generally, this section is a direct response to the requirements presented in the Technical Section of the RFP, and you will be requested in the instructions to follow the format of that section. For example, in an RFP to purchase an office automation system, the Technical Section will list and describe specific functions the equipment must perform; what type

Tip
The introduction reveals your insight into issues and how you can develop a business case for your solution.

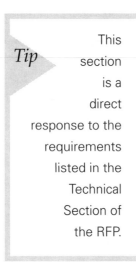

Tip This section is a direct response to the requirements listed in the Technical Section of the RFP.

of communications capabilities are needed based on the amount of traffic over the network; what is expected of the data server in terms of number of people connected to it; how much data storage is anticipated; what the response time should be; and what type of work is to be performed at the workstations, such as word processing, desktop publishing, spreadsheets and accounting, e-mail, etc. An excellent method for responding to this type of request is to repeat the requirement from the RFP and then respond to that requirement directly below it, as shown in Figure 6-1.

Responses to requirements should be brief, but provide enough information to satisfy the reader. Information that is more detailed or too detailed to be presented in this section can be included in an appendix, as discussed below.

FIGURE 6-1 Requirement/Response Format

3.4.1 System Security

RFP Requirement
The system must provide the capability to detect false log-ons and lock a workstation in which three efforts to log on have failed. Upon three failed attempts, the data server will lock the workstation, record the time and date, identify the workstation, and alert the system operator.

Response
The AJAX system is capable of detecting false log-on attempts, locking that workstation, recording the attempt in the system log, and notifying the system operator. The AJAX security system is user-programmable, with lockout periods assigned by the system operator. Lockout periods are defined at the time of system initiation and may be changed as a group or individually thereafter. The AJAX system will also allow the system administrator to define the number of log-on attempts before locking a terminal. These features are included in a simple user interface that makes customizing the program easy to revise and monitor.

See Appendix E, Operating System Security, for a detailed explanation of the security system features and options.

Notice that this proposal not only addresses the basic requirement in the RFP, but also provides additional functionality. The clear and concise description shows that product features and benefits more than satisfy the requirement. While not every sentence written in a proposal must conform to the need/feature/benefit style of writing, it is important to identify the requirements that may have additional evaluation weight and respond to them with added detail.

Product Descriptions

Product data sheets, manuals, brochures, and information gleaned from many other areas are the sources for data in your proposal. Many RFPs require product descriptions in the Technical Section, and this may create a problem. These descriptions can be very long, technical, and difficult to read. Although they relate to a requirement, such descriptions do not lend themselves to supporting the proposal themes and story. In many cases, long product descriptions can actually interrupt the narrative and themes in your proposal. It is not advisable to simply dump the contents of a data sheet or a product manual into your proposal in response to a particular requirement.

It is possible to satisfy all requirements by using short, summarized versions of the product descriptions for the Product Section, and placing the complete product description in an appendix. This approach has several benefits for both you and the reader. It allows you to tailor the short versions to the specific proposal being written by including pertinent, but not highly technical information about the proposed project, the customer, and your proposal themes. In addition, it saves the reader from having to read or skip over pages of heavy technical material that may not be relevant to the first reading of the proposal. If the reader requires more information, the full product description is available in the appendix.

Tip In the body of the text use short, summarized product descriptions and include more details in an appendix.

It is typical for the evaluation team to do a "quick read" of the proposals in an effort to eliminate proposals that are not compliant or do not provide adequate responses to requirements. By keeping the detail to a "responsive" level, you allow the evaluator a "quick read" of your proposal, and it will then be passed on to the second evaluation stage. Proposals making it to the second stage get a much closer reading and a more detailed evaluation.

By placing information that is highly technical in the appendix, you will be able to include more feature/benefit information in the product description than originally anticipated.

Proposal writers often condense product descriptions in an effort to make the proposal smaller and more readable. The result of this abbreviated product description is that the information is incomplete, and the reader may have to make assumptions about the product or submit a question to you and wait for your answer. Either way, you are not controlling the reader's expectations and this lessens the overall impact of your proposal. By providing the full version of technical material in the appendix, the reader is able to research questions and get answers without too much frustration or time spent. Condensing information without providing the full text can even lead the evaluator to consider your proposal nonresponsive.

Assumptions

Often, RFPs do not include sufficient information, whether due to oversight or lack of experience on the part of the authors, leaving you with many unanswered questions. However, it is possible the customer will not know all the answers and will ask you to make assumptions to fill in the information you need. It is also possible that, due to time constraints and unforeseen issues, you will be unable to ask questions and receive the information you need in time to finish your proposal. Making

Tip When making an assumption, be sure the reader understands what it is based on.

assumptions is a standard method for continuing to work on a proposal when some of the information is missing.

Assumptions should be based on your expertise in the subject area. Carefully document and support any assumptions in your proposal by providing as much information as needed to explain why you had to make an assumption and what information the assumption is based on.

Figure 6-2 is an example taken from an RFP that allowed assumptions under two conditions:

1. Lack of information about the project and the application
2. A choice between two methodologies

The first condition refers to the customer who is not a technical expert (as is often the case) and is depending on the vendors to provide the best solution or ask the right questions. Your solution may involve technology the customer is unfamiliar with, or your approach to the application design may be different from what the customer anticipated.

The second condition may be a result of the proposed technology. If, for example, an RFP requests personal computers capable of providing desktop publishing, accounting, word processing, and general office automation, there are at least three types of computers that could fulfill these requirements: Intel-based PCs, Apple computers, and UNIX-based personal computers.

If this were the case for your proposal, you would explore the three alternatives (including a "positives" and "negatives" discussion for each choice) and then make your recommendation. Your recommendation would be based on your knowledge of the customer, several assumptions about the long-term requirements, and the product fit.

Making assumptions can be risky however, if your knowledge of the customer or products involved is inadequate, or you're not totally sure what the customer

> *Tip* If your knowledge is inadequate or incorrect making assumptions can be risky.

FIGURE 6-2 Assumptions

This section of the proposal will provide a detailed description of the system solution proposed by the vendor. The section should include the following subsections:

A. *Understanding the Problem.* Vendors will demonstrate that they have fully understood the problems addressed in this RFP and on site visits. Each vendor must demonstrate a clear understanding of this industry, our needs in relation to this industry, and the needs of our customers. Vendors must also demonstrate that they have examined the present system volumes and the projected system volumes, and can discuss potential problems and what tradeoffs must be made—if any. Any assumptions made in making the overall system design should be stated and clarified. Clarification falls into two categories:

- Assumptions made due to a lack of information about the project and the application
- Assumptions made due to a choice between two methodologies

B. *Technical Solution.* This subsection will provide a complete definition of the vendor's proposed system solution. The proposal must address all phases of the proposed vendor-client relationship as follows:

- Detailed system design
- System development
- System integration
- Initial installation

The technical solution will be reviewed for scope and completeness. All areas detailed in Section 3 of the RFP must be addressed. The vendor will demonstrate how he will meet the business requirements of the proposed system.

wants. Basing a solution on a wrong assumption can contribute to losing the proposal. For example, one computer company based its solution on using previously installed equipment at the customer's site. The assumption was that because this equipment was still operational, the customer wanted to retain the equipment. Several proposal themes demonstrated how cost-effective the proposed solution would be, in addition to demonstrating technical ability to interface with the existing equipment. This proposal lost simply because the customer was looking for a solution that would replace existing equipment.

Summary

The primary goal of the Technical Section is to demonstrate your product's ability to meet the requirements set forth in the RFP. The demonstrated solution must be presented in such a manner that it is clear to people not familiar with your products and shown to be superior to the competition's proposals. (Remember, the RFP team is evaluating many proposals whose technology they may not be familiar with.)

The second goal of the Technical Section is to demonstrate your understanding of the customer's requirements, along with your ability to anticipate and resolve problems, complete the design, and provide a workable solution.

The third goal of the Technical Section is to showcase your product's features and benefits in such a way that your solution proves to be superior to other proposed products and solutions.

Although there are aspects to winning a proposal that are clearly outside of the RFP, such as account knowledge and familiarity, insider relationships and information, and company politics, you must have a basis for winning the proposal and that basis is the technical solution. If your solution is clearly superior to other solutions, you can overcome objections that relate to nontechnical aspects such as maintenance, training, company history, and a smaller installed base than your competitors are offering. Without a solid and technically correct solution, you lessen your ability to negotiate with the customer.

The Technical Section of your proposal can become an unusually difficult section to structure and write. While it contains the very heart of your proposal, it generally is not given the attention devoted to the Executive Summary or Pricing Section because fewer people understand the product at this level. And because fewer people are available to write it, and it is one of the larger sections of most proposals, this section often will take longer than planned to complete. The

Tip ▶ Without a technical solution, there is no chance of winning.

time factor becomes even more critical because you cannot finish other sections until the Technical Section is complete.

These potential problems may be compounded by circumstances that are outside of the proposal effort but directly influence the project. For example, a systems analyst who is responsible for customer accounts, presales calls, and other sales activities generally writes the Technical Section of a proposal for a computer system. This person is also responsible for customer-account management, including loading new software, trouble-shooting, and managing problems. These duties may require the analyst to be at a customer's site instead of writing the proposal. As these are unforeseen problems, it is wise to start the Technical Section as early as possible with the goal of having a rough draft well before the deadline. Once the rough draft is complete, others can help fine-tune, edit, and make corrections as needed.

The Technical Section must make liberal use of illustrations, graphics, charts, and other means of communicating what the product looks like, what it does, the technical trade-offs made, and other visual means of presenting your story. This is especially important because technical data tends to be densely written and dry. The illustrations will help to break up—and amplify the value of—your text.

Because this part of the proposal is very technical and difficult for the reader, it is important to continue weaving in your sales themes, benefits, and product superiority. In addition, a consistent style and method of responding to the requirements facilitate the reading of this section. Finally, do not overwrite the Technical Section by throwing in every datasheet or every bit of documentation you can find. Overwriting the Technical Section will frustrate the reader who is looking for straightforward answers.

Tip Add graphics to this section!

Management Section

The Management Section assures the buyer that you have the experience, facilities, personnel resources, and ability to provide and install what has been proposed. This section displays your understanding of complex issues such as site preparation, equipment installation, test procedures, and education of users.

The Management Section determines what personnel are required from both companies, defining their relationship (who has responsibility for which requirements) and how the work will be accomplished. In addition to the people required for the project, the Management Section provides insight into what physical resources will be required and who is responsible for supplying those resources.

This section is as important as the technical solution. If you are not able to install and service your equipment properly, the customer may pick another solution. This is true especially when proposing a solution that will become part of a company's line-of-business operation.

In short, the Management Section is a master project plan with added detail about the tasks and steps in the plan.

Who Reads the Management Section?

The RFP team reads the Management Section, and personnel concerned with training, testing, and maintenance may be among the reviewers. Once you have convinced the evaluators that your proposed solution is the correct solution, the next step is to convince them that you can install and maintain the system. The people reading the Management Section are now interested in *how* you are going to implement your product or service. In this regard, the Technical and Management Sections must work together in order to have a consistent theme.

For example, in one proposal by a major computer company, the technical volume stressed ease of installation, no requirements for a special computer room for

> *Tip* The Management Section provides insight into what physical resources will be required and who is responsible for supplying those resources.

Even service-based proposals can have a management plan. A service, such as a counseling service, may require such items as site preparation (the room in which the service takes place) and facilities preparation such as a telephone, furniture, etc. There will also be a schedule for various events that need to happen prior to the service being started.

cooling and cable runs, and some basic functionality once the system was running and tested. However, the Management Section stressed the need for a large and involved project team to oversee installation and testing of the equipment. The complexity of the management plan was not consistent with the technical volume's theme of simple installation. As a result, the vendor lost the project.

As with the Technical Section, the Management Section must stress your understanding of the problem (the need), and use the need/features/benefits style of writing to emphasize why your management planning is superior to that of other companies.

Development of the Management Section

Many RFPs do not require a Management Section, simply asking for information about your company's service or training. RFPs that do require a Management Section often make it a part of the Technical Section. The following examples show different requirements for the Management Section.

> *Management. This section should include a description of the bidding firm, including age of company, number of years in business, number of employees, sales for most recent year, and a description of at least three currently installed systems of similar size.*

Here we see a request for information about the vendor's management and company, but no request for

> *Tip* — Even if not required, you should consider including a project Management Section.

information about installation, testing, and acceptance. Though not specifically requested, it is still advisable to add details about how you will maintain and install your products.

Management Support and Experience. This section should describe how the vendor proposes to service and support the equipment being proposed. Vendors must provide five reference sites that have similar applications and equipment.

In this second example, the RFP is asking for a description of service and support, but does not mention installation, project planning, training, etc. In both examples, the system proposed was worth well over a million dollars and required a considerable amount of coordination between the vendor, subcontractors, and the customer.

This last example is from an RFP for a very large system that required more than a year of work before it was brought online.

Vendors must demonstrate in this subsection their approach to the design, development, and installation phases of the project. A description of each task proposed by the vendor to meet the requirements of this RFP must be included. The proposal must also include a summary and detailed schedule indicating task start and completion dates, total time to complete the task and the vendor resources required for the tasks. For each task identified, the total vendor days estimated to complete the task must be listed.

By asking for basic information about design, development, and installation phases, these instructions provide a clear outline for a Management Section. The vendor is being asked to think through his solution and plan for setbacks, delays, and conflicts, in addition to addressing the project at a task level. This degree of detail requires vendors to have an established project management group that is familiar with project planning and implementation services. Vendors who do not have this expertise will be quickly disqualified.

Below is a suggested outline for a Management Section. The outline is generic but does mirror the basic sections of a complete Management Section. At the minimum, this section should include an introduction to the proposed management plan, what your capabilities are, who is responsible for installation and acceptance, and what the customer's responsibilities are. It is possible to place descriptions of the service and maintenance plan, training classes, and corporate profile in this section.

- Introduction
- Project Management Approach
- Project Organization and Responsibilities
- Management of Subcontractors
- Project Plan
- Project Schedule
- Site Preparation Configuration
- Acceptance Testing and Sign-off
- Service and Maintenance Program
- Education and Training Program
- Project Personnel Resumes
- Corporate Reference Accounts
- Corporate History

Using Proposal Boilerplate Material

The management volume is a good place to make use of the prewritten materials known as boilerplate files. Many management documents can be developed, standardized, and incorporated in a boilerplate library ready for use in all proposal efforts. For RFPs that do require additional information not included in the boilerplate file, the document can be easily modified to suit each RFP effort. The following is a list of potential boilerplate documents:

- *Resumes.* Complete resumes for key company officers, account executives, project managers, lead engineers, and product developers who may be working on projects. You may also have resumes for senior management: presidents, vice presidents, CEOs, COOs, CIOs, etc.
- *Corporate profile.* A standard company description should be written to include such information as history, company goals, personnel, manufacturing locations, and major product lines.
- *Service department.* Normally, there are standard policies and contracts that state how a company maintains its products. Rewrite these policies and contracts to provide a general description of your maintenance department and the services it provides. Use this as a template when adding specific information in response to an RFP requirement.
- *Education department.* If your products require training, there will be a training department with class descriptions and dates. Write an overview of your training department to include such information as your training philosophy, description of classes and instructors (i.e., what types, and how much experience), and how professional course designers develop classes.

    Education is an important prerequisite for selling. Promote specialized training such as computer-based training (CBT), video-based training (VBT), or other unique methods of training—especially if your competition is behind in this area.
- *Reference accounts.* Most RFPs require that you provide at least three reference accounts. These references will be used to verify your product works as stated, your company's performance in such areas as installation and service, and overall performance as a company. This kind of material may include very brief histories of the referenced companies,

why your company was chosen, and what equipment or service is currently in place at the customer's facility. A designated contact, with name, title, phone number, and address, is also provided.

Choose reference accounts to match the proposed business application. For example, if you were bidding on an HR computer system, you would try to have references to similar HR applications that your company has provided.

- *Project Management.* Many companies that have project management departments develop or employ a standard methodology. Based on the standard organization and method employed, this file would contain a statement of work, the project plan, and a schedule.

Chapter 10, "Preparing and Managing Boilerplate Files," discusses suitable subject matter for prewritten material and includes samples of a resume, corporate profile, maintenance schedule, class description, reference account, and organization charts.

Having boilerplate files on standard business areas will save you enormous amounts of time. Imagine having to create from scratch three reference accounts, or tailoring the education department offerings by rekeying information from a brochure. Time can be better spent developing the solution or working on the pricing, which typically don't receive enough attention.

Installation and Implementation
Installation and implementation are closely related activities and are generally tied together in an RFP. Installation refers specifically to hardware/software/ product installation, what work is required before it can be installed, and what is needed during the installation. Implementation refers to the project in general and how the application is developed, how and when training occurs, how system cutover will be achieved, etc.

If your proposal requires installation of equipment, and certain prerequisites must be met, develop an installation plan as part of your proposal. Include a project schedule broken into task-level detail and relative dates. For example, if you are proposing a computer system that requires a special computer room, a controlled environment, filtered power lines, communication lines, and myriad other details, an installation schedule will be required if the system is to be installed on time. Generally, computer companies do not install computer rooms, which means that the customer is responsible for ensuring that computer facilities will be adequate for the system being purchased. However, it is your responsibility to provide the customer with the specifications for your equipment.

Many companies have an installation guide that outlines the exact operating specifications and all other requirements for their equipment. This guide is usually sent with the proposal as an appendix and referred to when writing the installation section.

Implementation takes a broader view of the project schedule. It is concerned with identifying all of the project tasks and listing those tasks in a complete project schedule. Although the actual scheduled dates may change, the task list should not—unless the project itself changes during final negotiations. The purpose of the implementation plan is to identify and break down the overall program into smaller, and hence more manageable, pieces. Once all tasks have been identified, they can be organized by related groups, interdependencies can be established, schedules developed, and work assignments made.

For example, if you were bidding on installing a computer system, you'd want to divide the implementation plan into major tasks, then subdivide those tasks into subtasks required to complete that piece of work. This task list and schedule will help you establish what tasks need to be performed before other tasks can be performed

Tip

It is important for the customer to know which work is his and when it needs to be completed.

(interdependencies), and what tasks can be performed simultaneously. Figure 6-3 shows a simplified task list and schedule for a computer project.

FIGURE 6-3 Sample Project Management Schedule

ID	Task Name
1	**Project Initiation & Control**
2	Organize Project
19	Project Control
25	Hardware Ordering and Acquisitions
29	Software Ordering and Acquisitions
34	Site Configuration and Site Survey
35	Schedule Site Survey
36	Obtain Facilities Layout
37	Obtain Detailed Writing Schematics
42	Installation Plan
43	Site Preparation Plan
44	Site Equipment Plan
45	Installation Schedule
46	Phase One—Backfile Conversion Muni and Superior Courts
47	Functional Design Stage
48	Conduct High-Level Application Analysis
60	Review Reporting Requirements
72	Finalize Workflow Application Requirements Definition
78	System Requirements Analysis
89	Technical Design Stage
103	Establish Security Rules
107	Develop Application
112	Application Interface Development
117	Hardware Installation/Platform Services
118	Receive HW for Internal Testing
119	Install HW for Internal Testing
120	Test Hardware
121	Verify Hardware Configuration
122	Ship HW to Marin Installation
123	Prepare Site for Hardware Installation
124	Verify Site Preparation
125	Install HW at Marin Site
126	Configure Hardware at Marin Site
127	Load All Third-Party Software

FIGURE 6-3 Sample Project Management Schedule, continued

ID	Task Name
128	Exercise and Tune all SW and Peripherals
129	Review/Accept HW Installation
130	Software Installation at Marin Site
131	Test and Verify Network Connectivity
132	Install Software
133	Establish Interface Terminal Emulation Connectivity
134	Full System Testing
135	System Acceptance and Test Plan
136	Prepare Draft of Acceptance Test Plan
141	Submit Final Test Plan to Marin
142	Perform System Acceptance Tests
143	System Acceptance
144	Sign Ready-for-Use
145	Backfile Conversion
148	Production Cutover
150	Develop Custom Reports
151	Review Technical Report Specifications
152	Present Custom Design for Approval
153	Develop and Test Reports
154	Verify Test Specifications
155	Document Custom Reports
156	Deliver Custom Reports
157	Develop Procedures and Documentation
158	Prepare System Administration Documentation
162	Deliver System Admin Documentation
163	Develop End-User Documentation
168	Deliver End-User Documentation
169	Develop Users' Manual
170	Training
171	Schedule System Admin Training
172	Deliver System Admin Training at Marin
173	Schedule End-User Training
174	Deliver End-User Training at Marin
175	Provide Training

This plan has been "collapsed" to just the major tasks and some of the subtasks, as you can see from the numbering. Your company might want to develop a "standard" project task list that can be customized for each project. The proposal would include the standard list customized as much as possible for the proposal.

Project Organization and Key Project Personnel

RFPs for large complex systems often require an organization chart and resumes for the personnel who will be involved in the project. The organization chart identifies the project leader and defines the structure of the program; it also identifies key personnel by name and position (see Figure 6-4).

Present the organizational relationship in two charts. The first identifies where the proposed project resides within your organization, and the second is the organization of the project. The customer is usually very interested in where the project resides within your organization and how close or far away it is from upper management. Even a simple diagram, as shown above, provides the customer with some sense of the project organization.

FIGURE 6-4 Sample Organizational Chart

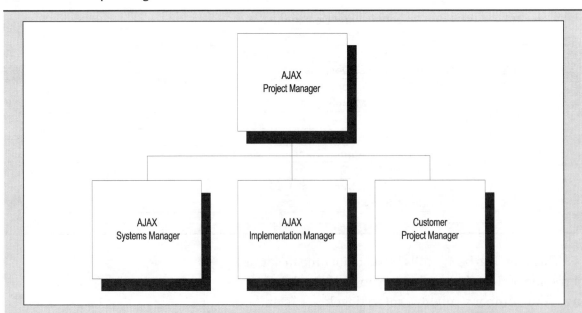

Resumes should be prepared in a standard format and generally be consistent in content (i.e., the depth of information provided). Rewrite resumes of project personnel to emphasize staff skills needed for the current project. A standard format may include

- name.
- title.
- corporate project experience.
- education.

Information about experience should begin with the last job completed, followed by a description of the person's role in the current project. This type of resume is not the same as a job applicant's resume. Chapter 10, Preparing and Managing Boilerplate Files, discusses formats for organization charts and resumes in detail.

Summary

Having a strong management volume can be a deciding factor in the evaluation of your proposal. Often, a technical evaluation staff recommends at least two companies whose solutions meet all requirements. If the prices are also similar, the evaluation may focus on the information in the management volume. Such requirements as project management, experience with similar applications, maintenance, education, references, or your company's financial profile may be stronger than the competition's and give you the extra points required to win. There may also be intangible benefits derived from a strong Management Section. For example, providing a project plan, complete with the names of the personnel involved, their positions, duties, and resumes, can strongly suggest to the customer that your company is well organized, with the ability to execute your plan.

Pricing Section

Rounding out the basic proposal format is the pricing section. This section is perhaps the most misunderstood,

> *Tip* Planning is a key indicator to the customer of our capabilities.

has the most misconceptions about it, and generates the most debate when talked about after a long day of writing. Its value and worth should not be underestimated.

Who Reads the Pricing Section?

The RFP team reads the Pricing Section and may be supported by purchasing and the accounting group if it is complex enough. However, everyone associated with the RFP, and some who are not, will look at this section. Pricing is often the first part of a proposal looked at and will be the first subject discussed by the RFP team.

Pricing is difficult to evaluate. A "price," which is the bottom line, is really composed of many parts, and the dollar amount in any one section will not directly compare to all other proposals.

Let's look at an example. You want to buy a car and you have a certain budget. You have narrowed the choices down to two cars from different manufacturers (the short list!). The higher-priced car does not have as many features as the lower-priced car, which features a larger engine, a sunroof, and leather seats. However, the higher-priced car offers a better warranty and a better service record. Based on looks, you could go with either car.

If you were to evaluate the differences, you might find that in the long run, the higher-priced car is less expensive because it will require less service over the life of the car. On the other hand, you really want the extra power and the leather seats.

In this case, salesmanship will make the deal. As with a proposal, the salesman has to help the customer make a decision and will try to influence the sale by homing in on what the real requirements are, based on his reading of the customer.

I bring this up because in many cases, the buyer will try to get down to a short list of two vendors whose proposals are roughly equal. The decision could go either way, but most likely it will come down to a comparison of features/benefits vs. price. While price may not have been a deciding factor in the initial evaluation, it becomes part of the deciding factor for the final decision.

While it is entirely possible that the higher-priced proposal may win, it would be because the buyer believes that he is getting a better value per dollar. Notice that *value* is the more important part of the equation.

In smaller, less formal companies that issue RFPs, evaluation of prices is often performed by the technical evaluators. This group may be less skilled in pricing analysis and value projections, and therefore their analysis may relate more directly to the established budget and comparative pricing.

If you can determine who will be reviewing your Pricing Section, it could influence the amount of information you provide, as well as your method of organizing and presenting the information.

Development of the Pricing Section

The content of the Pricing Section will vary widely. It may be as simple as an equipment list with prices, or so detailed as to include your cost-estimating techniques. Many proposals are delivered with standard unit pricing and extended pricing that is taken from the established price book. Even large multimillion-dollar proposals prepared for state or federal governments use prices directly from their established price guides.

If the RFP provides instructions for setting up the section, these instructions *must be followed*. They should be read and understood well before the proposals are due because they may necessitate work you had not anticipated. In addition, the pricing instructions are mixed together with contract instructions, which may require that you review the contract and provide feedback on any items you may question. The example below is a typical

Tip Guidelines for pricing vary widely. Be prepared to be creative.

request in a pricing instruction that requires you to provide more than a simple lump-sum price.

Vendors shall provide purchase prices and installation costs for each equipment item, software product, and service proposed. All elements of recurring and nonrecurring costs which must be borne by ACME Banking shall be identified. This includes, but is not limited to, hardware maintenance, system engineering, manuals and documentation, consultation, training, conversion services, shipping charges, installation costs, acceptance testing, and taxes.

The Pricing Section is known for its complexity and may require considerable thought and calculation to arrive at a price. For example, if the project is for developing a computer system that requires custom code, the effort to price this code may take several weeks and involve personnel from engineering, project management, contracts, and pricing. Pricing is difficult because it is often the case that you can't price the item until programming has been estimated, and the programming estimation may come only after the proposal team decides exactly what is to be built.

Generally speaking, companies that have established products with part numbers and commercially available established prices are not asked to break products into component parts and then justify how the costs for individual parts were determined. This type of pricing is requested only in RFPs that require the vendor to build unique one-time-only products. For example, when pricing a PC, the vendor would not normally be asked to price the Ethernet card or the SCSI card separately.

If you are bidding for state or federal contracts, the pricing may be based on the General Services Administration (GSA) price list. A GSA price list is used by the federal government to establish your lowest price for each product. Once you have established pricing for the GSA, you must be very cautious when bidding prices go lower than those established, whether to a commercial customer or to another federal customer.

A careful reading and understanding of the GSA contract is required for anyone writing proposals in the federal sector. If you have a GSA contract but do not completely understand it, ask for an appointment at your local federal contracting office.

Organization of the Pricing Section

The Pricing Section generally contains

- product/service/equipment and license-price breakdown.
- services and education.
- totals.
- shipping schedules.
- payment schedules.
- standard terms and conditions.

Tip Review and follow all RFP instructions.

If your proposal is sufficiently detailed to warrant an in-depth Pricing Section, but the RFP does not ask for detailed responses, you can use the pricing outline in Figure 6-5 as a guide. This outline comes from an RFP that was released to procure a very large computer system. If your proposal includes project management, acceptance testing, and other tasks that you normally charge for, it may be difficult to find a place in the RFP's pricing model for these prices. The pricing model you build for your proposal must meet, at a minimum, the model requested in the RFP. The outline in Figure 6-5 exemplifies a well-organized pricing section, and may provide you with additional ideas to include in your proposal's Pricing Section.

Remember that it's a good idea to provide the customer with a separate price volume so that people who evaluate the proposal are not influenced by the price. It is wise, even if not requested, to create a separately bound price volume, mark it as such, and if possible, give it to

FIGURE 6-5 Pricing Outline

Product Description	Total Price	Annual Maintenance	Annual License
System Hardware			
System Software			
Application Software (Product)			
Application Development			
Project Management/Integration			
Training			
Documentation			
Miscellaneous (Detail provided below.)			
Shipping			
Taxes			
Total			

Example only, supplier to complete.

the purchasing agent. Make only one copy and mark it *CONFIDENTIAL and PROPRIETARY*—unless, of course, you are asked to provide pricing with the main proposal. Meticulously follow the instructions provided in the RFP.

It is also possible and *sometimes* allowed to turn in the cost volume one or two weeks after the main proposal is due. This is because pricing a large proposal often cannot be completed until the configuration, equipment lists, and personnel requirements are finalized. These may not be ready far enough in advance to allow the pricing volume to be complete at the same time as the main technical sections. Discuss this possibility with the purchasing agent designated in the RFP.

Government RFPs, whether state or federal, sometimes provide you with a series of forms that constitute the price volume. These are fill-in-the-blanks forms, and you have no choice but to comply. Figure 6-6 is a sample pricing for PCs.

FIGURE 6-6 Sample Pricing for PCs

Item	Quantity	Unit Price	Extended Price	Maintenance Price/Year
PC	5	3000.00	15,000.00	150.00
Monitor	5	600.00		
SCSI	5	50.00		
Hard drive	10	150.00		
Ethernet	5	25.00		

Pricing Strategies for Your Proposal

It is often difficult, if not impossible, to determine the budget for the project being proposed. Most often, the sales representative is asked, "What's their bogey? What do we have to come in at to be competitive?" Using this kind of "insider" information, the sales rep determines a figure, which becomes the target (or "bogey," in proposal-ese).

While it may not matter in some respects, the customer may have totally misjudged the amount of money he'd need for a project. (The misjudgment is rarely on the plus side!) So while the vendors' pricing may be within 10 percent of one another, it could also be 50 percent off from what was budgeted by the customer. Thus, it is equally important to understand how both the customer and the competition have determined their bogeys.

Inevitably, a certain amount of gamesmanship is displayed before completing the Pricing Section. The sales representative will want to have full list price for those items that he receives commission on, and a healthy discount on those items he does not receive commission on. And he will want to provide a number of things free, such as an extra training class, a no-charge project review, or an extra set of manuals.

These no-charge items, of course, come directly out of the training department's budget, or groups such as

Tip Estimated pricing is estimating what the customer thinks the budget will be.

This gets us back to qualifying the opportunity when the RFP is released. In one example, the customer put out an RFP for consulting services. Proposals came in at around $45,000 to $55,000, which is not too bad of a price spread for six vendors (especially considering the poorly written RFP). No contract was awarded! The customer had budgeted $20,000 for a $50,000 job. The difference was so great that even after reducing the requirements, vendors could not price below $30,000.

Tip > Creative thinking is often called for when pricing a proposal.

project management or manuals, which are considered profit centers. These groups are not willing to give their products away or even discount them because the margin made is often very small relative to the margin made on the primary products that the company makes and sells, such as hardware and software.

If the proposed price is too far out of range of the target, a price reduction has to occur if your proposal is to be considered competitive. Creative thinking is often called for to achieve the target price.

Discounting should not be the first option; it should be used last to arrive at the final target price, and only after all other "fat" has been trimmed from the proposed price. Your first consideration is the basic product that is being proposed. Using a computer system as an example, a thorough review of the hardware and software configuration frequently will turn up excess equipment to "cover the base." This excess is sometimes proposed to cover up a poor design or to provide an extra margin for specifications that are not completely understood. Sometimes excess equipment is proposed to dress up the system and add functionality that has not been requested and is not in the requirements.

After this excess equipment is taken out, turn your attention to the preliminary design for the project. Can the number of programmers be reduced without significant impact on the design itself or the delivery date?

Sometimes this can be achieved by rethinking the design schedule. Often, the application effort is overestimated because the RFP was not clear and a certain margin was built in to cover "project creep."

Revisit the RFP requirements that are suspect or not clear. Make an assumption, which is included in your proposal, and base your pricing on the assumption. This way, you can lower the price while leaving it open to negotiation if the customer disagrees with your assumption. Also, the idea of options may help reduce your costs by breaking big-cost items into component parts that the customer may select. Be careful with options because they may confuse the customer.

If the price is still high relative to the estimate, and as much excess as can comfortably be trimmed has been removed, then further price reductions may come from discounting.

Discounting has no common rules. The most frequently asked questions are: Do we just add a discount and not say anything? Do we attempt to explain it? What if the customer wants to know why? Several strategies may be used.

Tip High pricing often covers our lack of understanding of the RFP.

- *Large-quantity discount.* You explain that the customer qualifies for a quantity discount because he is buying more than X amount (usually ten).
- *New-account discount.* This discount is applied on a "one-time only" basis and applies only to new accounts.
- *Old-account discount.* This discount applies to "favored" customers who have consistently spent a large amount every year.
- *Showcase discount.* If the customer allows you to use the completed installation as a reference site for customer tours and verification of equipment operation, you will give them a discount.
- *Partnership-development discount.* This applies if you can convince the customer to allow you to beta test

a product or build a product that is unique to your product line and you "need customer input."

- *Try-and-buy discount.* If the customer is willing to give your product a chance for X amount of time, you will discount the basic product.
- *Straight discount.* You explain that this discount is used to get the business so you can meet your quota. The customer and salesperson win. The company may or may not win.

A note of caution: The practice of *selling discounts* instead of products can have long-range effects. A discount should have a reason and should be used for a single purchase only. *Discounting sets a precedent that is hard to overcome* once established, and can affect future relationships with a customer who comes to "expect" a lower price on everything, every time.

Tip	Discounting has no rules.

Summary

Because the Pricing Section is perhaps the most volatile portion of the proposal, it generally requires more time and effort than is normally expected—and at a time when everyone on the proposal team may be close to exhaustion or some sort of mayhem. This combination of factors can lead to a Pricing Section that is poorly written and carelessly conceived. On top of these problems, the Pricing Section is often the only one that gets management's attention (both yours and theirs). Frequently, your management will want a review of the Pricing Section, with detailed information about any deviations or discounts. Being bottom-line oriented, most managers take a critical look at the Pricing Section and are usually able to justify changing something. Such changes will further impact your ability to complete the section on time.

The only possible answer to these challenges is proper planning, strict adherence to a schedule, and the ability to be flexible and persevere.

- *Plan.* Having the pricing materials available and in place at the start of the proposal will help. If your company does not have any formal methodologies, at least collect several recently submitted proposals and copy what is applicable to yours. Be sure to follow RFP instructions on pricing and formatting.
- *Schedule.* Strictly adhere to a schedule that is functional and that includes time for management reviews.
- *Persevere.* Being in charge of a proposal is not always a popular task. Fellow workers tend to steer clear of you, managers can get very busy on other projects, and people in other departments often drift away because they do not directly report to you. If you have planned correctly, have kept to your schedule, and know this proposal is a winner, it is up to you to simply outlast everyone else to get the job done.

Finally, after you submit your proposal and make the short list, you must anticipate and be prepared for customer changes. These changes can take several forms: a customer may want to add or subtract equipment; she may strive for a price reduction at the expense of functionality; or some totally unexpected requests could arise, forcing you back to the drawing board. However, whatever the changes, they will affect your pricing schedule. This last stage may afford a good opportunity for you to win—if you outlast your competition and continue to provide quality and professional answers.

The Proposal Appendixes

An appendix is a separate section of your proposal that contains supplemental bulky information. Generally, this information is considered of value to an evaluator, but may be too detailed to be included in the main body of the proposal. For example, you may be writing about

Tip An appendix may provide more detailed information.

your software development methodology, but would not insert the "methodology manual" in the body of the proposal. If the manual is brief or a summary is available, you may refer the reader to "Appendix A, Summary of AJAX Software Development Methodology, for more complete details."

Some RFPs will require an appendix and will outline what material goes into the appendix. Most RFPs, however, do not require an appendix and therefore its inclusion is optional. As you did with other sections in your proposal, organize the appendix area early to minimize confusion.

Appendixes are named by letter, not number.

> Appendix A—Product Data Sheets
> Appendix B—Sample Contracts
> Appendix C—Training Schedule
> Appendix D—Maintenance Schedule
> Appendix E—Annual Report

The appendix section should be set up in the beginning stages of the proposal effort and a copy of its contents distributed with the proposal table of contents. If appendixes are established early, writers will be able to refer to the appropriate appendix letter as they write—"See Appendix C." In the absence of appendixes, writers might create their own, which may conflict with other appendixes and create confusion when the final version of the proposal is being read.

Any additional appendixes should be added to the end of the list and not inserted ahead of other letters. When an additional appendix is added ahead of other letters after the list has been established, there's always the chance that some writers will have already referred to the original list. Any writers who have not received the changed list will make incorrect references. Again, this may not be caught (if ever) until the proposal is being given a final review.

The appendix can provide any information that may be of value to your proposal. It can include separate

Tip Set up your appendix contents early to avoid confusion.

binders with technical manuals or nontechnical material such as

- annual and financial reports.
- company brochures and datasheets.
- reprints of articles about the company or product.
- industry surveys.
- industry analysts' reports.
- sample contracts.
- sample training class outlines.
- training schedules with places and dates.
- personnel policies and guidelines.
- unusual policies and procedures.
- whitepapers on your industry or company.

Although the appendix will help you organize material for your proposal, it should not contain information that is not directly related to your proposal. Each appendix should be referenced in the proposal and provide information that enhances or supplements the topic at hand. When an appendix is used to provide unrelated material, it lessens the impact of any material that does have value.

Unless requested in the RFP, material in an appendix may not be considered or read by the evaluators. Therefore, any material that is needed to satisfy a requirement in the RFP should be in the main body of the proposal. You should not depend on material in an appendix to satisfy requirements in an RFP.

Tip — Appendixes should not be used as dumping grounds for excess material. Material should be relevant and accessible.

Summary

We covered a lot of ground in this section. The proposal you submit should be well organized, information should flow naturally from one subject to the next, and the "sales pitch" should be understandable and supportable. Self-inflated claims such as ". . . the industry leader . . ." have little relevance and may do more harm than good. Boastful claims can mean that you are selling your company's image and not the product—most buyers will quickly see through this and consign your proposal to the "tossed" pile.

The sales message should be centered on features and benefits first, and comparisons to the competition second. Negative selling is never a wise course, but fair comparisons and assessments between competitive products have value. Remember that many product comparisons are meaningless unless the comparison treats the products equally on a feature-by-feature basis.

The proposal you write will be one of several read by evaluators. *Evaluators like proposals that make their job easy:* if your proposal follows the RFP instructions to the letter, it will be looked upon favorably. The more time an evaluator must put into searching for the answer to a requirement, the less time may be available for understanding whether the response is compliant or not.

If there are few or no proposal guidelines, use the general guidelines suggested in this section. When in doubt about this, always get clarification from the customer. When in doubt about the amount of writing needed, err on the light side. Too often proposals are so bloated that the real story never gets through.

FOLLOW THE SUBMISSION AND DELIVERY REQUIREMENTS

There are a number of items that must be reviewed when your proposal is ready for submission. These items are required by the RFP and include such activities as ensuring the specified proposal format has been complied with, correctly addressing the proposal package, and observing the delivery date.

Thoughtful attention to these matters is important enough to make the difference between winning and losing the contract. Generally speaking, there are two main areas of concern:

1. Submission criteria
2. Proposal delivery requirements

The following excerpt from an RFP explains why proposals have been disqualified by this company.

Many of the causes for rejection arose from either an incomplete understanding of the competitive bidding process or administrative oversight on the part of the bidders. The following examples are illustrative of the more common causes for rejection of bids:

- *A bid stated, "This proposal is not intended to be of a contractual nature."*
- *A bid was submitted that had not been signed by a properly authorized individual.*

I was in the top five remaining vendors when I made the most stupid mistake: I didn't correctly read an e-mail from the customer. Those of us who had made the first cut received an e-mail from the customer, requesting additional financial information. I misread the e-mail and sent the information, via e-mail, three hours after the requested time—on the same day! I asked if this would disqualify me. No answer. I waited, and the next week received a letter saying that I did not make the final cut. I called. "Yes," she said, "all other vendors sent their financial data in on time and we had to drop you from the final list." I lost this proposal because I didn't pay attention to the postproposal work.

- *A bid was delivered to the wrong office.*
- *A bid was delivered in an unsealed condition.*
- *A bid was submitted that was incomplete.*

A careful and experienced proposal writer understands the value and importance of sustaining the proposal effort beyond completion of the proposal itself. It is during the postproposal period that proposal team members are beginning to break apart and return to their "real" jobs. The team members are tired; they are concerned about work now awaiting them, and they want to get this proposal work behind them. However, if the same amount of effort as was given to proposal development is not spent in carefully attending to proposal submission requirements, control over meeting these requirements will be lost; details such as signing the requested documentation, packaging the proposal correctly, or even delivering it to the right address, will not be properly taken care of.

Tip There are several important postproposal activities not required by the RFP.

Submission Criteria

Most, if not all, RFPs contain simple, item-by-item instructions for format and content of your proposal. Often they're not read until the last minute when people need to have such information as how many copies are required and where they should be sent. The following topic headings have been taken from RFPs:

- Submission Criteria
- Vendor Instructions
- Proposal Preparation Instructions (PPI)
- Bidding Instructions
- Responsibilities of Vendor
- Appendix 1—Guidelines for Vendor's Proposal
- Section 11—General Instructions for Bidder
- Appendix B—Instructions for Technical Response

These instructions range in scope from very simple—indicating the name, address, and number of copies requested—to very complex. In one RFP, the instructions were included in an appendix that was more than 50 pages long and listed such details as the page length for each section and the size of the type. Missing the instructions or ignoring the submission criteria may result in the proposal being disqualified.

Sometimes the instructions are not found in a single section of the RFP but are spread throughout the RFP as part of the introductions to each major section When this is the case, there will be general instructions in the front of the RFP—name, place, time, number—but each section or volume will contain detailed information on the format for that section only. For example, the Cost Section or volume may contain detailed instructions for submitting costing information on an electronic spreadsheet.

These instructions provide information about working with the requestor: who the contact person is, how that person may be contacted, when and where the bidders' conference will be held, and whether attendance is mandatory. There is usually a paragraph that "expressly prohibits social or after-work invitations to personnel engaged in this Request for Proposals," and instructs that "all questions must be directed through the RFP administrator (name, address, etc.) and submitted in writing."

Tip Not reading all the instructions may result in your proposal being disqualified.

RFPs that require a standard format facilitate the evaluation process. Without these guidelines, there is often no adequate means of comparison among the many different proposals submitted. Proposals that follow the format guidelines offer evaluators an apples-to-apples comparison. This type of comparison allows your features and benefits to be more clearly understood because they can be easily compared to those of the competition.

General Submission Criteria

Before a proposal undergoes evaluation, it is checked into the system: copies are made, initial adherence to RFP submission criteria is checked, and there may also be an initial screening of the contents for conformance to required standards. Listed below are basic submission requirements that apply to all proposals. If proposal submission instructions are not provided, the following information should be requested from the customer:

- *Response due date and time.* If these are not provided, contact the person who released the request. Early submission of your proposal may not, in fact, be advantageous. Some companies and government agencies do not open the proposals or start the evaluation until all proposals are received. Early submission may increase the chance of your proposal being misplaced or even lost.

> *Tip* RFPs that require a standard format facilitate evaluation.

I was the RFP manager for a fairly large intranet project, and we had sent out our RFP to nine vendors. Since I wrote the RFP, the proposal preparation instructions were very clear and detailed. One particular instruction was that you could not "give" the RFP to another vendor or subcontractor without prior permission. One of the proposals received was from a company we did not send the RFP to, but this company was serving as the systems integrator for the company that actually received the bid. The RFP evaluation team agreed to disqualify that bid without reading it.

- *Number of copies.* The number of copies required will vary according to each RFP. Some companies ask for one master and then make their own duplicates of your proposal, and some request 15 or more. One RFP released by an international consortium required 125 copies of the proposal.

  An increasingly popular submission request is that you provide your proposal on a CD-ROM in addition to the hard copy. There are also requests to have proposals sent via e-mail or uploaded to an FTP (file transfer protocol) server site.

  This can all be quite complex if your proposal contains many different files, appendixes, and sales brochure materials. Be sure to read the submission instructions right away and be prepared to submit your proposal in a variety of formats. If you wait until the last minute, you may find that you can't e-mail your proposal, or that you don't have the necessary CD recording software.

- *Address.* A common question is: To whom do I address the proposal? Some sales reps have been in contact with a particular department manager but received the RFP from another manager in procurement. Even if you received the RFP as a result of your conversations with the RFP leader, *send your proposal to the name provided in the RFP.* If for some reason no name is given, write a question asking whom the proposal should be addressed to.

- *Packaging.* Depending on the size of your proposal and the number of copies requested, it may be possible to use a large envelope, or you may need to use multiple boxes. In all cases, though, the proposal *must be sealed.* Do not submit open binders with your business card stapled to the corner and a rubber band around the binder. (Believe it or not, this actually happened.)

Tip Be sure to seek clarification if you are not sure about the submission guidelines.

- *Markings.* Because most proposals are submitted to a procurement department, and held there until the RFP manager is ready to receive them, it is important to properly mark the proposal package with the RFP number and project name. This will help prevent a proposal from becoming misplaced or lost in the shuffle of proposals for other projects that are being submitted to the same office at the same time.

  Typical instructions might read: "All responses shall be marked with the solicitation number and the project name: Solicitation 92-057, 'Parts and Inventory Control Project.' Multiple packages shall be marked 'Box 1 of X.'" If you have three boxes, you would mark the first Box 1 of 3, the second Box 2 of 3, and the third Box 3 of 3. Each box will bear the RFP number and full address.

- *Price proposals.* Often, instructions will request that you separate the technical proposal from the price proposal and seal each in separate packages. The price proposal usually is analyzed by procurement personnel, and in many RFPs, the customer does not want the technical evaluators to be influenced by the price of the equipment. Unless specifically instructed otherwise, it is generally all right to submit the price and technical proposals in separate binders or envelopes.

- *Signature.* Most RFPs request: "All proposals shall be signed by a duly authorized officer and dated upon execution." The reason for this requirement is that should you win, your proposal will become part of the contract, and the contract will be legally binding. If there is any question as to who is "authorized," have your vice president sign the proposal.

Specific Nonstandard Criteria

The above requirements are basic to all proposals. However, some sections will have additional requirements

Tip ▶ Following the submission criteria will prevent your proposal from being misplaced, lost, or otherwise compromised.

of their own. Failure to comply with all requirements will result in two possibilities:

1. You may be disqualified before the evaluation begins.
2. If accepted for evaluation, your proposal will receive a lower score than those proposals that did follow the preparation instructions.

Below are some specific, nonstandard requirements taken from actual RFPs.

Vendors are required to submit one complete set of contracts with their proposal. Contracts should include purchase agreements, maintenance contracts, and licensing agreements for all software products proposed.

One problem common to most inexperienced people is not knowing what to look for when reading and outlining an RFP. Often, mandatory requirements are buried in narrative sections of the RFP, and in a casual reading, these requirements may not be noted as proposal deliverables.

The stipulation cited above was buried in a general section of an RFP and was not included in the preparation instructions. Conditions like this are frequently added at the last minute by the final RFP review team and are not placed in their appropriate sections. Careful reading of the RFP for words such as *required*, *shall*, or *must* reveals many requirements not apparent on the first reading.

All questions must be answered and cross-referenced to the relevant paragraph number. If a question is not applicable, it should be listed with the notation 'not applicable (N/A)' and a reasonable explanation of the exception included.

Some RFPs are written in question/answer format. A simple version may be just a list of questions; each question is numbered and accompanied by a corresponding number for your response. Some RFPs are written as a series of paragraphs with blanks for you to fill in. When

Tip Submission guidelines are often buried and not picked up in a casual reading. Consider a close reading, looking just for submission criteria.

you find a question or blank that is not applicable to your proposal, you must give a reasonable explanation. Be as specific as possible.

Instructions can be very specific regarding such items as number of volumes or sections, page count, number of copies, and number of binders. In the example cited below, the requestor is specifically limiting the size of the proposal and attempting to keep proposal boilerplate responses to a minimum.

> *Proposals will be page-limited to 100 pages, printed one side only, single column with one-inch borders. Type size is limited to 12-point Helvetica or similar.*

To avoid confusion and possibly being disqualified, and to ensure that your proposal receives all evaluation points possible, total compliance with the proposal preparation instructions is strongly recommended.

If, for example, you are page-limited and have exceeded the specified number of pages, include all information that is relevant—but not important enough to attach to the main body of the proposal—as an appendix. Usually, there is no limit to the amount of information or number of appendixes you can submit, and your customer may or may not choose to read everything in your proposal.

If you are not clear on a submission requirement or you want to include an appendix to a page-limited proposal, ask a formal question. Do not assume that it will be all right.

> *Tip* Words such as *shall* or *must* indicate a requirement in most RFPs.

Proposal Delivery Requirements
Delivery Date

Delivery dates should always be taken seriously. Following is an example of one RFP's deadline stipulations:

> *All proposals shall be received no later than 4:00 P.M. Pacific Standard Time, Friday, April 1, 200x. Proposals are to be mailed or delivered to: [the address]*

No proposals will be accepted after this date. No exceptions will be allowed. Proposals must be physically present. Postmarked dates will not satisfy the requirement to be physically present on the due date.

There have been occasions when weeks of hard work have been in vain because an inexperienced bidder thought the deadline was negotiable. Many companies actually clock proposals in and refuse to accept any that are late. However, it is not always advantageous to finish and submit a proposal early; proposals may not be opened until the due date and the evaluation team is assembled and given instructions.

If you find you are not going to meet the deadline, you may ask for a last-minute extension. If you realize only a few days before the proposal is due that you are not going to meet the deadline, call the contact point for the RFP, explain in detail why you are unable to keep your commitment, and inform him or her of when you can submit your proposal. If the call is made several days or a full week before the deadline, it is a reasonable request. It would not be reasonable to request an extension on the day the proposal is due. Having the request for extension granted depends entirely upon your relationship with the account, the number of other vendors, and the flexibility of the company's procurement department.

For example, a company requested an extension one week before a proposal was due and was turned down. The RFP manager felt no need to grant an extension because all other vendors were able to submit their proposals on time. The company making the request was unable to submit a proposal after three months of dedicated work.

If you have a physical problem that will delay the proposal, such as a postal strike, a flood, etc., call the RFP contact person, explain the problem, and commit to a date when the proposal will be delivered. If it is an "act of God" problem, you can generally expect an approval

Tip Proposals generally are not opened until the due date and after all proposals have been submitted.

for being late. In this kind of situation, if it is possible, offer to send your proposal via e-mail or FTP upload to show that it is actually finished.

Delivery Conditions

Your proposal should be delivered in a sealed envelope or box. The following example is from an RFP that clearly requires all proposals to be submitted under sealed cover:

> *All copies of proposals and bids must be under sealed cover, which is to be plainly marked with the program name and solicitation number. The sealed cover shall also be clearly marked CONFIDENTIAL and shall state the scheduled date and time for submission. Final bids not received by the date and time specified will be rejected. Proposals and bids submitted under improperly marked covers may be disqualified.*

There are many reasons customers ask that all proposals be delivered in sealed packages. One obvious and primary reason is to prevent accidental loss or disclosure of materials submitted in open packages. In proposal competitions there may be internal backers who favor a particular vendor and are willing to provide insider information on the other proposals. An unsealed proposal may be previewed by unauthorized personnel and information concerning solutions and pricing given to a favored vendor. Proper marking and sealing of the package will help prevent potential leaks.

Another reason has to do with internal management of the evaluation. Many companies want to hold the proposals in the procurement department until all have been checked in; there are no further requests for extension; and other administrative tasks, such as checking for required documentation, are completed. Once the procurement department is satisfied that the proposals meet minimum requirements, the evaluation committee is briefed on the proposals, rules for their evaluation are explained, and questions are answered.

Delivery Method

Finally, the proposal's destination, and how you plan to get it there, are important considerations. For proposals that are strategic opportunities and very important to your company, delivery in person should be considered. This ensures that your proposal is signed in and that you receive a receipt. If you cannot verify that your proposal has arrived on time and has been signed in, you may be disqualified for missing the deadline.

Another way of sending your proposal is via an overnight express company. As an added precaution, a separate copy of the proposal may be sent via another overnight courier. It's also possible to send one copy on a separate flight using an airline's counter-to-counter package service. This copy is then picked up at the airport by another representative of your company and hand-delivered to the customer.

If your proposal does not warrant personal delivery, overnight express services usually provide a safe and convenient method for transporting your proposal. In addition, they offer the ability to trace a shipment if it has not arrived. Also, be aware of the check-in time. If proposals are due at 10:00 A.M. and your delivery is slated for afternoon at 3:00 P.M., you may be disqualified. And even though these services guarantee delivery or your money back, $25 or $50 will not compensate for a contract you didn't win because your proposal was lost en route or delivered late.

Tip — Now is not the time to save pennies at the expense of losing a proposal.

You may be wondering why I am even discussing this issue. It may seem so obvious that it only deserves a passing mention. As an RFP manager I can only tell you that I typically receive at least one proposal that is late, mislabeled, or otherwise doesn't conform to the instructions—and you know the fate of these proposals!. Some of you out there may need this reminder.

Summary

Experienced RFP writers know that strong submission and delivery requirements will help them to review many proposals quickly, immediately disqualifying those that do not follow instructions. If you are missing key requested information or have not otherwise followed the submission requirements, you may be disqualified without further review. Many evaluators view this as the "first test," for if a vendor can't follow simple directions, what else can be expected of that vendor? Evaluators may have little patience for proposals that miss several of the criteria. Glaring errors like this may put them on the lookout for further problems, such as poor grammar, misspellings, typos, and minor infractions of the submission requirements. In other words, try your best not to get the evaluators irritated by minor offenses that may have major impact later on in the review cycle.

Just as important are the delivery requirements. Most federal and state evaluators have zero tolerance for vendors not following the requirements. If someone protests, and it is later found that they did not disqualify a vendor when required to, it may jeopardize the procurement (and their job). Public companies are not under as much pressure and may let minor problems slide, but many minor problems added together can become major problems.

As we have stressed throughout this book, it is best to follow the directions in the RFP exactly. These requirements are put in place to help the evaluation committee work faster by having all proposals conform to the same rules. These rules also allow the evaluation committee to disqualify vendors, thus lessening their workload.

ORGANIZE THE
POSTPROPOSAL ACTIVITIES

There are several activities that are not required by the RFP, but are nonetheless necessary to complete the proposal development process and "put it to bed." These include, but are not limited to, establishing and maintaining complete files of the RFP and any supplementary materials (such as page changes), an exchange of questions and answers during the proposal-writing period, planning for negotiations, and continued selling of the solution. Thoughtful attention to these matters is important enough to make the difference between winning and losing a contract. There are three main areas of concern:

1. Postdelivery considerations
2. Precontract steps
3. Interpreting postproposal feedback

Review Appendix G, Postproposal Checklist, for a list of typical activities.

Also, it is during this time that essential, difficult, and costly tasks, such as writing a presentation or building a product demonstration, must be undertaken. The same intense energy that was devoted to the proposal must now be directed to postproposal activities. Lack of attention to detail at this phase may jeopardize the success of the project.

Postdelivery Considerations

Once the proposal has been delivered, there is a natural tendency for people to sit back, take a day off, or begin calling on other accounts or working with existing accounts that they neglected during the proposal-writing period. However, *the job is not over yet.* It is during this postdelivery time that many tasks, such as organizing and filing all records, must be given proper attention.

Instituting good housekeeping practices before, during, and after the proposal is imperative. Both an electronic and paper filing system should be maintained throughout the proposal process. "Hard" records may be kept in folders marked by section and stored in a filing cabinet. All information relating to team decisions should be kept in a separate folder, with minutes of meetings, personal notes, and audit trails that lead to how decisions were reached. Decisions that might need to be tracked are those that would have to be justified to the customer, such as pricing models, equipment configurations, or anything that needs to be tracked internally, such as discount information.

As part of the postproposal cleanup, special attention should be paid to documents that explain

- how products were chosen.
- why certain products were not chosen.
- how the proposed solution was developed.
- what trade-offs were made in the development of the solution.
- who participated in these decisions.
- how pricing was developed.
- who was responsible for nonstandard pricing decisions.
- who was responsible for nonstandard discounts.
- who approved nonstandard pricing and discounts.

These papers and other related materials are collected in preparation for the time when the customer begins to ask questions and request clarifications of product descriptions, procedures, or prices.

When the proposal is finished, the original RFP and the final version of the proposal should be kept together

Tip — Analyzing why other proposals have been rejected can help you to avoid the same pitfalls.

in one file (if electronic). Added to this file would be any addenda, supplements, questions, answers, or other written communications between you and the customer. The file becomes the master record of the project and is a duplicate of the file kept by the customer and added to the contract as an exhibit. This will be the "public" file that would be reviewed by lawyers during contract negotiations and also serve as the beginning of the project notebook kept by the project leader.

The electronic file should contain all e-mail correspondence that has occurred between you and the customer and among RFP team members. If you have a document management system, an electronic file area should be established to capture all of the electronic files that have become part of the proposal. This may include such items as

Tip ▸ Develop an audit trail by organizing your proposal files and records.

- the final proposal sent to the customer, and versions of it.
- the sales contract (which could be in a PDF file).
- pricing spreadsheets and tables—e.g., Excel files.
- project management schedules such as MS Project.
- e-mail correspondence.
- notes and memos sent within the group.
- illustration files (all illustrations should be kept separately so that they may be located if needed for the project when it starts).

If your proposal wins, it will be copied many times (within your company) as new people are assigned to the project. It's likely that various departments—contracts, legal, accounting, manufacturing, engineering and development, customer support, and customer training—will need copies of the proposal. This will be a normal request if a department is going to support the project effort. Without this file, or with an incomplete file, the contract will be subject to the customer's interpretation of the facts. The file will also obviate the wasting of time spent in re-creating and justifying why equipment or services were proposed.

Depending on your company, it may be a good idea to have your proposal copied, or electronically distributed, and sent to the departments that will have a part in the project. Too often the training or service group begins to interact with the customer without having read the proposal. It can be discouraging to your customer to learn that your own people haven't read the proposal.

Another reason for keeping the files in order is to facilitate ongoing proposal activities before the contract is awarded. In many cases, there will be pre-award steps (described in detail below) such as questions and answers, demonstrations, factory visits, and oral presentations, that will require information from the proposal or even make use of parts of the proposal itself. Quite often illustrations from the proposal are used in the oral presentation instead of being redrawn. (Drawings may also have been lost, or so abused that they cannot be used and must be redrawn.)

In addition, as the contract award draws closer, it is possible that the customer will ask you to do some *what-if projections* and calculations. If these are successfully sold, and the customer is willing to accept them, a good audit trail must be established in order to substantiate the what-ifs at the time of the contract award. As an example, the customer might want to increase the number of workstations being proposed in order to receive a higher discount, or a customer may ask you to provide training at their facility instead of yours and want you to give "what-if" prices for the different facilities and different numbers of attendees.

It is often the case that when a contract is won, the team responsible for the proposal is not able to document why a decision was made, and what effect that decision had/has on the current state of the negotiations. Nor is it uncommon during contract negotiations for members of

> **Tip** Materials from your proposal are often used for the presentation and demos.

the proposal team to have either left the company or been transferred to another division—having left no notes or other material on why a decision was made.

The following examples highlight some problems that can occur by not keeping a well-organized and documented proposal file.

1. A company finished a long and difficult proposal that required the efforts of many people and company resources. The proposal team also included a third-party software supplier. This third-party group was not located in the same city as the proposal effort and therefore made many decisions at their corporate office. No consistent method was developed among the wide diversity of people and companies involved for tracking how certain decisions came to be made.

   Upon notification that they had lost the proposal, no attempt was made to consolidate files or put away proposal-related material in an orderly fashion. In addition, as proposal members learned of the loss, they threw away personal proposal material as they cleaned house, were transferred, or left the company. Several months after the contract award, the company was notified that the winning vendor had been dropped, and that their company was being asked to negotiate the contract. During the negotiation period, this company was unable to justify several price items and re-create most of the documentation required. Unprepared for negotiations, the company gave the customer a lower price than was originally proposed.

2. A sales representative who was managing a proposal created a project management section along with a project team, and quoted a price for these additional people and for installing the equipment. Before the contract was awarded, this sales rep, who had been responsible for writing and

pricing the proposal, left the company. During the negotiations, the customer wanted a detailed explanation of why a large project management group was required (and priced) to manage the installation of standard equipment. The customer thought installation of equipment was covered under the "installation charge" that was separate from the project management charge. Due to lack of documentation, the company was unable to resolve this issue, among others, to the customer's satisfaction, and the contract was awarded to the competitor.

3. A systems analyst, who was responsible for developing the system configuration (how many CPUs, disk drives, tape drives, etc.), left the company. Due to unforeseen circumstances, the contract award was delayed by several months. Upon award, the winning company belatedly began to develop a project team and organize the effort. Lacking records, the people in charge soon realized they did not understand how the proposed configuration was arrived at and, after much study and embarrassment, had to inform the customer that the configuration proposed did not include enough hardware. Fortunately, the customer changed the requirements and the equipment shortfall was covered under a new agreement.

Tip Writing the proposal is only one of the many steps toward winning the contract.

Precontract Steps

Generally, customers do not decide to award their contracts based solely on submitted proposals. There are many potential steps before the final decision is made. These steps may include the following:

- Question-and-Answer Period (to question vendor proposals)

- Oral Presentation
- Product Demonstration
- Reference Checking
- Reference-Site Visits
- Headquarters Visit
- Best and Final Offer (BAFO)
- Contract Negotiations
- Contract Award

Question-and-Answer Period

While your proposal is being reviewed and evaluated, there will be questions about your solution, your products, your price, or how you are going to administer the project. If your proposal is going to make the short list, or has made it, the customer will often reserve the right to request clarification of vendor responses, and request additional information as needed. *Generally, the customer also requires that questions and responses to questions be made in writing; oral responses are not acceptable.*

In this phase of the proposal evaluation, the customer is looking very seriously at your proposal and may develop a list of questions that you will have to answer. Just as you were allowed to ask questions concerning requirements in the RFP, and perhaps could not go on until you had the answers, customers have the same problem. Usually, you will receive one set of questions from the customer. However, if the proposal is very complex, your answers to the customer's first set of questions may generate more questions on their part.

Questions from the customer are a positive indication that you are being considered for the short list and that your proposal is being given serious consideration. It is important that you give these questions as much attention as you gave to the original proposal. Because questions indicate that something is not clearly understood,

> *Tip* Questions are a positive reaction from the customer.

you may lose the award by not being able to give clear, understandable responses.

These questions are a means of keeping the communication lines open as well as marking your progress through the evaluation cycle. By analyzing these questions, you will be able to determine what section of your proposal the evaluation team is having problems with and, therefore, what section you should be prepared to defend. This knowledge may help direct you in preparing for the oral presentation and the system demonstration.

If, for example, the proposal section that described the computer operating system provoked several questions and a request for additional information, it would be prudent not only to provide as much information as possible, but also to devote additional time to this subject in your oral presentation and demonstration.

Proposal Presentation

Being asked to make a presentation is a definite sign that your proposal has made the short list.

> *Selected vendors will be required to make a presentation of their proposal This presentation will be made to the evaluation and executive staff responsible for awarding this contract. This opportunity is given to allow vendors the chance to further define the primary features and benefits of their proposals, allow for clarification of proposal weak areas, and allow for limited questions from the review team. Presentation format is left to the discretion of the vendor; however, presentations should address the proposed solution and not address general marketing features and benefits.*

The presentation can be a simple affair in which you make a presentation to the evaluation committee and they ask questions about your proposal. Or, it can be an elaborate event involving the use of a presentation with a "canned" demonstration and written handouts of your

> *Tip*
>
> An oral presentation allows you to clarify any misconceptions and interact directly with the evaluation team.

presentation. If you are going to make a formal presentation with graphics and handouts, the planning stage must start before the proposal is due. A well-planned formal presentation requires

- a clear understanding of your proposal.
- knowledge of your weak areas.
- knowledge of your competition's strong areas.
- knowledge of your competition's weak areas.
- resources to write and produce the presentation.
- hours for rehearsal.
- additional time for unexpected requests.
- additional money for travel and equipment.

Ask the customer what is expected and who should be present for the presentation. Usually the sales representative gives the presentation while a technical representative is present to take the technical questions during and after the presentation. However, for a more detailed presentation, several people may present to the customer. A typical multiperson presentation may include

> *Tip* Remember that oral presentations require additional planning and resources.

- the sales representative providing introductions and covering the basic business features of your proposal, serving as the moderator for your company, and providing a summary and conclusion. If time permits and the occasion warrants, a brief overview of your company and products should be included.
- the technical analyst giving a detailed description of the solution.
- a project manager reviewing how the project will be implemented and managed.
- a regional manager providing insight into the pricing structure, if required.
- the sales representative making the concluding remarks.

Presentations give evaluators the opportunity to ask questions about your proposal before making a final

When two competitors are equal from a technical standpoint, many customers begin to look at the vendors from a "Can I work with this company?" point of view. You are always giving the customer subtle hints about your-self and your company, as when you follow up on time with a request, display professionalism, and always take responsibility for your actions.

decision. The presentation allows the evaluation staff to meet key participants in the proposal effort and affords them an opportunity to make nontechnical assessments of your company and its personnel. If you are running even with a competitor, your presentation, corporate deportment, and personal demeanor could be the deciding factors in winning the contract.

It cannot be overemphasized that pricing and technology are becoming less of a factor in decision making, while company-related considerations are assuming greater importance. In many cases, you and your competition may be bidding many of the same products, and it will be your ability to convince the customer that your company is the safer choice for on-time installation and project success that wins the contract. Company consideration may include

- company financial history.
- company stability and growth.
- ability to handle and implement the contract.
- quality of personnel (resumes and physical presentation).
- prior project history and successful implementations.

The presentation itself *should not be your standard canned presentation*. The presentation should be customized to the specific opportunity and should reemphasize your strong points and counter any weaknesses. The

Have you ever heard people say, "We don't sell products, we sell solutions"? It's this concept of solution selling that is the meat and potatoes of your proposal and presentation.

When you sell an accounting system, you are not selling a computer system with accounting functions, you are selling better accounting accuracy, easier input capability that saves time and money, better accounting trace ability for record keeping, and better audit-reporting capabilities.

The customers may be seeking this system because they just failed an audit by the IRS, could not provide certain documentation, and were required to reverse parts of the previous year's annual statement. These customers are not buying an accounting system; they are buying the solution to their accounting problem.

presentation should not simply review your proposal, but should review the business issues behind the RFP and how your proposal solves those business issues. If possible, time may be spent on a review of the cost justification and how confident you are that the numbers represent a true justification. Once the business issues are addressed, it would be best to spend time on how your proposal technically addresses and solves the business problem.

If you are competing with other companies bidding the same products, time should be devoted to your implementation strategy, past successes, and how your understanding of the customer's issues will make your implementation faster, smoother, and trouble-free—i.e., you have already experienced and solved problems your competition may not have encountered yet.

The presentation can be either a total success or a miserable failure, depending on how much preparation and effort you've put into it. Remember, during the presentation you have no place to hide when you don't know an answer. You are on stage live without the engineering department or marketing department to help. Be prepared by

Tip ▷ Be sensitive to customer feedback: it will give you hints on how to direct your presentation.

- knowing what was said in your proposal.
- knowing your product.
- fully understanding the business reasons for the RFP.
- knowing the RFP.

Product Demonstration

In conjunction with the presentation, or as a second step in the process, a demonstration of the proposed technology may be requested. This request by the customer might be very specific—asking for a demonstration of product and functionality—or it could simply state that a demonstration may be required.

> *This procurement may require a demonstration of the bidder's response to specific requirements (including benchmark requirements) before final selection in order to verify the claims made in the bid, corroborate the evaluation of the bid, and confirm that the hardware and software are actually in operation.*
>
> *The demonstration is the last phase for technically qualifying your solution and can be a deciding factor in your ability to win this procurement; a successful demonstration will allow you to move to the negotiation phase, but an unsuccessful demonstration may eliminate you from any further participation.*

Whether you are provided with a detailed script by the customer, the same amount of attention and effort must be given to planning, developing, and executing the demonstration. Some RFPs require that you explain in your proposal how you will demonstrate your offering.

> *Bidder must prepare and include in their bid a complete Demonstration Plan for the performance of all applicable products. The Plan must include a discussion of applicable hardware, software, and communications in your configuration. Failure of the bidder to demonstrate*

Tip ▶ Doing client product demonstrations can be costly and time-consuming.

*that the claims made by the bid, in response to the RFP
requirements, are in fact true, may be sufficient to cause
the bid to be deemed nonresponsive.*

A typical demonstration may include any or all of the
following equipment and physical resources:

- Proposed hardware and software in operation
- Custom-developed demonstration program of the
  application
- Additional in-house equipment
- Nonstandard equipment
- Adequate space to have the demonstration
- Reserved time for setup and rehearsal
- Additional personnel to support the demonstration
- Accelerated product development schedules (to
  demonstrate a partial solution)
- Sufficient reserve resources to meet unexpected
  needs

A demonstration of computer systems has the potential for being very costly in terms of facilities, hardware
and software, programming resources, and personnel. It
is not uncommon for a major demonstration to cost a
company $100,000 in equipment, time, and facilities.
Before beginning to undertake a major demonstration,
your senior management should approve a budget and
plan. If adequate resources are not made available or
provided, the demonstration is almost certain to be infe-
rior and potentially cause your company to lose the
competition.

Most proposals are not won outright. During the
postproposal period, selling, positioning, and negotiat-
ing are constantly occurring. Throughout the demonstration, there will be steady interaction between you and the
customer. This interaction should sharpen your awareness of your position, showing whether your proposal
and demonstration are being accepted by the customer.

Tip

During
the
demo
there will
be steady
interaction
between you
and the
customer.

As an RFP manager, I requested the final two vendors to provide a runoff demonstration that tested their software. The project was for a corporate search engine, and I provided both vendors with exactly the same test database after they had set up their software on two identical servers.

After several hours of searching for data using a variety of methods, it was clear that one of the vendors could not support his claims while the other one provided excellent results. Needless to say, the vendor with the most accurate search engine was given the project.

It became clear that the losing vendor had overstated his company's capabilities. By requesting a demonstration, we were able to clearly see that their product was not as capable as the other product.

The message: Be accurate in your sales pitch and claims, as they may be challenged and tested.

Tip

Many customers are naive in their understanding of what can be accomplished in a demonstration.

For example, in one situation, a company was in the middle of a demonstration when the customer took documentation from her briefcase and asked the vendor to work with this new material instead of the material already selected for the demo. The new material was used and the equipment failed to process it as required. The demonstration was stopped and a lengthy meeting ensued. The result of this meeting was that the demonstration would be rerun at a later date—the first being a "mistrial"—with the second demonstration using the new documentation. The second demonstration was successfully run. However, if this company and the customer hadn't already established a good working relationship, and the sales representative did not continue to sell and negotiate, the project would have ended with the failure of the first demonstration.

Demonstration Plan and Agenda

Once you have been selected for a demonstration, it is important that you work with the customers to ensure that they will see what they expect to see. If a customer has an agenda, follow it and make agreed-upon changes that suit your company and products. Remember, the original agenda was prepared to cover all the vendors and potential technologies. Your solution may not exactly fit that agenda, so don't be shy about speaking up.

Also, be cautious about accepting the customer's agenda without careful consideration and review. Many customers naively think that you can demonstrate your whole solution "out of the box" when, in fact, considerable programming and other work must be done to make the application work. If you are in a proposal/demonstration situation in which the customer wants you to demonstrate a solution, you have to explain that that capability will take weeks/months to build—i.e., refer to your implementation plan and the amount of time you have proposed to program the application. (This is similar, in a sense, to an Excel spreadsheet. It has many functions out of the box, but these functions don't work until you write—program—a macro to demonstrate the function.)

Instead, focus the customer's attention on the functional aspects of your software and hardware. If you say that your scanner can scan 40 documents per minute, the demonstration should prove that functional specification. If your database can handle 200 transactions per minute, set up a demonstration that loads the database with transactions, and show the customer some type of report that demonstrates the transaction throughput.

It is imperative that you and your customer have the same expectations of what your demonstration will accomplish. If this is not negotiated and agreed to up front, you may seriously underestimate what your customer expects and (perhaps wrongly) find yourself eliminated from the competition.

Tip — Reference visits are used to verify your claims.

Checking References
One of the final steps in the proposal review process is to check the customer references that were listed in your

proposal. The evaluators may request a visit to a customer site where your equipment is installed and even request a visit to your headquarters and manufacturing areas.

The purpose of the customer-reference requirement is to provide the evaluation committee with the ability to verify the claims made in the bid by the vendor. The bidder must provide a list of five customers who presently have the proposed equipment installed and operating.

The customer will contact your references and usually arrange to visit only one of the sites. The purpose of the reference-checking and site visits is twofold: the first is to see and verify that your equipment is working at a customer's site; the second is to speak candidly with your customers about your company's qualifications, reputation, and capabilities.

Customers may also ask for a factory visit. This request will include a company tour, a meeting with your executives, and an overview of your company and its future direction. In short, the customer is trying to get a firsthand impression of your company and to decide whether he wants to do business with you, the sales representative, and your company.

During this visit, the customer will want to verify that your company is stable and able to perform successfully against the contract.

Prior to award of contract, we must be assured that the vendor selected has all the resources and experience required to successfully perform under this contract. This includes, but is not limited to, personnel in the numbers and with the skills required, equipment of appropriate type and in sufficient quantity, financial resources sufficient to complete performance under the contract, and experience in similar endeavors. If we are unable to assure ourselves of the vendor's ability to perform under this contract, additional information such as credit ratings,

Tip A factory tour will give your potential customers a firsthand impression of your company.

credit letters, or performance bonds may be requested. If these are found to be insufficient, we reserve the right to reject the bid and discontinue further negotiations.

Only vendors in the final stages of being accepted will undergo a company visit. This means that the customer is still torn between two companies (it's usually only two); the technological solutions are equal, and they are trying to find that "deciding factor." It is at this point that you, the sales rep, and your company can make the decision in your favor by careful attention to detail, professionalism, and common sense.

Best and Final Offer (BAFO)[1]

The BAFO stage is the final phase of a procurement and negotiation. The purpose is to allow bidders to review equipment, schedules, management, organization, and pricing in light of requirement changes, and to supplement their proposal one final time. These modifications are allowed because requirements have changed due to

- the length of the procurement process.
- availability of new technology.
- modification of requirements by the customer, during the question-and-answer period.
- inability to meet original requirements.
- change in contract requirements by the customer.

Being invited to a BAFO is another definite sign that you are on the short list or have won agreement to these final changes. BAFOs are sometimes considered a prenegotiation stage in which the customer is clearing away any remaining technical or implementation problems that

> *Tip* — The BAFO takes time and resources.

---

[1] Note: BAFOs have lost favor with the Federal Government, but they have become more common with commercial industry. The term BAFO may not always be used, but the option to have a final price and/or quantity adjustment is always present. We use BAFO as a catchall for the final negotiation phase.

BAFO was originally a federal government procurement term, but the concept is still valid and is now also used by commercial companies. The federal government's Federal Acquisition Regulations (FARs) were changed to eliminate the strict BAFO procedure and replace it with a more open procedure allowing the contracting officer (CO) to request final pricing and proposals from different vendors at different times. The concept is, however, the same in that it allows final adjustments to be made to a proposal after extensive talks and clarifications have taken place between the buyer and the seller. The government now calls the BAFO phase simply, final proposal revisions.

may result in an unsuccessful negotiation. BAFOs are interactive sessions in which the customer asks a series of questions, makes statements about the proposal, defines and lists any problems with your solution, and finally, tells you if your price is not in line with the budget.

When you attend a BAFO session, you should be accompanied by the technical and financial people who were part of the proposal effort, in addition to your contract negotiator. Generally, you are not asked to make decisions at the meeting, but are allowed to respond in writing after a designated time. It's a good idea to have several people taking notes, so that you all "hear" the same thing.

Federal and state governments generally have BAFOs. Although unusual, commercial RFPs are beginning to incorporate formal BAFOs as part of the RFP cycle. The difference between a government BAFO and a commercial-account BAFO is that the government is bound by the Federal Acquisition Regulations (FARs), whereas a commercial customer is not bound by any laws or regulations. Therefore, the federal BAFO is subject to and in compliance with the FARs. If you lose, it is possible to protest the award. Protesting the awarding of a commercial contract is difficult and generally without benefit of legal precedent.

It is important to note that you can lose the proposal at this point by not being responsive to BAFO requests, not being prepared for questions raised during the BAFO, and not reading between the lines to come up with the correct solution/price.

Contract Negotiation

Contract negotiation is the final step before you are awarded the contract. The purpose of this step is to reach agreement as to an exact and specific statement of work (SOW) that spells out who is responsible for what work, and when it will be done. In addition to the SOW, contracts are concerned with administrative tasks such as the FOB point, payment terms, recourse for mistakes and deficiencies, and how simple paperwork is to be transmitted between the two companies.

Because negotiation is defined as the bargaining between two parties, it is important to remember that *both* parties are needed to negotiate. Some customers try to dominate the negotiation session so that most of the concessions are made by you and your company.

The key to successful contract negotiations is to be prepared to explain and defend your solution and price. If you are unable to explain why project management staff is required, or to defend the cost of one, the customer may not buy the idea, and will prevent that portion of the proposal from being written into the contract. On the other hand, if the customer is unable to provide you with specific information that is required to properly size your configuration, he will have to concede to your proposed configuration.

It is important for both parties to understand what is being purchased and what it will and will not do. If this understanding is not reached and agreed to, the contract will be a constant problem as both vendor and customer point fingers at each other in an effort to

Tip Be flexible, and let the customers do the talking because the ball is in their court.

assign blame for products and services that do not meet expectations.

In rare cases, it may be better to refuse a contract if you and your customer cannot agree on certain key items. Some customers may still not fully understand the technology and the solution you are proposing. This can result in a dissatisfied customer and a contract loss for your company. Let the competition have this customer.

As an example, a vendor bid on and won a contract, but the value of the contract was lower than the vendor had expected. To compensate for the low dollar value, the vendor cut corners on the project plan, and over-charged for travel costs. In addition, this contract fell to the "bottom of the stack," and higher-value contracts were given more attention. Needless to say, the customer balked at this lack of attention and cancelled the contract, forcing the vendor to accept returned equipment and pay for time lost. (I doubt that they carefully read the contract terms and the "liquidated damages" clause.)

In the final analysis, the vendor lost not only a contract, but good will and good-name recognition with this customer. The customer was one of nine campuses in a state university system; therefore, the vendor lost the potential to supply eight additional campuses with the same software application.

> *Tip* ▷ The good news is, we won the contract. The bad news is, we won the contract. So goes an old proverb.

Interpreting Postproposal Data

After your proposal is submitted, your oral presentation complete, and your best and final offer is made, your proposal responsibilities are still not over. Now is the time to assess the signals and cues given by the customer. These signals are sometimes obvious but more often are obscure. Sometimes they are called "buying signals," indications of the customer's readiness to think of you as the winning vendor.

For example, the customer may be concerned about delivery times and the first-possible date for completion of the installation. The customer may be asking about the possibility of a 30- or 60-day delivery instead of the 90 days that were quoted.

Other signals are less apparent, but you may have a general feeling that things are going well—confident that you might win. If it is possible to pinpoint why you have this feeling, you may be able to develop a postproposal selling plan that capitalizes on your strengths and draws attention away from your weaknesses. Similarly, if you think you are losing the proposal, an analysis of the signs from the customer may reveal your flaws.

Imagine that you've been given questions to answer and are invited to give a presentation. Several questions are directed at the Management Section and ask, more or less, who will actually be responsible for the project and what place that person occupies in your company's chain of command. This could be a subtle cue from the customer, telling you indirectly that the sales rep is not the appropriate person to handle the postaward account.

If you work out of a small office, you might restructure the project so that the technical analyst acts as the project manager and the sales representative continues in his capacity as the account manager. In any event, it seems highly likely that the potential customer is not satisfied, and this may affect the award.

From the beginning of the proposal effort, the sales rep should keep track of any hints given by the customer. These generally come from

- very detailed questions about your proposed technology.
- questions about why you chose one product over another.
- questions about your implementation plan.
- questions about delivery and installation.
- questions about your company and its stability.

> *Tip* ▷ Now is the time to assess the signals and cues given by the customer.

Summary

If you pay attention to details, it is possible to assemble some facts that will guide you through the postsubmission phase. Assuming you have put your best effort into the proposal, now is not the time to relax! If anything, hope that your competitors have slackened in their efforts, *while you continue to drive home every point whenever possible.*

It is this principle of continuing to sell and build a good working relationship with the customer that will reap the most benefits. The situation in the second example of this chapter, in which the company proposed but could not substantiate a project management charge to the customer, could have been turned around if better relations had been established with the customer, and the salesman had better data to present. Unfortunately, the company writing the proposal had no previous contact with the customer and had no knowledge that an RFP was to be issued. Compounded by the change in sales reps in the middle of the process, circumstances were far from favorable for winning the contract.

Savvy sales reps find ways to keep in contact with their customers during the postproposal phase. They use this contact to judge how they are faring against the competition, and try to offer additional information whenever possible. For example, an industry analyst published a false and misleading report about a company that was vying with other vendors for a contract. The competition was quick to capitalize on this by forwarding a copy of the report to the project leader for the RFP. When the maligned company was not invited to provide a demonstration, it asked for a debriefing with the customer and was told that both its product and the company were given low ratings, and that the report had influenced their decision.

Of course, the company that had received the low rating knew of this report. The author was advised that he

> *Tip* Now is not the time to relax!

was mistaken, and that the report was very misleading. When a retraction appeared in his next report, it was immediately given to the customer. The company also used this opportunity to deliver a well-written and very powerful letter from its president. Placed back on the potential winners' list, the company was given the chance to provide a demonstration, and in the end was awarded the contract.

If your company is in the midst of change while you have proposals that are still out there being evaluated, be proactive, and let your customers know what is happening and why. Changes are typically beneficial, and these benefits should be brought to their attention. Be prepared to counteract the competition's use of any misrepresentations about your company's changes that would sound the alarm bell in your customers' ears, activating the FUD principle of *"Fear, Uncertainty, and Doubt."*

We have covered a lot of ground in this chapter and hope that you will put as much effort into postproposal activities as you did into the proposal itself. Postproposal activities follow the proposal as day follows night: each step, presentation, demonstration, and negotiation brings you that much closer to winning. Don't stumble!

PRINT AND DELIVER YOUR PROPOSAL

Printing, which may mean traditional paper printing or electronic printing, is the last step in producing your proposal. In some ways, printing is one of the most difficult steps because of limited time and, usually, an inflexible due date. Even though you may have planned thoroughly in the beginning when the original schedule was made, there is always some time slippage as the proposal progresses—unforeseen problems are invariably encountered. Sometimes the four or five "extra" days you may have originally planned for are lost, and you are suddenly behind schedule.

This section is devoted to familiarizing you with the printing process so you can complete this phase as quickly and efficiently as possible. We will cover

- methods of printing and binding.
- what parts of the proposal are specially printed, including a discussion of binder tabs.
- selecting a printer and knowing what is expected of you as well as what you can expect from him.
- how to physically organize and assemble the proposal.

See Appendix D for a checklist of printing activities.

Methods of Printing

The vocabulary of different industries is important to understand. A familiar story concerns a man who had never been to an auction before and unintentionally bought a $5,000 vase when he raised his hand to scratch his head. I encountered a similar situation at one of our field offices. The first day I arrived, the sales personnel and I had a meeting with the printer they had selected. As we talked, it seemed we were talking about the same thing—but not the same thing! We soon discovered the printer was a book publisher and was treating our 250-page proposal as if it were a book, with plans for a special binding. (We wanted three-ring binders.) When he came up with his rock-bottom price of $30,000 for typesetting the proposal, we stopped right there. He didn't understand what a sales proposal was and the field-office people knew nothing about printing.

In the context of proposals, the word *printer* is used loosely to mean anyone who agrees to reproduce your proposal, regardless of the method used. It is unlikely that you will use the services of an offset printer, as that term normally implies a company that uses large letterpress or offset printing equipment. If you do not have special requirements for such items as photographs or continuous-tone artwork (i.e., artwork that has graduated fine shading), you will probably use printing processes such as photocopying or laser printing.

Therefore, we will spend most of our time on photocopy-type reproduction and the laser printer. However, there are a few pieces that you might consider having professionally printed, such as the cover, tabs, and other color inserts.

Tip Covers and tabs may require special printing.

Specialty Printing

Certain parts of the proposal, such as covers and binder tabs (also called index tabs), may need to be specially printed at a venue other than a photocopy shop.

Covers. If you have original cover art drawn by an illustrator, it is best to have the cover art and text handled

FIGURE 9-1 Sample Cover Design

Corporate Intranet

Workstation

IBM Compatible

Electronic Document Management
Systems (EDMS) Project

Submitted by:
AJAX, Inc.
June 1, 20xx

Laptop computer

professionally. The proposal cover may require the most time to print; therefore, it should be taken to the printer as soon as the information for the cover is determined. The cover text will need to be typeset, proofread, corrected (possibly), and approved before the final copies are printed. This only applies if you have had original artwork created for your covers, whether it be one-time-only covers or covers used as boilerplate.

If your cover art is done on a PC or graphics workstation, it may be printed on a color printer (laser or inkjet), or the electronic file can be transferred via modem or taken to a color reproduction shop.

The above also applies to any binder spines that are being created. Binder spines are strips of paper that are slid into the presentation-binder spine. The spine usually displays the customer's project name, or your company name. The spines will be cut to fit the binder, and you will need to know the thickness of the binder.

Having a printed cover and spine gives your proposal a professional look. In Figure 9-1, created from a commercial-drawing software program, the cover features a grouping of computers because the project is a computer system. The printed spine could carry company name AJAX Inc.

Binder Tabs. Custom-printed binder tabs are very professional in appearance but are the most expensive and time-consuming to prepare. A more complete discussion of other alternatives, as well as what is involved in ordering custom-printed tabs, follows.

Binder Tabs

Binder tabs are available in several formats. Below are listed the most common types:

- *Preprinted.* These are available at most stationers and are the least expensive and most convenient to use as no preparation is required. They consist of a package of preprinted tabs bearing numbers or letters and are simply inserted in front of the appropriate section after the proposal is complete. Their main drawback is that they don't indicate the titles of the sections. Also, refrain from using colored tabs and stick with black and white.
- *Blank tabs.* You can buy blank manila tabs from a good office supply store and then type right on the tab. This allows you to specify section titles and gives the proposal a custom feel. You can purchase clear stick-on labels that are printed with your laser printer and placed on the tab. However, they are much more work—especially if you have to submit multiple copies—and may not always stay on the tab with heavy use.
- *Clear plastic tabs.* You can buy tabs with clear or colored plastic holders into which you insert a typed piece of paper with the section number and title. However, these are not very professional-looking and tend to look amateurish.

FIGURE 9-2 Sample Binder Tab

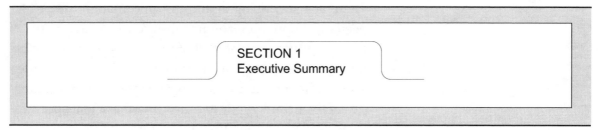

- *Professionally printed tabs.* The most professional-looking are custom-printed tabs. A very important proposal is worth the extra money. If you decide to use this type, be sure to allow enough time to have them printed; tabs should be turned in to the printer at the same time as the cover. Figure 9-2 is an example.

General Information

Binder tabs are called out by cuts. The cuts indicate how many tabs appear across. Tabs usually come in standard three-cut, five-cut, or seven-cut banks (sets). A five-cut bank is shown in Figure 9-3.

A three-cut gives you the most room to type information (it has a larger tab area), but a five- or seven-cut may be better for very large proposals. The information on a tab is the section number and title as shown in Figure 9-2.

FIGURE 9-3 Sample Five-Cut Bank of Binder Tabs

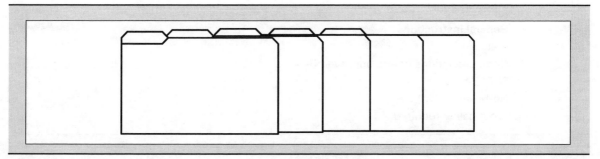

Ordering Tabs

There is a surprising amount of information the printer needs to know about your tabs. You can save yourself and the printer a great deal of time and grief if you specify all the required information at the time of the order. The information falls into three general categories: identity of the printer; your identity; and the actual specifications (called specs). Prepare a form or checklist (see Figure 9-4) that you can use over and over. Be sure to make a copy of the completed form for your files in the event of a dispute between you and the printer.

FIGURE 9-4 Sample Binder Tab Order

Binder Tab Order

To:	John Brown
Print Shop:	Quick Print
Phone:	123-4567
Ajax:	P O 45678
Date:	July 1, 2003
Contact:	Jane Smith (408) 555-1212
Needed by:	July 15, 2003

Specs

Tab banks:	5-cut
No. sets:	15
Font (face and size):	9-pt. Helvetica bold all caps for section no., 10-pt. Helvetica medium upper & lower case for section title
Alignment:	Left
Position on tab:	centered top and bottom, left and right
Ink color:	Black
Paper stock:	Standard manila card stock, off-white
Sides printed:	1

General Instructions

Collate

No abbreviations unless approved by Ajax

5/16" 3-hole drilled

No Mylar

Proof galley required

Note the request at the bottom of the checklist: *Proof galley required*. The galley is the typeset text that will be printed on the tabs. It is very important to proof it for typographical errors and conformance with your requirements before it is printed on the tabs.

Tabs are often given a coat of clear Mylar to protect and strengthen them. Unless offered at no extra cost, this is not needed, as proposals have a very limited shelf life.

In addition to the specific information on your checklist, you may be asked by the printer to provide additional information. Note: If your company has an in-house print shop, check with them first to see if they can print the tabs for you rather than ordering them outside; most company print shops can handle this kind of job.

Preparing Instructions for the Printer

The following instructions apply if you are reproducing the proposal at a print or photocopy shop. It is essential that printers be given specific instructions so they can copy the proposal according to your needs.

This may not appear to be especially difficult, but in some cases the pagination can be complex if you are printing on two sides. Briefly, you would want your first-section page to start as a right-hand page. Right pages have the binding on the left side and are the odd-numbered pages, i.e., the first page of a book, "1," is odd. The second page, which is on the left-hand side, is even.

Because the last-printed page may be a right page, the printer needs to know to insert a blank left page as the next page; otherwise, your next section would be printed on the backside of the last section, which you probably would not want. This may not be consistent, as some sections may end on a left page.

Printing One-Sided or Two
Consider first whether the proposal pages will be printed on one or two sides. Several factors should be taken into

Tip ▷ Be sure to outline your instructions to the printer.

account. If your proposal is long, printing on two sides will cut the actual size in half. If your proposal is only 50 pages, you may want to print on one side only. Printing two-sided gives your proposal a more professional appearance, but one-sided is usually acceptable. Occasionally, the RFP will specify whether you must print one- or two-sided.

If not, the decision should be based on the need, time, expense, binding method, and your own experience. In most cases, printing on two sides is preferable. If you choose this format, some of the page information will need special attention. For example, if you normally print your page number on the bottom right, when you print two-sided, the page number on the back side will appear on the bottom near the binding, rather than on the bottom left where it should be. Also, the margins must be alternated if you have the margin near the spine wider than the margin at the outside of the page. Centering the text on the page, and centering the page number at the bottom of the page eliminates these problems. Most word processors today have the capability to alternate "left" and "right" pages and when selected, will automatically set the page margins, headers, and footers for left and right printing.

Preparing the Dummy

The next step is to complete what is called a printer's dummy. As shown in Figure 9-5, the dummy gives the printer a road map of how you want your proposal printed. It also shows how many pages there are in each section, as well as how many and where tabs, photos, or other artwork will be inserted. Without this information, the printer, or you, may lose a sheet unknowingly.

By convention, pages on the right side of a book are odd-numbered and are called front pages; those on the left side are even-numbered and are known as back pages.

> *Tip* The dummy sheet provides the printer with a road map to your proposal.

FIGURE 9-5 Sample Dummy Sheet

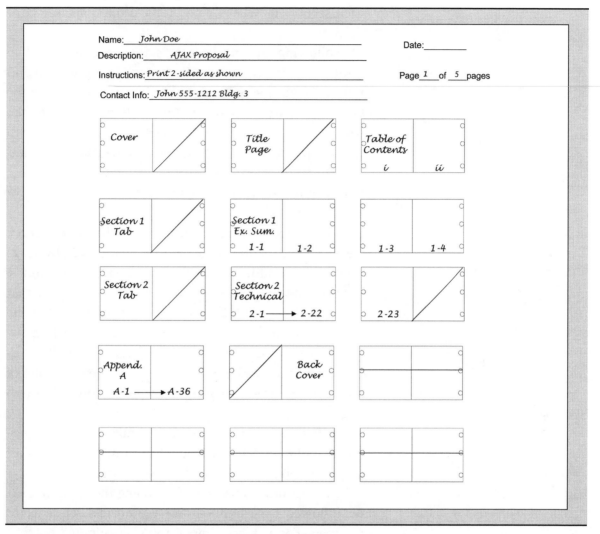

Figure 9-5 shows how to fill in the dummy layout for a proposal that is to be printed on both sides of the page. At the top of the form is general information. The page ___ of ___ is important to fill in because this indicates how many pages of the dummy there are. For example, if your dummy is five pages long, you would write page 1 of 5, page 2 of 5, etc. Remember, once you turn the material in to a print shop, they will not have time to call you and ask for such information as how many pages are in each section, or whether you have a one- or three-page dummy sheet.

Following the blocks across the page from left to right, you will see that the first page is a right page and is indicated as the cover and a slash is drawn through the back page to reinforce that there is nothing printed on the back. The next page, a right page, is the title page with nothing printed on the back, and also has no page number. The third page starts the table of contents; notice that it is paginated by Roman numerals (lower case), not Arabic numerals.

The proposal proper starts with the first section. Generally the section begins with a tab followed by a section title page, although both are not needed. Sometimes, in very long proposals, a mini table of contents for that section only is printed on the back of the tab or on the section title page. Page 1-4 is the last page of Section 1.

For long proposals, you do not need to actually indicate each page. Notice in Figure 9-5 that the beginning of section two starts on page 2-1 and goes in order through page 2-23.

If there were special printing requirements or pages, they would be called out on the dummy as "foldout page" or "photograph" to alert the printer.

An appendix is paginated by using the appendix letter followed by a hyphen and the normal sequence of numbers. For instance, Appendix A is paginated A-1, etc. The last block on the dummy indicates to the printer that there is a back cover with nothing printed on the inside. The remaining pages are lined out so that every page on the dummy is accounted for.

Special Treatment

If you have special illustrations, photographs, foldouts, or anything that is out of the ordinary, be sure to alert the printer as well as indicating it on the dummy. The printer

Tip

Check with your printer first for his version of the dummy.

may need to subcontract such work as making a photograph into a halftone. In the case of foldouts, the print shop will separate them from the rest of the material and print them on a special machine. The dummy then helps in reassembling the proposal.

To save money, suppose you are going to assemble the proposal yourself, and are not asking the printer to insert tabs, foldouts, etc., or to place the completed proposal in a binder. You will get a separate stack of foldouts from the printer that may not be collated. To help you put the foldouts in the text, colored papers called slipsheets may be used. Indicate on the dummy where slipsheets are to be inserted so the printer can prepare the manuscript accordingly.

Most printers have their own version of the dummy sheet and may want you to use the one they provide. Also, each printer will have different customs and methods for noting special needs. The best approach is to discuss the entire job with the printer before preparing the dummy.

Types of Binding

Before having your proposal printed, you must consider how it will be bound. There are several methods commonly used that are acceptable, depending on your situation. The following is a list and explanation of the types of binding that are suitable for proposal work.

Three-Ring Binder

The three-ring binder is probably the easiest binding method and allows for instant change when needed. In addition, it has the advantage of being able to stand up on a shelf; if you have your company's name and the requester's name on the spine, it will be easy for the evaluator to pick out your proposal from the others. Also, it lies flat when open, which is convenient for the evaluators.

Tip Three-ring binders are recommended.

If you use a binder, it is best to use a presentation or view binder that has clear plastic slip pockets on the front, spine, and back. With the slip pocket, you can insert custom covers and put your company's name on the spine. However, for a really special proposal, you can contact a company that makes binders and have your logo; proposal project name; and other information, including an illustration, printed right on the binder itself. Although this is costly and time-consuming, it can make a compelling statement!

Generally on the inside front cover of a presentation binder there is a plastic half-slip pocket that may be used to insert additional preprinted material such as an annual report, data sheets, brochures, reprinted articles, or your business card.

Binders usually come in one-half-inch increments, starting at one-half inch and going to three inches. Anything more than three inches is not advisable, as the sheer weight of that much paper becomes a problem to work with. Binders generally hold 100 sheets of paper (including binder tabs) per one-half inch. As a tip, if you do decide to use a three-ring binder, ask the printer to punch your paper with the larger, five-sixteenths-inch hole rather than the standard one-quarter inch. This larger hole makes the pages easier to turn and helps prevent tearing around the holes.

Any binders other than three-ring are not recommended. There are binders with more than three rings, but if you use them, you will encounter problems when making corrections—unless you have a 16- or 32-hole punch.

ACCO® Fastener

The ACCO type of binding is a two-piece metal fastener that uses three-hole-punched paper. ACCO binding is almost as flexible as the three-ring binder, allowing spot changes to be made. Like the three-ring binder, ACCO allows you to assemble the proposal in your office instead of paying a printer to do it for you.

ACCO binding does, however, lack several key features of the three-ring binder:

- It doesn't have a spine on which your company name and the proposal program name can be printed.
- It can't stand upright on a shelf.
- Pages cannot lie flat when open.
- It lacks the substantial feel of a binder.
- It doesn't look as professional as a three-ring binder.

Plastic Comb Binding

The plastic comb is a spiral strip of plastic with teeth that are inserted into the page and bind the paper by various methods. Perhaps the most commonly known type is made by the General Binding Corporation (GBC). It is commonly referred to as the GBC 19-hole, or simply comb binding.

This type of binding is more permanent than the first two because once bound, the pages cannot easily be separated. Also, unless you own a machine, the proposal will have to be assembled and bound by a printer. Once this is done, the proposal can only be changed at additional expense and time, as the old comb will have to be cut and a new one inserted. It is possible to remove the comb yourself and change pages, if the new pages are punched and you are willing to spend some time inserting the comb by hand. Otherwise you will need the machine for opening the comb binding.

Comb binding can give your proposal a professional look and you will be able to use your custom-made covers. However, comb bindings normally do not have information printed on the spine, although it is possible to have your company name and logo specially printed if you are ordering large quantities. Comb bindings do not stand upright on a shelf.

Stapling Your Proposal

Stapling is an unacceptable and unprofessional method of binding your proposal. Never staple your proposal!

Selecting a Printer or Reproduction Shop

Your selection of a printer will depend on your location and the type of proposal you are writing. For many people, the company reproduction department will more than satisfy their needs. However, in a field sales office with an important account, the office copy machine may not do. You could print the whole proposal on a laser printer, but this would be time-consuming and costly when printing 200 pages and six copies.

Start by looking up several printers in the Yellow Pages under Printers. Choose those that are close to your office. Driving across town in rush-hour traffic to get your proposal or make last-minute changes before the printer closes is much too risky.

If your proposal is basically simple and small, a quick-print shop is adequate. The quick-print shops, also called instant-press shops, are not equipped to provide services other than high-speed photocopy reproduction from your masters.

For more complex requirements, select full-service printers that are capable of providing typesetting, photographic work, paste-up, offset printing, binding, and possibly two-color work, in addition to special handling for covers and assembly.

Once you have selected several printers, arrange to visit their shops. Have them show you around and explain how they operate. Ask what they expect you to provide and what things cause them problems. Have them show you samples of their work. If they have an illustration department, ask to see it and meet the illustrators and typesetters.

Here are some of the basic qualities to look for in a printer and his printing.

- Can the printer handle all of your needs such as typesetting, binder tabs, photographic work, and complicated reproduction work for covers and special artwork?
- Is the printer well organized and able to meet your deadlines? It is critical that the printer understand up front the importance of having your job done on time.
- Is the print itself clear and sharp?
- Is the paper clean, with no roller marks or shadow lines?
- Are halftones sharp and with good contrast?
- Can the printer provide the appropriate kind of paper for your job?
- Does the printer offer advice and assistance in preparing the job?
- Does the printer suggest cost-saving alternatives for reproduction?
- Is the printer willing to handle small jobs? Some printers may believe that your small jobs are not a cost-effective way to do business.
- Is the printer willing to work overtime or on weekends if necessary?

Finding and keeping a good printer will be invaluable to you. For most nondeadline work, such as printing in-house forms or making copies of expendable data sheets, almost any printer is probably satisfactory. But for proposals, you need to establish a good rapport with a printer who is willing to hold his pressrun for an incoming job that might be several hours late, or who will add extra pages at the last minute for an additional, unexpected appendix.

You need someone who will do favors for you, and be willing to put up with totally outrageous demands and deadlines. If you are lucky enough to find a printer like this, do everything in your power to show your appreciation—just paying rush charges is not enough.

Also, check to see if the printer can handle the files electronically. You may be able to e-mail the files, or for larger proposals, FTP (file transfer protocol) them to a printer's FTP site. The printer receives the files and may download them to a printer without printing the file or making a master set of printed files.

If you have a printer with this capability, you would, of course, pay careful attention to how the files are transferred and how they need to be organized so that the printer can print directly without opening and manipulating the file itself.

And you should always pick up the proposal at the print shop so that you can review the work and have time to make any corrections, if necessary. It is inadvisable to have the printer package and mail your proposal without your review and signing of the cover letter.

Final Assembly

If you, and not the printer, will be doing the final assembly of multiple copies, here are some suggestions to make your job easier. The assumption is that you will be using three-ring binders.

Open all the binders and lay them out on a large table. Stack all the special graphics, foldouts, photos, etc., in sets in the order in which they will appear in the proposal. Stack all the binder tabs in sets. Organize the proposal by sections (front matter, main sections, appendixes) in individually labeled folders and stack these in the same manner.

Insert the front, back, and spine first, as binders may get heavy after they have been stuffed. Place the front matter in all the binders. Next, insert each section with its binder tab. Once all the printed matter is inserted, take each set of graphics, foldouts, photos, etc., and go through the binders one at a time, inserting this material where it belongs. By setting up this assembly-line procedure, you are less likely to overlook some material in some of the binders. The more methodical you are, the less likely you are to leave something out.

Finally, if possible, have another person check the binders for completeness. Often, a "fresh pair of eyes" can spot something you overlooked. At this point, you can't be too careful.

After all, this is the final moment when you are ready to present the winning proposal you have worked so hard to develop and prepare.

PREPARING AND MANAGING BOILERPLATE FILES

The term *boilerplate* refers to standard contract terms and conditions (Ts&Cs) in a written document. For example, payment terms such as *NET 30* or *F.O.B. Destination* are standard boilerplate. In recent years, boilerplate has evolved to mean anything, whether text or illustrations, that is standard material representing your products or contracts. For example, a product description such as a datasheet or a standard product illustration is a boilerplate file.

Boilerplate files can become an important part of your proposal program and one of the more useful tools for writing proposals. Be prepared, however, for resistance to preparing boilerplate files, as some people see them as being "canned" text that avoids addressing the real issues. This argument has some merit in that boilerplates can be overused at the expense of fresh, solution-oriented proposal writing. It is up to the individual proposal manager or writer to properly use boilerplate files.

If set up correctly, maintained, and supported, boilerplate files can help in many ways.

- Having at least 50 percent of a proposal prewritten affords the sales team more time to keep in contact with the customer.
- Boilerplate files give headquarters some margin of control over, and ensure consistency of, the information in a proposal.
- Boilerplate files enable you to respond more efficiently to an RFP, in addition to producing a better, more complete document.

However, there are potential problems in using boilerplate files that should be constantly monitored. *Prewritten material can be as dangerous as it is helpful if not kept current.* Because most proposals become an attachment to a successful contract, obsolete or incorrect information will become part of the contract.

Keep in mind that the purpose of a proposal is to tell a potential customer that you understand his requirements, you have a solution to those requirements, and you are able to address all the issues in your proposal; it is a written personal commitment to meeting his unique needs. Using boilerplate files exclusively in generating a proposal involves (and achieves) little more than stapling a few datasheets together and attaching a cover letter. Think of a proposal in terms of modules of information, and the prewritten boilerplate files as completed modules ready to be inserted in the appropriate places.

The purpose of this section is to help you develop ready-to-use materials about your company, products, and services; how to use them to your best advantage; how to organize and index them; how to get them to the people who will be using them; and how to maintain the files to ensure they are always current. Two types of boilerplate files are considered: written text that is stored online or in reproducible masters, and artwork in the form of illustrations, tables, and photographs.

This section will also discuss how to use the Internet and intranet, as well as collaborative software for distributing proposal information and working on proposals.

Later in this section, we will discuss developing, distributing, and maintaining the boilerplate files. Your corporation should have a department responsible for ensuring that boilerplate files are accurate and current. *Having old or outdated information is worse than no information.*

Developing Boilerplate Files

Undertaking the development of a boilerplate library is a sizeable task. Development of the files requires a dedicated effort to convert existing information about products and

---

Tip Boilerplate files should be an important part of your proposal development efforts.

WRITING KILLER SALES PROPOSALS

services, write new files as needed, and continually maintain those files.

Why have boilerplate, other than as a convenience? If you are a company with scattered or centralized offices, and have to respond to many RFPs to win business, there is a chance that your proposal writers are

- retyping company data and information each time.
- using past proposals as a basis for new proposals.
- using datasheets and other materials that are out of date.
- not responding well to certain sections of the RFP due to lack of comprehensive information.

Without adequate product descriptions, your company may be losing proposals because they are poorly written and not representative of your true product capabilities. Also, if a proposal is won, it may have been based on obsolete or out-of-date product information, which now forces you to renegotiate what is being provided.

Product and service boilerplates enable your corporation to centrally control the information used in a proposal and, therefore, ensure that the product information is current and correct. By eliminating the burden of searching for and typing information that already exists, good boilerplate files allow sales and technical personnel to concentrate on defining and developing the solution.

Having good boilerplates allow the proposal team to concentrate on putting together an attractive and appealing proposal that is interesting to read.

How are proposals written today in your company? Chances are that without any formal support, proposal material is taken from datasheets, press releases, old "successful" proposals, and other information gleaned from the corporate databanks. Lifting information from old proposals is common practice because the office administrator may have the last proposal written in hard

Tip Never use boilerplate files exclusively when writing a proposal.

CHAPTER 10 / PREPARING AND MANAGING BOILERPLATE FILES / 233

In my previous life as a manager of proposal development at a high-tech company, I was asked to go to a field office to review a proposal for a major effort that was underway. Reading the proposal, I began to realize that the product information was out of date and that a key new training class was not included. Researching the matter, I found that they were using a downloaded version of the corporate boilerplate that was more than six months old. Instead of getting the files fresh from the corporate database each time they were needed, they had downloaded the whole set of files six months ago and were continuing to use them without checking for updates. This is a prime example of how boilerplates, if not used correctly, can cause problems.

> *Tip* Make sure you scrub boilerplate taken from an old proposal.

copy or electronic versions. This copy is taken by the sales rep and cannibalized as needed for the new proposal. Because this old proposal may in fact be one or two generations removed from the original proposal written a year ago, it is highly likely that basic information is no longer correct.

While you would expect a sales rep to catch mistakes, it is almost impossible to catch all the mistakes or all outdated information. Thus, a proposal may be submitted with wrong product names, or worse yet, names of previous customers left in because a global search and replace for Bank of America did not catch BankAmerica or some other variation of the name.

Old proposals may contain products that have been superseded or become obsolete. Product specifications may have changed from 10 megabytes per second to 100 megabytes per second, and new features, benefits, and selling themes may not be included. Even in a well-run office, these problems occur.

Returning to the original theme of this chapter, how and where are proposal boilerplate files created and maintained? Most typically, the job of creating and maintaining the files belongs to the marketing organization.

Marketing is generally responsible for supporting sales and creating the sales collateral and basic themes that are published. However, some of the boilerplate needs to go beyond marketing material; therefore, marketing must have access to documentation in training, maintenance, and engineering. For the following reasons, it would be too much to expect each of these areas to maintain the boilerplate files:

- It is not generally in their charter.
- The files would not be consistent in writing and appearance.
- The collection would be distributed, making it harder to access and choose files from a central database.

Along with the files, there is a need to provide assistance when new products or sales themes are being generated. The field should have a consistent set of people to work with.

Another possibility is to have the sales department support the proposal files, because they are the ones who use them. This can work well if the sales department has the appropriately skilled people and can obtain the resources necessary to maintain the files. Sales would have, perhaps, better access to recent proposals, and could adapt parts of them as boilerplates—parts such as an excellent Executive Summary or a section on why your product XYZ is better than the competition's.

Establishing boilerplate files gives your company a chance to develop its own distinct proposal writing style and a winning proposal format style. This is important: Proposals from XYZ Company will always have a professional look and feel to them that many proposals simply will not.

Most people who write proposals are competent in their own particular areas, but not everyone is a competent writer. Few people are also good at setting up effective

Tip Old proposals may contain outdated data.

When desktop publishing software first appeared on the market, I quickly convinced my company to buy the software and get the people in my proposal department trained. We won one of our first proposals using the new software! When I debriefed the customer on why we won, he said part of the reason was that our proposal looked so professionally printed compared to those of other vendors. He was so impressed with the design and layout of the proposal that he asked me to recommend the software we used and to help him integrate it into his own company.

Tip

It is a total waste of time to have someone rekey a datasheet or training class description instead of having it already prepared.

page layout and design that complements the writing and adds value to a proposal.

Using professional writers and graphics people for the initial setup and design of the boilerplate files will help you to develop a consistent, professional, and appealing look for your proposal. Once a style is established, with perhaps a sample formatted page or two in the boilerplates, many writers will be able to adopt it in their own writing.

Text Boilerplate Files

One way to keep control of the proposal process is to have as much material as possible already written. The following is a description of standard material that can be already written, formatted, and ready for use when preparing a proposal. A common question is how much or how little should be written. It is advisable to always provide as much information as possible, since it is much easier to delete than to write something new at the last minute.

Descriptions of Products or Services

If your company sells products, such as equipment, machinery, or computer software or hardware, existing datasheets for your products can be edited, reformatted, and used as boilerplate material. If the product is a service, such as Internet development, boilerplates can be developed from existing product sheets and other literature.

Boilerplates can be derived from many different sources available to you, such as

- datasheets.
- brochures.
- Web sites/Internet material.
- service descriptions.
- contracts.
- product manuals.
- training manuals/presentation/classroom instruction materials.
- other proposals. (Be sure they are current and that the information is accurate.)

Material from all sources above may be combined to create a single boilerplate file. Of course, you can also interview people associated with the product and develop freshly written material.

Although marketing material seems easy and straightforward to use, some of it may not be suitable for proposals, and will need to be extensively edited. The problem is that marketing copy tends to be of an advertising nature whereas proposals are more technical and conservative. Watch out for inconsistencies in style, presentation, and level of detail that may result from combining sales literature modules with technical material taken from manuals or datasheets.

If your company provides services, use existing descriptions of those services and how clients are benefiting from them. This may include descriptions of the services, personnel profiles, and any unique products used to enhance service. In this case, service is the product that is being proposed. If there is no existing copy that is suitable for boilerplate files, have a marketing writer prepare new material to add to the boilerplate files, or try to write the product description yourself.

Tip A common question is, how much or how little needs to be written?

RFP requirements are not presented in such a way that you can drop a whole section into a response requirement. For example, your boilerplate on a personal computer may include everything from the monitor specifications to the floppy-drive specifications and individual components inside. In Figure 10-1, the RFP requirements call out each component of the personal computer as unique requirements. It would be inappropriate for you to drop in a complete boilerplate file as a response to these singular requirements, forcing the evaluator to find the information.

In the example of Figure 10-1, you would have to "cut and paste" the boilerplate file into the appropriate response section. While this may cause you more work, it facilitates the evaluation and ensures that all complementary features and benefits are properly described.

If you were to simply dump your workstation boilerplate into this RFP section, chances are you would lose points for not following RFP guidelines, even if your equipment met the specs. Dropping a complete boilerplate into sections like the above, instead of answering

> *Tip* RFPs may present a series of questions, allowing you to cut and paste your boilerplate responses.

FIGURE 10-1 Example RFP Specifications

Desktop System Description

Our system requirements for monitors are as follows:

1. Color monitor
2. Resolution 1600x1200
3. 21-inch screen
4. The CPU should be 5 GHz or better.
5. The hard drive must be 100 gigabytes.
6. Must contain a DVD rewriteable drive.
7. The Ethernet card must handle 100 Mb/s.

each requirement individually, could be interpreted as nonresponsive, and result in lost evaluation points, or even disqualification.

Company Services Provided

Services vary, of course, from company to company. If yours is a typical technology company, you may provide the following services that are normally proposed to your customers:

- System implementation
- Project management
- Site installation of hardware
- Training
- Maintenance
- Consulting

These services are usually centered around providing a product. However, if your product is a service itself, such as consulting, you would still need to describe how you conduct the consulting service once you have won the project.

Maintenance and training are common to most companies and lend themselves well to boilerplate files. The items below can be described in detail, stored as separate files, and combined during the proposal effort.

As a consultant, I must write proposals to win my business. Since consulting is a service, I include as part of my proposal, whether asked for or not, a description of how I will begin the consulting engagement and what my customer will need to have or make available to me when the project starts. In other words, I don't just show up on Monday without any prior preparation. Part of my "implementation plan" includes what the customer must prepare prior to my arrival onsite, and such things as office space, telephone, communications access, etc. Depending on the engagement, I may include in my proposal a checklist of items that the customer must accomplish prior to my arrival.

- Service hours
- Normal hours
- Outside-of-normal hours
- Response time to repair
- Normal response time
- Faster-than-normal response time
- Location of repair depots
- Location of spare-parts depots
- Need for spare parts on site
- Ability to meet special requests
- Normal repair procedures
- Preventive-maintenance program
- Normal inspection visits
- Special services offered

Maintenance and Hours of Service

Perhaps the most important question in an RFP is how the product will be serviced after purchase. This section should be more detailed than the information outlined in the contract Ts&Cs. Tables, such as the one in Figure 10-2, are very useful, easily maintained, and provide information that can be used in a variety of places.

Training and Education

The second common service offered is training and education. Most companies offer some type of training program

FIGURE 10-2 Sample Table for Maintenance Response Time

Table B-1. Extended-Hour Maintenance Coverage

Day	Coverage Time	Charge
Saturday or Sunday	8 hours	Add 5.0% to BMMC*
Saturday or Sunday	12 hours	Add 10.0% to BMMC
Monday-Friday	16 hours	Add 25.0% to BMMC
Monday-Friday	24 hours	Add 40.0% to BMMC
Monday-Friday	12 hours	Add 15.0% to BMMC

*Basic Monthly Maintenance Charge

that customers will pay for. Therefore, describe your training program and classes in detail. If your company has standard classes and training facilities, describe all classes (see Figure 10-3) and the facilities. (That is, from the boilerplate file, you would only include those classes

FIGURE 10-3 Sample Training Description

Administration Training

Course Title:	Ajax Workstation Administration
Duration:	5 days
Instructional	
Materials:	1. Workstation Administration Student Guide
	2. Book, Workstation Administration, by Jones and Wiley
	3. System Command Summary

Course Description

This course is designed for anyone assuming total responsibility for the administration of an Ajax workstation system. It is an advanced course that focuses on the fundamental skills required to maintain the Ajax workstation system environment.

It includes information on management of the database and management of the workstations.

Topics are presented using a problem-solving approach. Guided by the instructor, students are expected to refer to the manuals to determine the steps necessary to accomplish administrative tasks.

Maximum number of students per session is ten. Additional courses may be scheduled at prevailing rates.

Course Outline

1. Editor use
2. Documentation
3. System start-up and shut-down
4. File system management
5. User setup and control
6. Backups
7. Device configuration
8. Workstation operations
9. Database operations
10. Preventive maintenance procedures

that apply to the products being proposed.) If your company provides training through other companies or self-paced tutorials, describe each one.

- Introduction and overview of the training organization
- Description of training philosophy
- Description of training facilities
  - Classroom atmosphere
  - Online training capabilities
  - Internal facilities
  - Lunchroom
  - Workshops available
  - Laboratories
- Resume of typical instructor
- Location of training facilities
- On-site training requirements and description
- Materials supplied/materials needed
- Descriptions of all classes
- Instruction methodology
  - Self-paced workbook instruction
  - Stand-up lecture
  - Computer-based training
- Ability to provide customized training
- Ability to respond to special requirements

Corporate and Project Management Descriptions

Often, an RFP requires a description of your corporation, resumes for the people who will be working on the project, a statement of project management methodology, and what, if anything, the customer is responsible for during the implementation period. Relationships are easily depicted and revised by developing a hierarchical organization chart. This is a very good place to describe any unique equipment or facilities that will differentiate your company from other companies.

Tip

Corporate descriptions are provided to allay any fears that your company is too small to handle the project.

A corporate profile is a basic short description of your company and what it does. Annual reports and marketing brochures are good sources for this material.

Corporate Profile

The corporate profile may include, but should not be limited to, the following information:

- Primary objective/mission and date company was founded
- Major product line and any other equipment and services offered
- Number of people employed
- Personnel functions expressed as a percentage (sales 20 percent, service 40 percent, R&D 20 percent, management 20 percent)
- Description of special laboratories, equipment, and processes
- Primary locations of manufacturing plants, repair depots, sales offices, service offices, and other significant locations
- Basic company organization and organization charts
- What countries you are located in
- Reporting relationships—if you are owned by another company

Below is an example of a typical corporate introduction.

ACME Information Solutions is a Fortune 500 company that has one of the largest networks of information-conversion service centers in the world. With more than 35 years of experience providing image capture and processing services, ACME is a leading provider of integrated information-management services, transforming data into effective business communications through capturing, transforming, and activating critical documents. ACME has more than 150 operations offices in the

United States, Canada, Mexico, India, and Europe. Within the United States, the company has more than 50 multifunctional imaging centers serving more than 9,000 customers nationwide and operates more than 60 facility-management sites located on customers' premises. Throughout these facilities, ACME scans more than 200 million pages per month and prints more than 150 million pages per month—worldwide. ACME's services support customer acquisition and customer-service activities throughout the health-care, financial, utility, manufacturing, energy, and telecommunications markets.

The above corporate profile provides a good, but brief, overview of the company. Remember that you can provide more detail in an appendix and that additional corporate detail will appear in the annual report and company brochures.

Project Management
Project management may or may not be a factor in your proposal, depending on the size and type of business you are bidding. If, however, you do bid on large jobs that require project management, try to collect old proposals and talk to current project managers to get the information. This is usually a sensitive area and care must be taken not to overstate your abilities or describe services that are not normally provided. These files, in particular, should provide an outline of possibilities and should be reviewed and revised for each new proposal by the designated project manager.

A project management file may include the following:

- Project management approach
- General project principles applied
- Project team organization
- Project staffing and duties
- Project leader and duties
- Project plan

> *Tip* A well-written project management plan could be the difference between winning and losing in tight competition.

- Project deliverables
- Vendor's responsibilities
- Customer's responsibilities

The project plan should be your first attempt at putting together what you perceive to be the major steps of the implementation effort. While this plan may not be accurate or even close to the final plan, it gives the customer something to review and consider. There is a fair chance that your competition will be too lazy to do this and will only talk about putting together a plan ". . . after contracts have been signed . . . ."

It is important to emphasize that putting a plan together, even for the smallest project, will help you to

- think through the steps involved—for your own benefit.
- provide the customer with a "better than a guess" idea of what is involved in installing and maintaining your equipment.
- provide the customer with a subject in your proposal about which he may ask questions and begin a dialogue with you about the project.

Figure 10-4 gives an abbreviated example of a project management plan that provides the customer with some basic tasks. These tasks will be reviewed and finalized during the first meetings after the contract is awarded.

Personnel
Other corporate descriptions that can be prewritten are resumes of leading company officers, engineers, and product developers who may be part of the project (see Figure 10-5). Once the format is developed, it will be easier to write resumes for everyone involved in the project. *Many RFPs require resumes* for the project personnel.

Reference Account Descriptions
One important boilerplate file describes past projects or customers who are successfully using your product and

FIGURE 10-4 Sample Project Plan

ID	Task Name
1	Project Initiation and Control
2	Organize project
3	Define project scope
4	Finalize implementation plan
5	Orient project team
6	Review implementation plan
7	Hold kickoff meeting
8	Project Control
9	Establish project meeting schedule
10	Establish project reporting schedule
11	Develop contingency plans
12	Prepare status reports
13	Hardware Ordering
14	Complete purchase requisitions
15	Monitor Project Schedule
16	Hold project team meeting
17	Software Ordering
18	Complete purchase acquisition
19	Schedule receipt of SW
20	Schedule Hardware Installation
21	Software Development
22	Begin software development
23	Site Configuration
24	Schedule site survey
25	Obtain facilities layout
26	Installation plan
27	Prepare detailed installation plan

can be used as references in the proposal. Keep in mind that any time you list a reference in a proposal, the RFP team could request to interview that reference. Be sure that any reference you list 1) consents to be listed and 2) is willing to be called.

FIGURE 10-5 Sample Resume

Name:	Mary Smith
Title:	Project Manager
Education:	MBA, EE, Computer Science
Experience:	Ms. Smith has been with AJAX for ten years. Her last assignment was project manager for the Pacific Bank project. This project involved $10 million in hardware and software, custom application software, and integrating and managing four subcontractors. The Pacific Bank project was completed on time and within the specified budget.

For the ACME project, Ms. Smith will assume the role of project manager. She will be responsible for the following functions:

- Hardware integration and source selection
- System software integration
- Custom application software
- Customer interface

The reference account file should include at least the following information:

- Name and address of company
- Type of business or industry
- Contact name, address, and telephone number
- Contract number (if there is one)
- Length of contract or performance period
- Dollar amount of contract
- Description of project or application
- Description of equipment installed

This type of boilerplate file is very useful, but also very sensitive. The most powerful type of reference account description is one in which you can actually name the account and a person within the account to contact. It is also impressive to be able to visit that account if a site visit is requested in the RFP. On the other hand, few sales reps feel comfortable with potential customers calling existing customers directly if there is a chance that the reference account has experienced any problems. Figure 10-6 is a reference account description.

Another problem with reference accounts is that they tend to change—not only from good to bad, but from one level of equipment or service to another. It is especially important to maintain and update reference account files.

The actual types of reference accounts that should be in your boilerplate files depend on your business. For example, a large software company might have several markets for its business, such as banking, communications networking, retail point-of-sale, and perhaps a library system. In this case, the software company would maintain one or more references for each line of business. If your business were service-related, the references would be two or three of the largest and best-run accounts.

The actual format for writing project description could be as follows:

- Introduction and description of service performed
- Situation at account before your company
- Situation that led to the change
- Situation after your service
- Description of services performed
- List of equipment used to perform the job
- Amount of work being performed by the above equipment
- Appropriate high-level customer quotation

A reference account is most useful if the work being performed is similar to the type and size being proposed. That way, the potential customer can see your work and relate that work to his job. Customer references with demonstrable products that are installed and working—not future or intended products still on the drawing board—lend more credibility to your proposal.

Reference accounts should be cross-indexed by the application (work being accomplished), the name of the

Tip Be sure that your reference accounts are current and still in good standing.

FIGURE 10-6 Sample Reference Account

Name: ACME Bank
Location: St. Louis, MO
Project Leader: Jessica Crawford
                     1919 State Street
                     St. Louis, MO
                     (312) 555-1212
Contract: FP091765
Type: Fixed Price
Performance Period: 1/4/2003–1/4/2005

Description: AJAX was responsible for supplying a turnkey computer system to automate ACME Bank's Customer Information System (CIS). This system is fully installed and is currently handling 500 transactions per hour per branch. There are 50 branches throughout the United States.

AJAX provided all system hardware, system software, peripheral devices, and the communications network. AJAX also provided, through a subcontractor, the CIS applications software. The application involved working with ACME clerks and customers in the design of each screen, the acceptable response time, and additional functions.

AJAX also was responsible for the system training, end-user training, and system maintenance. This system has met and exceeded all requirements and has increased bank activity by 22 percent.

Current plans require installation of new branch sites, upgrading the current computer to the next performance model, and developing new services based around current installations.

ACME currently has the following installed equipment:

   4 ea. Bonus Computer Systems, model 11-21

   4 ea. Interface modules

   20 ea. Alpine ATMs, model 50

   10 ea. X.25 gateways and communications peripherals

account, and the size of the account (whether in dollars, workstations, lines of code, etc.). Most customers like to read about jobs similar to their own for a number of reasons:

- They like to know that you, the vendor, speak their language. There is nothing worse than paying a vendor and having to teach him "the business."

- Many customers don't want to be the "beta" site for your first effort at developing a new application.
- A second- or third-generation customer is going to benefit from your pervious experience—especially in fast-moving technology fields.

Corporate Capabilities and Facilities

A capabilities and facilities section reinforces your ability to handle a contract by demonstrating that you have the resources needed and that they are available. These resources will vary according to the type of company, but typically would include

Tip Providing capabilities and facilities information will distinguish your company from the competition.

- description of corporate facilities, including number of personnel and total square footage available.
- description of facilities, factories, assembly areas, warehouses, and parts and remanufacturing depots.
- descriptions of unique equipment or custom-built facilities such as a custom-design microchip manufacturing plant, a special satellite acoustic test area, or a wind tunnel.
- capabilities of facilities to perform work, e.g., microchips per hour or total build capacity.
- ability to meet or exceed increasing demands or peak work abilities.
- ability to build new facilities or increase capacity of existing facilities.

Providing this type of information, whether required or not, may help distinguish your company and proposal from the competition.

For example, a new service company bidding on a large contract must demonstrate to the potential customer that it does have the resources to handle the contract. Perhaps it is a large landscaping project for a city park, and your company is a new landscaping business. For a large job, the city (that wrote the RFP) knows that to meet the time requirement, the winner will have to move so many cubic yards of earth per hour, and in order to do that, they will have to utilize the appropriate number and type of earthmovers.

If yours is a new company that doesn't already own the requisite equipment, you will have to show the city that you have the capability to rent or lease more equipment and hire additional resources in order to complete the contract. Then you will have to convince the city that you can do the work with these newly acquired resources. Remember, there may be a larger company competing with you that already has all the equipment and resources needed to handle the project.

Previous Proposals

In addition to the basic material collected from headquarters' sources, there are also proposals written in the field that may yield some excellent material for proposal boilerplates. Parts of these proposals can be cannibalized and turned into boilerplates. Below are some examples and ideas.

Tip Previous proposals are a good source of material but they must be scrubbed before use.

- *Application-specific Executive Summary.* Often an Executive Summary is written by an industry expert, whether it's the sales rep or a consultant brought in to help. It is a good idea to warehouse proposals that deal with vertical industry applications, such as transportation, pharmaceutical, insurance, etc. These Executive Summaries can be "scrubbed" (for lack of a better term) by the proposal boilerplate team to eliminate customer references but retain industry-specific insights.
- *Product-specific write-ups.* As discussed in previous sections, an RFP can be made up of a list of questions to be answered. It is a safe assumption that if one customer asks a question, it will be asked again in the future. This is similar, in a sense, to the Internet FAQ (frequently asked questions) file.

Most companies know from experience that there are certain questions that are asked over and over. Having ready-made answers to these questions will greatly enhance the proposal effort and potentially provide more accurate answers.

- *Product comparisons.* RFPs often want you to compare two products, such as two servers, and explain why you would choose one over the other. For example, you give the customer a choice between ACME and Widgets servers, and they want to know the differences and trade-offs.

- *Third-party or partner proposals.* Depending on how you operate as a business, you may team or subcontract with a system integrator or value-added reseller. Third parties often specialize in a vertical market area, such as insurance, and their proposals may provide a wealth of detail that you would not normally have access to. Careful review of final third-party proposals, and permission to "copy," should be a regular exercise for the boilerplate team.

These are just some of the subject areas to consider for your boilerplate files; they should not limit your thinking but provide a starting point. As a reminder and note of caution, boilerplate files must be maintained and kept up-to-date. This can become a challenging and full-time effort for a large set of files; however, the benefits can be significant when writing a proposal.

Illustration Boilerplate Files

Illustrations should play a vital role in any proposal; however, because they are even more difficult and time-consuming than writing text, illustrations are not used to advantage, or used at all. Like boilerplate text, illustrations that are common to your company can be prepared in advance, indexed, filed, and made available for use in any proposal. These illustrations can serve all

Tip   Illustrations of all types play a vital role in a proposal.

field offices and provide the same benefits as boilerplate text.

Remember that illustrations, like text files, can become out of date. Using old illustrations may technologically date your proposal and provide data that is inaccurate.

Following are descriptions of the types of illustrations that should be in the files. Most illustrations can be found in existing company literature. Review product brochures, training files, and product manuals for sources of illustrations. If you can't find any, new illustrations can be drawn, or photographs taken.

Many illustrations are electronically generated and may already be available from other corporate resources. With the availability of word processor programs to handle illustrations, and the profusion of illustration software packages, it has never been easier to put illustrations into a proposal. Many illustration software programs come with extensive clip art resources that can be used to generate diagrams of computer systems, computer networks, architectural layouts and designs, and many other business applications.

Clip art figures can be enhanced with drawings made specifically for your company by skilled graphic illustrators. In addition to drawings, other forms of artwork can be incorporated electronically, such as digital photographs and scanned images. Digital cameras make it easy for you to take a picture of a facility and insert it into your proposal without the support of an art department or other groups. A scanner can digitally copy almost any image—from photographs to drawings—and enable you to insert that image into your proposal. This means that even if there is a detailed illustration in a manual and you don't have access to the original, it is possible to scan and insert that drawing.

There are many other electronic tools available that will enhance your proposal by providing graphics or illustrations. Here are just a few:

Tip Your graphics program may already have boilerplate drawings.

- *Drawing software.* This type of software ranges from simple to extremely complex. The most useful programs are those with predrawn illustrations of computers, networks, office furniture, buildings, high-technology objects such as satellites, etc. These predrawn illustrations can usually be linked with arrows, circles, network clouds, and many other connectors. The average user no longer has be an artist to put together a reasonably good diagram.
- *Organization software.* These programs generally are designed to build organization charts and other charts that show placement of personnel within a company.
- *Workflow software.* Workflow may be specialized for certain industries, but in general, the software shows how a work process moves from one step to another. The workflow diagrams can be cut and pasted into a proposal.
- *Project management software.* This allows the user to develop and build a project. The completed project task list can be shown as a written task list or a chart with tasks connected. The completed project, whether written or drawn, can be inserted into the proposal.
- *Screen capture software.* Screen capture software allows you to capture what is on your computer monitor and save it. The saved image can be pasted into the proposal in the appropriate place. A screen shot may be taken to show proposed application screens or work that has been competed for other customers.
- *Spreadsheet software.* Spreadsheet programs can provide everything from simple tables to graphical charts and illustrations.
- *Internet.* While this is not a software package, many types of illustrations, charts, photographs, and

Tip A wide range of software tools will help you to illustrate your proposal.

other graphics can be downloaded from Internet sites. Care should be taken to properly recognize copyrighted material or original authors.

Products or Equipment

Manuals are a good place to start in developing your illustration boilerplate files. If your company has a graphics or technical art department, the original illustrations from manuals will be kept there. The idea for boilerplate illustrations should be discussed with the manager of the department and a plan for obtaining the required illustrations should be formed before any work is started. This plan should include keeping the illustrations current.

After obtaining a complete set of manuals for the products you will be writing proposals for, start searching for illustrations, making notes of the manual and page numbers. When a manual is thoroughly searched, copy the marked pages on a photocopier and write the manual number and page on the back of the copy. The art department will need this information when they begin to search their files for the illustrations you are requesting. Illustrations for products or equipment may include:

Tip Product illustrations can be found in many areas of the company.

- screen shots of product designs.
- screen shots of products used.
- photographs of products.
- line drawings of products.
- wiring diagrams and schematics.
- cross-section and cutaway drawings.
- parts breakouts.
- unique-features diagrams.

Figure 10-7 is an example of a stock boilerplate illustration that may be used to support text descriptions of products.

FIGURE 10-7 Typical Boilerplate Illustration

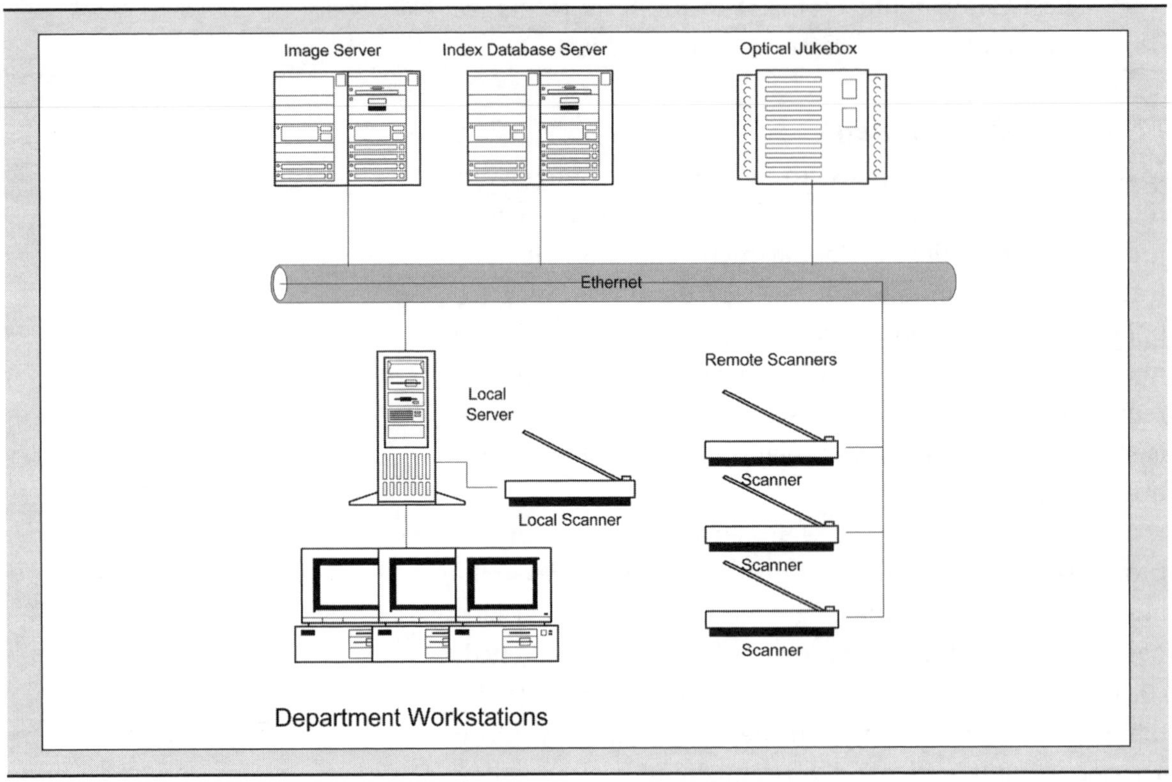

Facilities

In proposals, facilities are often described but not illustrated in any manner. For example, if your company is in the aerospace business and you have a special vacuum chamber, a photograph of the facility and several photographs inside the chamber add credibility to the text.

Types of facilities are

- headquarters buildings.
- typical training classrooms.
- research laboratories.
- personnel at workstations.
- special equipment.
- special tools designed and used.
- manufacturing buildings.

- manufacturing assembly areas.
- quality control areas.
- clean-room areas.
- unique transportation facilities.

Photographs increase credibility and should be used instead of line drawings or architectural renderings for facilities with working equipment or special features. For maximum impact, these illustrations should be placed as close to the text as possible. Photographs may be difficult to use in a proposal because of their size.

However, a picture of a clean room lends credibility to your proposal and gives the reader some assurance that you have experience in this area.

Headquarters Organization and Personnel Resumes

In an RFP that requires the Management Section to provide an example of a program implementation plan, the RFP will usually ask for a management organization chart and resumes of key personnel. Existing and newly created corporate organization charts are used to demonstrate where a project fits into the overall corporate structure and who will be managing the project.

The first diagram might illustrate how your company or division fits into a larger holding company, if that is applicable. Or, as shown by the chart in Figure 10-8, you might start with top management of your company and chart down to the vice president's level. Next, start with the vice president responsible for your division or group and branch down to the line managers who will be working on this particular project.

This sequential breakdown of your management organization lets you use all the charts or just the one closest to the project. It also complements the text if your company is large and the relationships are complex. The primary purpose of an organization chart is to show the

Tip Org charts visually show the customer who will manage the project.

potential customer how close his project will be to top management.

As part of a management plan, the RFP may ask for the resumes of key personnel on the project. If not already developed, resumes of key project personnel can be easily written and kept in a boilerplate file. A project resume should highlight a person's skills, similar project history and experience, and education. Including a photograph of the person is optional; however, a picture has the benefit of connecting a name to a face.

These organizational charts are easily developed with current software packages. The software program to

FIGURE 10-8 Management Organization Charts

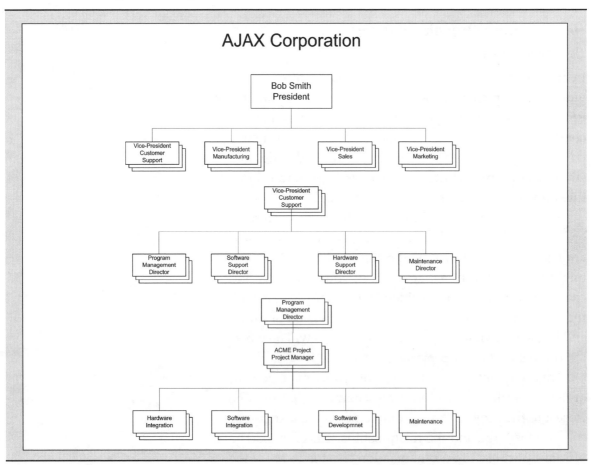

build an organizational chart is available in most word processing packages and can be used by almost anyone on the proposal team.

Reference Accounts

Many RFPs request that reference account descriptions be provided in the proposal. Depending on your product or service, the text for these accounts can be enhanced by providing photographs of working installations or of your product or service being used by a customer. This will reinforce for the evaluator that your company's products are actually operating in the field—as opposed to companies that may still be in the design stage, with no working product or reference.

These illustrations will be strategically placed with the text in your proposal. Illustrations can range from photographs of installations to computer screen shots of operating software designs.

Cost/Pricing Information

Some companies have standard forms for pricing equipment in a proposal. These forms may contain standard costing breakdowns for direct, indirect, or overhead information. This level and type of breakdown are often requested in an RFP. If it's available as boilerplate material, the finance group at headquarters will be better able to control the information than if the information is generated in the field.

However, if you use a basic spreadsheet program for pricing, the output can be easily cut and pasted directly into your proposal. When describing certain parts of your pricing, such as development costs, the spreadsheet model can be inserted into the text, underscoring the discussion. Diagrams and charts that show such things as return on investment periods can easily be used to illustrate your pricing numbers.

> *Tip* Use standard forms if available. Otherwise, develop a spreadsheet.

Cover Artwork and Illustrations

Given professional resources, a company can develop specialized covers for its proposals. The covers may reflect the application or the vertical industry for which the proposal is being written. Standard cover art could be developed for the following areas:

- Accounts payable
- Human resources
- Purchasing
- Manufacturing

Examples of vertical industries are:

- Banking
- Insurance
- Health care
- Transportation

Covers may be designed by professional illustrators to reflect your company's overall look and feel. If your company's logo and graphics are ultra-modern, for example, the covers should convey that same look and feel.

Using modern networks and communications, the covers can become part of the boilerplate files. The cover might come with an instruction page that specifies how to set up copy on the cover, such as "AJAX SEEP Program," along with the date of the proposal.

Covers can even be designed in color and prepared for printing on local color printers; the completed cover file (illustration and insert type) may also be delivered or transmitted to a color-copy vendor.

Using Boilerplate Files

A proposal should be as personalized to your customer and his requirements as it can be. This leads the customer to believe that you really spent time thinking about his needs and problems and have arrived at a

Tip Cover art adds a sense of professionalism to your proposal.

unique solution. Your boilerplate files allow you and your sales team to spend more time being creative, because the bulk of the work has been done beforehand and is available to you in the form of prewritten material.

There is, however, one pitfall to avoid: Don't think that because you have boilerplate files handy that you don't have to start as soon as you would have without them. It's easy to procrastinate when you know you have ready-to-use materials at hand. You may think you have plenty of time, and then realize too late that the proposal is more complex than you thought; or you may suddenly discover that you need to have approval and pricing for some special service requirements. Don't be lulled into a false sense of security! The result of this kind of casual effort can be as bad or worse than any achieved without boilerplate material.

Boilerplate files are best used as skeletons to be fleshed out. They may provide all or nearly all the core information, but it is up to you and the proposal team to bring these files together as a cohesive whole. This means custom introductions to sections must be written, bridges must be built between boilerplate facts and the customer's needs, and in general, the boilerplate material must be tailored and personalized as much as possible.

If possible, boilerplate should be broken down into individual units that reflect the whole product. As in the above example of the personal computer, requirements often force you to describe a system component-by-component, instead of as a whole unit. Therefore, if your boilerplate topic was AJAX Personal Computer, the subtopics to the file might include:

- Monitors
- CPU types
- Hard drive options
- Communications options
- Keyboard/Pointer device options

Tip — Boiler-plate files are best used as skeletons to be fleshed out.

With this kind of "componentization," files are easier to use and to update.

Indexing Files

For you and others to readily access your boilerplate files, you need to develop a method for indexing them. There are three key considerations:

1. The indexing/numbering system must be understandable and easy to use.
2. The system should allow for new files to be inserted with minimal effort.
3. The index number should show whether the files are current with the latest product revisions.

Written Files

The first step in developing an index system for text files is to establish categories such as products, services, education, corporate history and organization, account references, and other general files.

One very simple method is to have the index number composed of eight characters in two parts: the first part signifies the year the file was released (designated by an *R*), and the second is the sequential number of the file (designated by an *S*). For example, R03S063 indicates that the year of release was 2003 and the file is number 63.

After assigning the numbers, file the material alphabetically by category. A typical index might look like this:

Corporate		
	History	R03S001
	Organization	R03S002
Maintenance		
	System maintenance	R03S021
	System operation	R03S014

This method lets you insert a new file in front of others without having to renumber the files from the new file forward. In addition, it helps you to determine if the file is up-to-date. If a product was updated in 2003 and the release date in the index number is 2002, you will know the file is not current.

Illustrations

Assigning categories to illustrations is similar to categorizing text files. Depending on the type of product or services your company offers, illustrations may be separated into categories such as equipment, facilities, organization charts, reference accounts, cost charts and graphs, diagrams, and system configurations.

There are many types of illustrations.

- *Line art.* Line drawings can be created in pen-and-ink, pencil, or any other medium. They may also be computer-generated. They can depict anything from a piece of equipment to a wiring schematic.
- *Photographs.* File photographs may be original glossies or digital photos ready for production.
- *Screen shots.* Screen shots are images from a computer screen and can be used for a variety of purposes.
- *Computer-generated illustrations.* These may range from workflow diagrams to spreadsheet charts.

You can number the files just like the text files, but add a *P* or *D* or *C* to indicate whether an illustration is a photograph, a drawing, or computer-generated. The illustrations can then be filed alphabetically by category, such as products, corporate organization, facilities, etc.

Once established, the index can be kept online on a network that is accessible to all users, or a copy of the index could be sent to the field offices and updated as needed. Remote users would then cite the reference number when requesting illustrations.

However, with today's networking capabilities—the Internet, intranet, and private networks—it is most convenient to provide the proposal boilerplate files online. Proposal writers and teams are apt to be working around the clock.

Communication networks and universal access, with proper security (of course), will provide a tremendous boon to your company's proposal-writing efforts and success.

Dissemination of Material

After text and illustrations are indexed and ready for use, the most important consideration is how to make the material available to the users. If you are working out of a single office and developing the files for your own office, it remains fairly simple to keep the files available on a local server or PC. However, if you are working at headquarters and the boilerplate library is being developed for multiple field offices, the problem of distribution needs to be considered.

The best approach to keeping boilerplate text files available for users, as well as for update, is to keep them on a network server. This also applies to any computer-generated art. If the boilerplate files are available online, they should be on a network-accessible server that has 24-hour connection service. This gives users independent access at all times.

The reason for this type of access, besides being useful, is that you may want to prevent users from downloading the database to their own servers. If users have the database locally, they may not remember to update it periodically and may not have the most current information. If the information and product specifications change and they are using old data, it's very possible they will turn in a proposal that commits you to an outdated product.

Depending on your company's capabilities, it might be possible to periodically disseminate a copy of the

> *Tip* Security is a primary concern with boilerplate.

database to all field offices via the company network. This provides the field office with the latest version of the files; by offering local access, it also reduces traffic on the network, if that is a concern. Updating individual files via network download, you ensure that the latest product boilerplate is correct. If this is your method, don't forget to update the index file. All of this should be transparent to the user.

In terms of security, it may be better having the files on a central server with greater control of access. Field offices may not exercise sufficient control over the files. It may be impossible to prevent employees from leaving with a copy of the data; however, good security would prevent them from logging on to the network after they have left the company. Security should be considered and reviewed with the appropriate personnel.

As mentioned before, it is essential for the boilerplate material to be kept current and accessible to the people who need it the most; if not, they will simply ignore it and go back to using old proposals and outdated material. Boilerplate files must also be easy to use, easily accessible, and easily changed to fit unique proposal needs.

> *Tip* The proposal boilerplate should be updated with the regular product updates.

Maintenance of the Boilerplate Library

Maintenance includes several functions: adding files as new products are developed or new material is written, drawn, or photographed; determining the category for new pieces and assigning index numbers; updating existing files; filing the material itself; and informing all interested parties of changes to the boilerplate library or its index.

New products, whether major or minor, need to be researched and added to the library. If boilerplates are not maintained and up-to-date, the field users will find a way to get the information on their own. Thus begins a cycle of duplicated effort in which the keepers of the boilerplate library will become frustrated and ineffectual. The boilerplate team must be *pro*active instead of *re*active.

The team should maintain links to various parts of the company such as education, training, and engineering to ensure that they are informed of the release schedule for new products. Proposal files should be updated on the day the new product is released. It is very probable that proposals will be written based on upcoming products, and therefore the request for this material will be made by the field.

The boilerplate team should have access to, or be aware of, major proposals being written in the field. These proposals can become a tremendous source of new boilerplate material in areas that may not be covered in normal product literature.

The boilerplate team should also be receptive to suggestions for additions and/or changes to the boilerplates. It must be remembered that field personnel are using these files constantly, and if something is missing or doesn't work, they should have an open channel to the boilerplate team.

By keeping the boilerplate files modular, by subject and file, they can be updated individually, or new files added, without renumbering existing files or having to update the whole database with each new release. This means that the database will not have to be taken offline for updates, and users will always have the most current files when they access the database.

It is also helpful to indicate in the boilerplate index the most recent update date and file(s). This way, proposal teams can periodically log on to the boilerplate database and see if new usable files have been added. Otherwise, they would somehow have to search the database or index and try to determine if a new file had been added. For example, think of how manuals are updated with a list of changes and changed pages described in a general cover letter.

Developing and maintaining boilerplate material is a demanding, time-consuming task; but you will find that establishing and supporting a library of well-written text files and quality illustrations is well worth the effort and will contribute to winning more contracts.

Summary

Having a current, standardized boilerplate library will save the proposal team members hundreds of hours of work, providing more accurate and timely information than they could locate on their own. Material from these files can add a professional look to proposals and perhaps provide that extra information needed to win. Of course, color photographs and bells-and-whistles product features will not be why a customer selects your company; it is basic product functionality that counts. However, keep in mind that disorganized, hastily written proposals with sketchy grammar and poor spelling may be immediately eliminated.

Boilerplates can be extracted from data sheets, manuals, training materials, marketing literature, and even from field-written proposals. Companies usually have a wealth of material to be mined when you're gathering information. The material can be creatively used to make response files that range from general product descriptions to files that respond to individual technical questions.

With proper maintenance and dedicated resources, boilerplate files can help standardize the information content and format. And the more that can be standardized, the better your thinking and writing will be.

DEVELOPING ILLUSTRATIONS FOR YOUR PROPOSAL

The value of incorporating illustrations into a proposal cannot be overemphasized. Through graphic representation, products assume greater reality in readers' minds, and complex concepts become more meaningful. Text that is devoid of illustrations, especially in technical documents, is difficult to understand without the benefit of visual assistance.

Illustrations can be powerful tools for conveying information in a proposal. They serve as visual anchors or points of reference for product descriptions, offering an authenticity not available from written descriptions alone. In addition, illustrations help the reader to better assimilate the message by providing relief to the eye—especially appreciated when the reader is faced with several hundred pages of complex technical description and jargon. Seeing illustrations that complement the text may help evaluators differentiate your proposal from the others, thus increasing your score for professionalism.

However, like the writing they support, illustrations are subject to misuse and abuse. All illustrations in a proposal should directly relate to and clarify the subject matter. Illustrations used merely as embellishments or gimmicks will lessen the overall impact of the proposal by creating confusion and distracting the reader. A misleading or irrelevant illustration may cause the reader to misunderstand your product's capabilities or the services you are selling, and therefore lessen your chances of winning the contract.

On the other hand, a well-illustrated proposal not only helps describe your products and services, but also reflects well on you and your company by demonstrating that you have a clear grasp of the problem and can illustrate a viable solution. Because your proposal may be an evaluator's first communication from your company, it is imperative that the first impression be positive—or there may not be a second chance. In one sense, your proposal is the first "product" the customer is given, and how this product is received will set the stage for all communications to follow.

The purpose of this chapter is to provide a guide for distinguishing among different types of graphics; suggestions for sources of ready-to-use art; some tools, techniques, and standards you will need to be familiar with; and how to organize it all.

This section will focus on graphics that can be electronically generated and inserted into a proposal. The prevalence and quality of these programs almost guarantees high-quality illustrations.

Tip All illustrations should directly relate to and clarify the subject matter.

The Art of Illustrations

The term *illustration* refers to a variety of graphics such as line drawings, scanned images, or photographs of such things as system configurations, equipment, places, or people. Illustrations include charts, graphs, or maps. In a proposal, illustrations are referred to as figures. However, illustrations need not be confined to the text alone; a good drawing or photograph can make an appealing cover that arouses the interest of your reader, or may be inserted facing the title page to introduce your product. Statistical material is presented in tables, which are not strictly illustrations. However, for simplicity's sake, both tables and figures are referred to as illustrations in this book.

Types of Illustrations

Line Art

Line art is the basic figure drawn to resemble the actual product. Line art can be anything that you draw, such as your computer workstation, a satellite antenna, or a workflow diagram describing how a business process is being reengineered.

Line art is generally called a "Figure" in the proposal and is labeled with a figure number and caption at the bottom of the figure. The figure number may be a simple sequential number as in Figure 1, 2, 3 . . . . or it may be numbered with the section number preceding the sequential number, as in Figure 5-1, 5-2, etc. The figure caption should be short and descriptive (see Figure 11-1).

Tip Line art represents a product or service.

FIGURE 11-1 System Overview

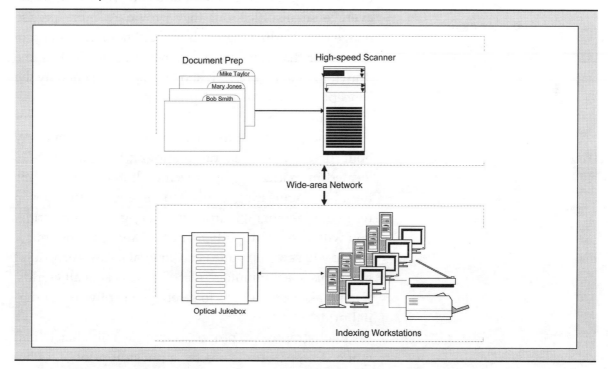

The caption should not be a long sentence or descriptive paragraph. The figure itself should illustrate and complement the subject of the text. The caption below it should be flush left with the margin. The word "Figure" and the number appear in bold, while the caption appears in italics. The caption should use initial caps. See Figure 11-1 for an example of line art and the placement of the figure caption. When used in the text to reference an illustration, the word "figure" has an initial cap.

An illustration callout should always appear before the illustration itself appears in the text. Illustrations that have been called out in the text should appear on that same page, if possible, or on the page following the callout.

Photographs

Without giving a short course in photography, suffice it to say that photographs are harder to work with in the average small office, but they provide a more precise image of a product than a drawing. Photographs assure the reader that your product is real and finished. A line drawing, as in Figure 11-1, above, may represent only the concept, and not the actual product.

Photographs may be taken specifically for a proposal and project but may also be available in company boilerplate files. General photographs are typically located in marketing, but specific photographs may be found in engineering, education, or service. In order to receive a photograph from marketing or engineering, you will have to properly identify it and give the source where you saw it, if there is no general index. Also, don't make this a last-minute request; in the best of all worlds, it may take several days to receive your physical or digital print.

Photographs in proposals are usually black and white. To reproduce correctly, a physical print of a photograph (not a digital photo, which is already formatted

Tip ▷ Photographs can be effective but are more difficult to work with.

correctly) must be made into a halftone. A halftone is made by shooting a photograph through a line screen that separates the image into black dots and clear areas. The more lines (or dots per square inch), the finer the texture of the halftone. A very coarse screen is used in newspaper printing. If you look at any newspaper photograph carefully, you can see the dots that make up the image.

If you use photographs that are film-based (not digital), a professional print shop should be consulted. The print shop will be able to convert the photograph to a halftone for printing and then size it to fit the page or space. The print shop can reduce or enlarge the picture to meet your needs, so be sure to measure the space for your photograph when you take it in to the print shop. Make sure you are organized and do not make these requests at the last minute. Print shops may take several days to produce a halftone.

You can also scan (digitize) the photograph on a scanner; the resulting digital image is then ready for electronic insertion into the page or space provided. You may wish to keep the scanned photograph on your hard drive, not yet inserted into the proposal, until the final review and printing. Otherwise, a section with many photographs could become difficult to manipulate because of the file size.

Digital camera photos are another, and perhaps the best, option. They should be taken by a professional

I once wrote a proposal that included many photographs of work areas, file rooms, file cabinets, and people working with files. The file became so large that I could not send the proposal electronically (as requested) and had to upload it to a CD and hand-deliver the CD. Fortunately, I was in the same city or I would have had to break the file into smaller files and send each one individually, which would have been an inconvenience for the client. So be careful and aware of your proposal file size.

photographer to ensure proper lighting and the highest-quality result. Pictures that are dark or amateurish may have a negative overall effect on your proposal.

Review all the prints and select only the best for inclusion. Like a scanned photograph, the file size of a digital image is large (even when compressed) and should be withheld from the proposal text file until final printing.

For both scanned and digital (which are really the same format), it is best to name the file with a sequential number, if you keep an art log, or name the photograph file with the figure number that applies to your photograph. The art log is discussed later in this section. (The problem with naming the photo with the figure caption number is that these numbers may change as figures are added or subtracted. Therefore having a neutral number helps in maintaining the placement and order.)

If you use an art log and assign a sequential number, the number given to a particular illustration should be placed on an empty line above the figure caption, shown below:

Tip Color art is not usually necessary.

(15)

Figure 5-1. *Workflow Process*

Color illustrations or photographs are not necessary but, if included, may require considerably more time and money for printing. If color photographs are to be featured, they must be sent to the printer for screening and color separation—a very expensive process. Usually, color illustrations do not warrant the extra time and expense.

It is also possible to use scanned color photographs that can be inserted digitally into your proposal. If you are using color photographs or other digital color work, the proposal page(s) will have to be printed on a color printer. To ensure consistent print quality for both text and illustrations, it may be best to have the complete proposal printed on the same printer. Copies can be made using either the printer or a color photocopy machine.

Note that if you print only the color pages on a color printer and the rest of the proposal on a laser printer, the print density, type, and page format of the printers may not match. Compare two pages closely and determine whether the match is close enough. If not, review your options and either print the whole proposal on one machine, or reassess whether color usage is warranted. You may consider placing the color page(s) in an appendix so that the difference in the print quality is not as noticeable.

Remember, many RFPs admonish against excessively elaborate materials and may even discourage the use of color.

Note of Caution

While photographs (physical, not digital) do enhance your proposal and can be more effective than a line drawing, they are awkward and cumbersome to use. If the photo is a halftone, it will have to be manually pasted into the blank space left in a paragraph or page, and special care must be taken during the reproduction process. This can be time consuming, and the results may not equal the effort if less than professionally done.

If the photograph is digital, the work is much easier because it is done electronically, with the printing performed on a laser printer. However, large photographs, or sections with many photographs, can become difficult because they make the word processor file very large—perhaps on the order of hundreds of megabytes. This can make the file cumbersome to work with during the proposal writing period, and difficult to transmit if going to an off-site printer or to the company that wrote the RFP.

If using digital photographs, consider holding them as separate files until you are ready to print. Some word processor programs can actually call the file when needed, but otherwise it is not integrated into the file.

Tip

Be careful when printing on two types of printers.

Tables

A table is a compact list of details or related facts arranged in an orderly sequence—usually in rows and columns—for convenience of reference. Tables, since they are set in type rather than reproduced from artwork, are not considered illustrations. They are listed separately from figures and are separately numbered. Table numbers and titles are centered at the top of the page or table as shown in Figure 11-2. As with figures, table titles use initial caps.

Tables should be used extensively whenever possible. They can present an enormous amount of information that describes an issue better than a detailed narrative. Tables can also be presented in graphic form when the table is presented as a chart or graph of the data. Charts and graphs can quickly display the data by showing a line

Tip Tables are a shorthand way of presenting information.

FIGURE 11-2 Example Table and Callouts

Table 5-1.

Estimates of Paper Volumes by Division

Division	# Files	# Pages	Method
Division 1	12836	351220	Count
Division 2	14967	314311	Count
Division 3	21821	458241	Estimate
Division 4	12836	397916	Estimate
Division 5	579	8685	Count
Division 6	1484	71232	Estimate
Division 7	298	8344	Estimate
Division 8	443	12404	Estimate
Division 9	2819	68482	Count
Division 10	1430	14299	Count
Division 11	16799	203280	Count
Division 12	18975	412419	Estimate
Total:	105287	2320833	

FIGURE 11-3 Tabular Information Presented as a Chart

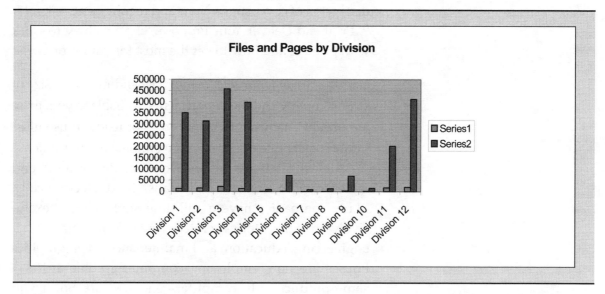

or bar chart of results. Figure 11-3 presents the charted information of Figure 11-2 as a graph.

Covers

It is very useful to have a standard cover that depicts your company's logo and product or service. Covers—front, back, and spine (if you use a three-ring presentation binder)—add a degree of professionalism to your proposal that your competition may lack. Covers may be inserted into a three-ring presentation binder or added to whichever type of binding you are using.

Cover art may be created electronically and stored on a central server. As suggested in Chapter 5, a cover can be a simple text cover with the essential information or a graphic that in some way illustrates your product or service.

If yours is a small company with limited resources, it may be better to use a plain text-based cover. However, if you have skills and the software to create an appropriate image, it may be worth the time to put together a graphic cover.

See Chapter 5, Format the Proposal, for an in-depth discussion of cover suggestions and requirements. Chapter 9, Print and Deliver Your Proposal, explains how to work with printers and how to get the most for your money.

Sources of ready-to-use illustrations. Depending on the size of your company and the departments available to you, there are usually many sources and types of ready-to-use illustrations, elaborate or simple, conventional or electronic.

Almost all types of line-drawing illustrations and tables can be created and transmitted electronically. Many companies have a full-time staff devoted exclusively to computer-generated artwork for marketing, engineering, education, and maintenance. Most graphics houses are now employing computer-graphic artists—some produce only computer-generated art. So, if you are equipped for and knowledgeable in desktop publishing, consider your electronic options.

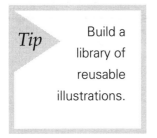

Tip Build a library of reusable illustrations.

If you decide to pursue this avenue, start building a library of illustrations that represent various hardware components, products, services, or equipment, depending on your line of business. These illustrations can be arranged and rearranged to represent different configurations. Using the same drawings for different illustrations has the advantage of giving your illustrations uniformity of style. Figure 11-4 is an example of computer-generated

FIGURE 11-4 Sample of Computer-Generated Illustration

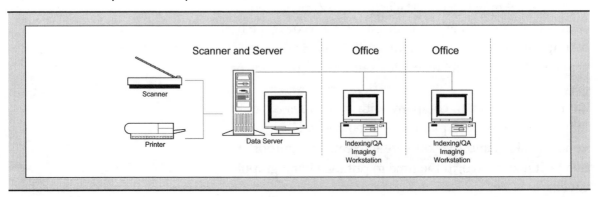

art composed of predrawn images that have been put together with a graphics program.

In-House Sources

If you work in a large company that has a technical illustrations department, you can arrange with that department's manager to supply your department with boilerplate graphics that you can keep on file. You should have an agreement with the manager early on—the main point of the agreement being that, in addition to being supplied with boilerplate art, you will be requiring a fast (meaning *very* fast) turnaround time for custom requests. If your art department manager is aware of the quick turnaround times you may require for a proposal, he will be better prepared to give your work priority.

If your art department manager is not familiar with proposal work, it is best to work closely with him on initial proposals. Draw the manager into the proposal so that the urgency can be experienced firsthand.

If you do not have a technical illustrations department in your company, or you are in a field sales office without direct access to this type of material, you might check with your engineering or technical manuals department to see if there are usable drawings of your products that can be added to your boilerplate files. Other internal sources of illustrations are datasheets, technical manuals, training manuals, and marketing brochures.

Tip Clip art will save you time and expense.

Clip Art

Electronic clip art is composed of electronic predrawn images that are available from many sources.

The word processing program that you use may offer built-in clip art. This art generally ranges from excellent quality to poor quality. Always do a trial run printing prior to making a final commitment to using this art.

Clip art may be purchased from companies that specialize in clip art. Like the offerings on your word processor, the quality of these drawings is variable. Often the files also contain photographs and other illustrations in various formats. Before purchasing, ensure that your word processor can read the files, as they may be stored in a proprietary format.

Illustrations and graphic-software programs usually feature a large number of predrawn illustrations that can be used as a single illustration or combined to complete a picture. Before purchasing, be sure that your word processor is able to accept this type of file format.

Online clip art services. Some companies specialize in clip art and photographs. Their quality is generally very good and prices vary.

Once you have decided on an illustrations program, any of the sources above can contribute to your storehouse of electronic illustrations. If you are collecting these illustrations for future use, it may be best to copy them from the original source into a directory that can be easily accessed and cataloged. Additional illustrations may be added at any time. Even complex drawings from your most current proposal may be kept as a separate file instead of redrawing the illustration.

Tip Remember that illustrations complement text.

Illustration Formats

When dealing with illustrations and tables, there are a few basic principles that should be followed. One of the most important is allowing for ample space around the illustration and providing sufficient space between the illustrations and their titles and/or captions. Keep in mind that for both illustrations and tables, all related information should be of the same orientation as the material itself, regardless of the type of page it appears on.

Illustrations are presented in various ways. Make sure all artwork is properly aligned with the paper edges (i.e., check to see if it is straight). And remember, the purpose of the illustrations is to enhance and clarify the text, so they need to be clearly, cleanly, and carefully presented.

Landscape vs. Portrait Orientation

Illustrations may be mounted vertically or horizontally on the page. A horizontal illustration is sometimes called a landscape or turn-page illustration because it is mounted in such a way that the proposal must be turned in order to see it properly. This type of illustration is called for when the drawing would have to be reduced so much in order to fit on the page that it wouldn't remain legible. If you have a turn-page, you must also ensure that the illustration fits within the margins and that there is space for the title. The turn-page illustration should be mounted so that the illustration is readable when the proposal is turned clockwise. The title should be flush left, with the left margin along the long side of the paper, not placed as it would be for a vertical illustration.

Tip Small in-text graphics help make your point.

In-Text Graphics

An in-text graphic is usually an example, using special text or a small illustration that does not warrant being a figure or a table by itself. The example is embedded within a paragraph and separated from the text by spacing. In-text illustrations do not have captions, are not numbered, and do not appear in the list of illustrations. The following paragraph features an in-text graphic:

> Developing and maintaining a library of icons, such as the ones shown here, is essential for effective electronic desktop publishing.

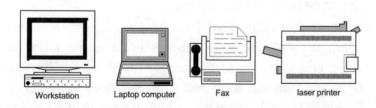

Workstation   Laptop computer   Fax   laser printer

These icons can be combined in many ways to produce a variety of configurations for your product or services.

A second example of an in-text graphic is a small table or graph that provides a visual representation of the subject at hand. In this case, the accompanying copy might read:

The graph below measures the spread of document imaging technology throughout the business community. It appears that the Eastern sector of the United States . . . .

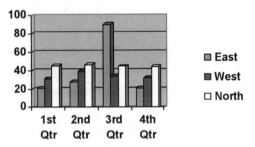

Stand-alone illustrations can be put into a number of different positions so that the text wraps around the illustration. If you are using two-column text, it may be essential to have this capability. However, in the interest of time and clarity, an illustration inserted between paragraphs, as above, with adequate spacing, is generally good enough.

It is not necessary to make your proposal look like a professionally published magazine or manual (unless that is your product). Clean and readable text is is your main goal.

Illustration Standards

To show that your proposal is the product of one united company, it is necessary to set illustration standards early. Following these standards will give your illustrations a consistent look and a professional appearance. The standards listed below should be considered—but

> *Tip* Setting standards makes the proposal look as though it came from one company.

not necessarily incorporated, if your company already has a standard. The key is to be consistent in the appearance and placement of illustrations. The word "illustrations" refers to both figures and tables.

The suggestions below should be modified according to your own company standards, and included in a proposal style sheet. Having your illustrations rendered in a consistent way will save you many hours at the last minute, when you need the time for final review, not final work.

Boxing Illustrations

There is probably a 50–50 chance that your company places boxes around all illustrations. Boxing illustrations is a convention, but it is not followed industry-wide. If the decision is to box, all illustrations, including tables, must be boxed for consistency.

Type Styles

Illustrations with many different sizes and styles of type tend to have less impact. A rule of thumb is to never use more than three sizes of type or two styles within any given drawing. If you use 12-point Helvetica bold for the title of a table, use 12-point Helvetica bold for all tables. Of course, this is also true for all figures. Use initial capital letters for words within an illustration.

Line Weights

Line weights refer to the thickness of the lines in an illustration. Generally, lines that are of medium-light weight tend to be more pleasing to the eye than heavy, bold lines. However, be sure the lines are not so thin that they will drop out (not reproduce) when printed. As with type styles, the general rule is to use no more than two line weights for any given drawing. Try to have all the drawings appear to have the same line weights and try to be consistent.

> *Tip*
>
> An effective proposal contains a consistency of typeface and drawing style.

Figure and Table Numbers

Illustrations are usually assigned two numbers: the section number and the sequential number of the figure within the section. Figures are numbered on the bottom while tables are numbered at the top. Callouts are flush left with the margin of the drawing. It is acceptable to number your illustrations with one number, Figure 1, Figure 2, Figure 9, but tables will have their own numbers, Table 1-1, Table 2-3, etc. For more complex proposals in which the sections or chapters are numbered, such as Section 4, you may also consider numbering the figures in conjunction with the section number. For Section 4, for example, the figures would be Figure 4-1, 4-2, etc. Either style is acceptable.

Illustration References

Two rules of referencing illustrations are as follows:

1. An illustration must be referred to in the text before it appears.
2. Illustrations should appear as close to the reference as possible. Do not save all the illustrations and place them at the back of the section or book.

When referencing figures and tables, avoid describing them in the reference when the illustration is obvious: "Table 5-1 is a list of . . . ." The best way to refer to a figure or table is by simple use of its number: "See Table 5-1." Remember, the text should not be describing the figure; the figure should be clarifying the text.

Titles and Captions

Titles and captions are words that help describe an illustration and are part of the illustration itself—titles and captions are not the figure or table number (see Figure 11-5).

While there are no "standards" for this type of work, and each company may do things differently, what is

Tip Illustrations should be near the text with which they are associated.

important is to have a consistent look and feel to your proposal and its illustrations.

Punctuation

- Figure and table numbers are followed by a period.
- No periods are used in the illustration caption unless it comprises several sentences.

While the above rules could all be incorporated as standards, you may already have your own company standards. Being flexible but consistent is key to getting a proposal finished on time while also maintaining a professional appearance.

Illustration Consistency and Orientation

One potential problem with using illustrations from many different sources is that they may not look the same in terms of line weights, detail, and orientation.

Tip The treatment of illustration elements is not dictated by hard-and-fast rules—it is consistency that counts.

FIGURE 11-5 Sample of Titles and Captions for an Illustration

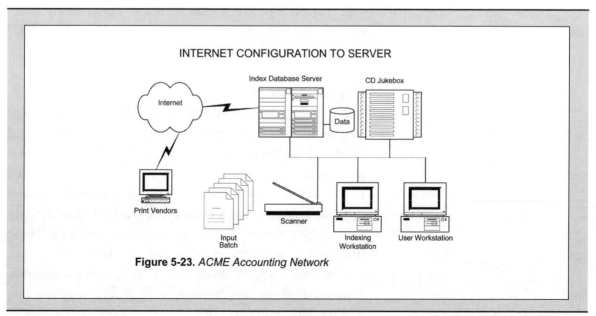

Figure 5-23. *ACME Accounting Network*

Thickness of the lines used may vary from drawing to drawing, giving some drawings a dark and heavy look while others are very light. This detail should be reviewed prior to using the drawings.

The amount of detail should be similar among the different packages. Some PC drawings may provide the least amount of detail while others may be very detailed. The amount and type of detail should be relatively constant (just like the text of your proposal).

Consistency should also include orientation of the drawings. Do your illustrations face head-on or do they face left or right? Do some face left while others face right? Are the views from the top? Side? Some other view? Readers may notice this type of inconsistency and it may have a negative effect if the differences are too pronounced.

While it may be easy to find and use electronic art, it can be tricky for the average user to make the illustrations look consistent. If you do not have a professional illustrator and/or guidance, use common sense and review your finished product with a critical eye. Having illustrations is worth the time and effort, but they should not look amateurish.

Tip — Try not to mix drawing styles and programs.

Organization

Using illustrations in a proposal requires a high degree of organization. The more you work with proposals and illustrations, the more you will find that artwork or photographic work must begin when you start writing the text. A single new drawing may take five full working days to complete. A photograph, even if it is already taken, will require several days of processing time. These illustrations need to be cataloged and kept where they can be easily accessed during the proposal preparation process. This section contains suggestions for indexing and tracking your artwork.

The key issue is: Will you generate or have boiler-plate illustrations in a corporate library, or will you simply generate illustrations on demand at the time of the proposal effort?

If you do have a library of illustrations, or want to start one, each piece should be indexed so that users may peruse the library and download the illustrations selected. The library may have a preview function allowing users to see a thumbnail of the illustration, or the index must be sufficiently documented to ensure receipt of the desired drawing. Users will not want to have to download many drawings in order to get just one or two.

Once downloaded, the illustrations can be renamed to reflect the illustration number assigned in the proposal.

If you do not have a library of illustrations but create them on the fly, they still must be assigned an illustration number and placed in a directory for ease of access. There may also come a time when the illustration is "roughed-out" by hand, and someone else is in charge of putting the illustration together using an illustrations package.

Numbering and Indexing Artwork

How you number and index your artwork depends on the source of the artwork itself. If you are using illustrations from an existing technical publication, or boiler-plate artwork supplied by your illustrations department, the art will most likely already have been assigned a number. Though you may want to keep this number, it's probably wiser to assign an index number of your own and cross-reference it to its original number in a log (in case you want more of the same from the original source). This log is independent of the proposal and is simply a reference for your own convenience. If you are having artwork custom created, assign your own new index number.

Tip Illustration preparation should begin when you start writing text.

The boilerplate illustration files will now have a unique indexing system that allows all users to quickly identify and request art from your files.

Figure 11-6 shows a log form for keeping track of illustrations. The first column stores the number for the illustrations library (a reference to the source document). This is important because you may change the original but want to change it back at some point—or download it a second time.

The second column shows the sequential number assigned to the drawing and is the number put into the blank space left for the drawing if not loaded into the text during the writing period. The sequential number is used because the figure or table number may change over time, potentially summoning the wrong drawing to that place.

The third column holds the assigned figure or table number. This number may change as drawings are inserted before the current number, so that Figure 5-1 would then become Figure 5-3, etc.

The art log allows you to see at a glance whether the art has been completed and approved. As the deadline draws near, you will want to hurry the completion of any outstanding illustrations.

The author column should be filled in for quick reference. A large proposal may have several authors working on it and producing illustrations. When a question arises, or an approval is needed, knowing whom to go to is helpful.

The last two columns are self-explanatory. For any given drawing, do not make an entry until work on the drawing has actually begun. You will be able to tell at a glance which illustrations are not being prepared, which are in progress, and which are completed. Note: logged entries should be made in pencil or kept electronically.

Tip Indexing helps you track and monitor the artwork.

FIGURE 11-6 Example Art Log

Index Number	Ref. Number	Figure Number	Title	Author	Status: Draft Complete	
HW027	1	1-1	Hardware Architecture	Bud P-R	6-23	7-3
HW009	2	1-2	Workstation	Bud P-R	6-15	7-3
ED015	3	1-3	Training Schedule	Mike M.	?	?
DI007	4	1-4	Project Org. Chart	Mary E.	6-12	7-3
	5					
	6					
	7					
	8					
	9					

This log is only an example. Your log may be more complex and have many more columns for dates and data. You may want to make a separate log for any tables that are being generated.

Master Proposal Illustration File

After your indexing system is established, the next step is to set up a master proposal illustration file on your network. This file is simply a place for the illustrations to reside while the proposal is being developed. For example, a section author could go to the illustration's log and view an illustration while he or she is writing the text. (Remember that illustrations, photographs in particular, can cause difficulties if inserted into the text during the drafting stages.)

This, of course, hinges on whether you store the art separately from the proposal, have professional illustrations being created, or are using clip art from a purchased source. If the art is being created, there is a good chance that it will change as it is being reviewed and the proposal story unfolds. Therefore, it is best to keep it on a shared drive or accessible to the illustrator and the user over a network. The art log illustrated above could serve as a simple check-in/check-out log. However, more sophisticated document management programs will provide library facilities for both the text and the illustrations.

How and where the files are stored, both text and illustration, must be decided during the initial stages of the proposal development process. Authors must have access to these files at all times; even when traveling, they should have access over the network.

Storage of Illustrations

Storage is an important part of developing a proposal and a proposal development program. Like boilerplate, if the illustration files cannot be located and used, they will rapidly become obsolete; people will also lose time looking for something that is already available. A file system is necessary for both the large company with a distributed set of offices and the local office with several people using the files.

Having a standard file location and support group allows you to continue building the illustration database as new files become available. New files can come from new products being developed as well as from in-progress proposals for which new illustrations are being drawn or acquired. People from the field can submit new illustrations to the team for inclusion in the database (and you should actively encourage this), which would not normally become available to other field offices.

Illustration files should be categorized and numbered as part of the illustration database. Categorizing will put the file into the proper topic heading such as

Tip Illustrations should be available over a shared drive or on a server.

hardware, software, education, etc. Each major category may have a unique identifier, coupled with a sequential number. For example, files in the hardware section may begin with HW and be numbered HW001, HW002, etc. Having unique identifiers allows the user to rapidly identify the files and file type after they have been downloaded from the database. A file entry in the database may look like this:

Illustration Number	Description	Original Date	Revised Date
HW015 XYZ	Server—Front view	3/18/20xx	12/05/20xx
HW016	RAID Storage 97G	4/01/20xx	9/07/20xx

For the single office or single user, the same system may be employed to track illustrations created for other proposals. The database may be nothing more than a spreadsheet, or it may be a more complex library-type program. The key is ease of use and access to materials. It is amazing that we sometimes spend more time looking for "lost" illustrations in old proposals than it would have taken to draw a new one.

Tip Final art should be indexed and saved for the next proposal.

Summary

In a proposal, illustrations are an especially powerful means of communication. Good supporting illustrations clarify your text, ensuring that what is being read is also being understood. Of course, illustrations add a professional touch to your proposal, but their real function is to help the reader understand complex technical concepts.

With the excellent illustration programs available today, along with extensive clip art files, there is no reason proposals should not have strong illustrations. Even a simple drawing will serve to break up dense text and help the reader to visualize what has just been described. However, be careful not to toss in an illustration that has little or no meaning and does not clarify the text. After a few instances of this, the reader may become annoyed at the superfluous information and disregard the illustrations that matter.

In addition to helping the reader, illustrations sharpen the writer's focus on the ideas that are being conveyed, which in turn may provide greater insight into the concept or subject itself. Many large government contractors, with adequate personnel to support the methodology, instruct their proposal writers to concentrate on developing illustrations before they write the text. This helps the writer to thoroughly understand the concept first, which leads to better writing and illustrations that are excellent complements to the text.

Finally, if you are in doubt about the power of illustrations and their place in a proposal, review any technical manual and try to read it without looking at the illustrations. The text becomes cumbersome as you try to visualize what is being described, and your focus and attention tend to wander from the subject. Also, do you want to "chance it" that your readers will incorrectly visualize the concepts you are trying to relate?

APPENDIXES

Introduction to the Appendixes

The checklists that follow will help you with preproposal activities, proposal activities, and postproposal activities. These checklists include work items that you may consider while writing and developing a proposal response. I encourage you to use, modify, and customize these checklists to meet your own unique needs.

Appendix I is not a checklist but a way of organizing and tracking your proposal effort and what happens once the proposal is won or lost. Too often we do not track why proposals are won and lost and how that information may best be used for future proposal efforts.

These checklists are valuable during the heat of proposal writing when you are most likely to forget to include something, such as your annual report or your references.

Appendix A—General Preproposal Checklist
Appendix B—Proposal Writing Checklist
Appendix C—Presubmission Checklist
Appendix D—Printing Checklist
Appendix E—Evaluation Checklist
Appendix F—Proposal Submission Checklist
Appendix G—Postproposal Checklist
Appendix H—Bid/No-Bid Checklist
Appendix I—Proposal Status Sheet
Appendix J—Cost Justification Whitepaper

A

GENERAL PREPROPOSAL CHECKLIST

	Item	Notes
❏	RFI/RFP received	
❏	Qualify opportunity	
❏	First analysis of RFP opportunity	
❏	Acknowledge receipt of RFP	
❏	Attend bidders' conference	
❏	Support	
	❏ Sales support	
	❏ Technical support	
	❏ Management support	
❏	Copy RFP and distribute	
❏	Bid/no-bid decision	
	❏ Technical	
	❏ Marketing	
	❏ Cost	
	❏ Timing	
❏	Send no-bid letter?	
❏	Send intent-to-bid letter?	
❏	Establish proposal schedule	
❏	Internal management presentation	
❏	Terms and conditions to contracts	
❏	Outline RFP	
	❏ Standard equipment	
	❏ Standard service	
	❏ Custom equipment	
	❏ Custom services	

	Item	Notes
❏	Plan kickoff meeting	
❏	Establish proposal resources	
	❏ Sales and marketing	
	❏ Technical/engineering	
	❏ Project management	
	❏ Service and maintenance	
	❏ Education and training	
	❏ Legal review	
	❏ Editing and illustrations	
	❏ Reproduction	
	❏ Word processing	
❏	Secure working space	
	❏ War room	
	❏ PCs	
	❏ Software	
	❏ Materials	
❏	Assign cost/pricing team	
	❏ Standard equipment	
	❏ Standard services	
	❏ Custom equipment	
	❏ Custom services	
❏	Assign internal review team	
	❏ Technical	
	❏ Management	
	❏ Cost	
	❏ Sales and marketing	
❏	Do competitive analysis	
❏	Develop marketing strategy	
	❏ Customer politics	
	❏ Primary business problem	
	❏ Develop marketing themes	
❏	Develop technical approach	
❏	Marketing strategy approval	
❏	Technical approach approval	
❏	Develop first RFP questions	
❏	Hold kickoff meeting	

PROPOSAL WRITING CHECKLIST

	Item	Notes
❑	Cover letter	
❑	Executive summary	
	❑ Marketing themes	
	❑ Technical approach	
	❑ Assumptions	
	❑ Implementation schedule	
	❑ Project management	
	❑ Facilities and capabilities	
	❑ Service and support themes	
	❑ Educational themes	
	❑ Company history	
	❑ Exceptions to requirements	
	❑ Develop illustrations	
❑	Technical volume	
	❑ Technical themes	
	❑ List of assumptions	
	❑ Product descriptions	
	❑ Implementation schedule	
	❑ Quality control	
	❑ Subcontractor's role	
	❑ Subcontractor's products	
	❑ Exceptions to requirements	
	❑ Develop illustrations	

	Item	Notes
❑	Management volume	
	❑ Marketing themes	
	❑ Resumes of key personnel	
	❑ Facilities and capabilities	
	❑ Related experience	
	❑ Subcontractor's role	
	❑ Service and support	
	❑ Education	
	❑ Exception to requirements	
	❑ Develop illustrations	
❑	Cost volume	
	❑ Introduction to cost	
	❑ Equipment totals and summary	
	❑ Standard hardware	
	❑ Standard software	
	❑ Custom hardware	
	❑ Custom software	
	❑ Project management	
	❑ Service	
	❑ Education	
	❑ Installation	
	❑ Licenses	
	❑ Payment schedules	
	❑ Discounts	
	❑ Tax	

PRESUBMISSION CHECKLIST

	Item	Notes
❏	Proposal cover	
❏	Title page	
❏	Proprietary notice	
❏	Signature papers	
	❏ Bid bond	
	❏ Performance bond	
	❏ Buy USA statement	
	❏ EEO documentation	
	❏ Small business qualification	
	❏ Minority business qualification	
❏	Table of contents	
❏	List of illustrations	
❏	Proposal road map	
❏	Executive summary	
❏	Technical volume	
❏	Management volume	
❏	Cost volume	
❏	Glossary	
❏	Appendixes	
	❏ Compliance matrix	
	❏ Exceptions list	
	❏ Supporting brochures	
	❏ Datasheets	
	❏ Annual report	

	Item	Notes
❑	Supporting manuals	
❑	Supplementary technical data	
❑	Industry whitepapers	

PRINTING CHECKLIST

	Item	Notes
❏	Printer/reproduction selected	
❏	Cover sent to printer	
❏	Tabs sent to printer	
❏	Printing format selected	
❏	Binding method selected	
	❏ Three-ring binder	
	❏ ACCO fastener	
	❏ Comb binding	
	❏ Other	
❏	Final art prepared for printing	
❏	Final text master printed	
❏	Dummy sheet prepared	
❏	Page masters to printer	
❏	Proposal assembled	
❏	Cover illustrations inserted	
❏	Final review	

EVALUATION CHECKLIST

	Item	Notes
❏	Evaluation team formed	
	❏ Sales and marketing	
	❏ Technical/engineering	
	❏ Project management	
	❏ Pricing team	
❏	Date and time established	
❏	RFP distributed to team	
❏	Space established	
❏	Team assembled for evaluation	
❏	Proposal distributed	
❏	Evaluation forms distributed	
❏	Review debriefing	
❏	Evaluations reviewed	
❏	Results reviewed	
❏	Proposal revised	
❏	Evaluation criteria determined	
	❏ RFP stated criteria	
	❏ Sales reps' input	
	❏ Engineering input	
	❏ Team's input	
❏	Evaluation criteria reviewed	
❏	Evaluation "weights" posted	
❏	Estimated technical points	

	Item	Notes
❏	Estimated management points	
❏	Estimated pricing points	
❏	Total estimated points awarded	
❏	Proposal scoring reviewed	
❏	Proposal scoring accepted/not accepted and proposed changes	
❏	Competitor 1 estimated	
❏	Competitor 2 estimated	
❏	Competitor 3 estimated	

PROPOSAL SUBMISSION CHECKLIST

	Item	Notes
❑	Proposal instructions reviewed	
❑	Due date and time	
❑	Number of copies	
❑	Address and name	
❑	Sealed wrapping	
❑	Box markings	
❑	Delivery method established	
❑	Authorized signature on proposal	
❑	Signature papers included	
❑	Separate cost volume?	
❑	Final review	
❑	Submit proposal	
❑	Proposal party	

POSTPROPOSAL CHECKLIST

	Item	Notes
❏	Store proposal and documentation	
❏	Respond to customer questions	
❏	Prepare for customer demonstration	
	❏ Demo room and facilities	
	❏ Demo equipment	
	❏ Demo script prepared	
❏	Prepare for headquarters visit	
❏	Prepare presentation	
❏	Prepare for reference-site visit	
❏	Respond to contract questions	
❏	Prepare for negotiations	
❏	Prepare contracts	
❏	Make requested proposal changes	
❏	Make requested price changes	
❏	Negotiate contract	
❏	New account celebration	

BID/NO-BID CHECKLIST

ACCOUNT INFORMATION

	Item	Notes
❏	Account information	
	❏ Sales rep in acct?	
	❏ How long in acct?	
	❏ Did we help write the RFP?	
	❏ What department is the RFP from?	
	❏ Who are the decision makers?	
	❏ Is the project funded?	
	❏ What is the funding amount?	
❏	Account technology base	
	❏ Has a study been completed?	
	❏ Who did the study?	
	❏ Do we have a copy?	
	❏ Are consultants involved?	
	❏ Is the account knowledgeable?	
	❏ Are other vendors installed?	
	❏ Who are the vendors?	
	❏ Describe current system	

BIDDING STRATEGIES

	Item	Notes
❏	Competition	
	❏ List the competition	
	❏ Did they write the RFP?	

	Item	Notes
	❑ What are their strengths?	
	❑ What are their weaknesses?	
❑	Why should we bid on this RFP?	
	❑ What is the RFPs application?	
	❑ Can we use standard products?	
	❑ What custom work is needed?	
	❑ Is this a technology fit?	
	❑ Is this a strategic opportunity?	
	❑ Any negative possibilities?	
	❑ List negatives and comment	
❑	What is our bid strategy?	
❑	What is our leverage?	
❑	What are our strengths?	
❑	What are our weaknesses?	

SOLUTIONS/STRATEGIES

	Item	Notes
❑	Describe basic solution	
	❑ Standard hardware	
	❑ Standard software	
	❑ Custom hardware	
	❑ Custom software	
	❑ Scope of development	
	❑ Standard maintenance?	
	❑ Standard education?	
❑	Contract	
	❑ Contract with RFP?	
	❑ If not, can we get a copy?	
	❑ Standard contract?	
	❑ Describe unusual terms	
	❑ Can these be negotiated?	
❑	Overall opinion of opportunity?	
❑	Recommendations	
❑	Bid or no-bid?	

PROPOSAL DEVELOPMENT COSTS

	Item	Notes
❏	Proposal resources outlined	
	❏ Proposal manager	
	❏ Technical team	
	❏ Management team	
	❏ Sales/marketing	
	❏ Pricing	
❏	Administrative resources	
	❏ Word processing	
	❏ Illustrations	
	❏ Administrative support	
❏	Facilities resources	
	❏ War room required	
	❏ Equipment	
	❏ Software	
❏	Site visits?	
❏	Headquarters visit?	

PROPOSAL STATUS SHEET

Customer Information

Customer Name: _____

Project Name:_____

Project Description:_____

_____

_____

Proposal Team Information

Salesperson: _____

System Analyst:_____

Manager: _____

Key RFP Dates

RFP Issued:_____	RFP Due: _____
RFP Extension: _____	Questions Due: _____
Bid Conference: _____	Oral Presentation: _____
Demonstration:_____	Benchmark: _____
RFP Award:_____	First Ship: _____
Initial Revenue $: _____	Total Revenue $: _____

Key Proposal Dates

Activity	Date	Room	Who
Planning Meeting:	_____	_____	_____
Bid/No-Bid Meeting:	_____	_____	_____
Kickoff Meeting:	_____	_____	_____
First Review:	_____	_____	_____
Final Review:	_____	_____	_____
Ship Date:	_____	_____	_____

Comments: _____

_____

_____

_____

_____

_____

_____

TECHNICAL AND BUSINESS REVIEW

Client: _____

Sales Rep: _____   Date: _____

Comments: _____

_____

_____

Sales Analyst: _____   Date: _____

Comments: _____

_____

_____

Marketing: _____   Date: _____

Comment: _____

_____

_____

Engineering: _____   Date: _____

Comments: _____

_____

_____

Decision

Refer to Bid/No-Bid Committee: _____   Date: _____

No-Bid Letter: _____   Date: _____

Comments: _____

_____

_____

PROPOSAL SIGN-OFF

Client: _____

Sales Rep: _____   Date: _____

Comments: _____

_____

_____

Sales Analyst: _____   Date: _____

Comments: _____

_____

_____

VP Sales: _____   Date: _____

Comment: _____

_____

_____

VP Marketing: _____   Date: _____

Comments: _____

_____

_____

VP Engineering: _____   Date: _____

Comments: _____

_____

_____

VP Finance: _____   Date: _____

Comments: _____

_____

_____

PROPOSAL DISPOSITION

Client: _____

Win/Loss Review: _____ Date: _____

Sales Rep: _____ Date: _____

Comments: _____

_____

Sales Analyst: _____ Date: _____

Comments: _____

_____

Primary Win/Loss Factors

Business Solution: _____

_____

Technical Solution: _____

_____

Pricing: _____

_____

Project Management: _____

_____

Maintenance: _____

_____

Education: _____

_____

Exceptions: _____

_____

PROPOSAL DISPOSITION, continued

Win/Loss Review Notes

_____
_____
_____
_____
_____
_____
_____
_____
_____
_____
_____
_____

Corrective Recommendations

_____
_____
_____
_____
_____
_____
_____
_____
_____
_____
_____
_____
_____
_____

PROPOSAL DISPOSITION, continued

Customer Comments

_____

_____

_____

_____

_____

_____

_____

_____

_____

_____

_____

_____

_____

_____

_____

_____

_____

_____

_____

_____

Cost Justification Whitepaper

Introduction

It is a rare exception when a project is authorized without a budget. The problem that is typically faced by the RFP team is how to establish the budget initially and, once established, determining how credible it is. While it may be possible to simply poll vendors and ask the cost of their equipment, it is generally not that easy because you also need to factor in installation and ongoing maintenance costs. Then you must determine if the return on investment analysis will be positive enough to make your project attractive to management.

Companies typically compare a capital acquisition project against all other projects vying for company funding. In addition to being compared against each other, the projects must have the potential to meet or exceed what a company will make on its capital if the capital is left in current investment programs.

The following brief review of the cost justification process is meant only as a general guideline. Each company has its own process and guidelines that should be followed.

Many projects are funded because of the savings that can be generated. If the project-investment costs can be repaid through capital savings, then the project is a good candidate to receive funding. However, depending on the project itself and whether equipment is being purchased, the "payback" time is generally expected to be within two years—faster is considered better. But payback time might be only one of the criteria set for capital acquisitions, with other financial indicators—such as net present value (NPV) and return on investment (ROI)—also being considered.

Prior to beginning work, the project leader should confer with the company's financial group, typically the chief financial officer (CFO), to understand what information is needed and how projects are evaluated from a financial point of view. The project leader should be in agreement with the CFO as to what is being measured and how that measure is calculated.

All materials compiled for the cost justification can be used later to develop a credible project budget and technical requirements section, assuming the cost justification is positive and the project moves forward. Other sections of the study can be sanitized and used as background information in the proposal appendixes.

Cost justifications typically fall into two primary categories. The first is hard-dollar savings in which the new project allows a company to realize actual cost reductions in their operating budget. Hard-dollar savings usually result from having tangible and identifiable reductions in expenses. For example, after a project is complete, the payroll for that department may be reduced from $2 million per year to $1 million per year. The $1 million reduction equals actual savings or cost reductions to the company. Hard-dollar savings may be realized from

- reduction in personnel.
- reduction in business operating costs (photocopying, postal mailing, telephone bills, and support personnel such as HR and IT).
- reduction in facilities costs (sell a building, or an "averted cost" in not renewing a lease).
- reduction in computer system costs (fewer and more efficient computers, less IT overhead, etc.).

The second type of cost justification revolves around soft-dollar savings in which benefits are realized but may not easily translate into verifiable hard-dollar cost reductions. For example, a new customer-support system allows you to offer better customer service, but the system does not reduce overall operating costs for the department. Soft-dollar savings may be identified in the following areas:

- Improved customer service

- Increased competitive advantage
- Better and faster access to information
- Faster internal communications

While hard-dollar savings are preferred because you can calculate the system payback time, soft-dollar savings can also be persuasive. How many "irate" customers can you tolerate, how do unhappy employees affect company spirit, and how do you not justify a system that will give you a competitive advantage? (But it may take 12 to 18 months before you realize whether it actually works or not.)

An example of a soft-dollar presentation may go something like this:

Each person using our corporate intranet takes approximately two minutes to locate the information that he or she is looking for. Out of 10,000 employees, approximately 3,500 use the intranet once each day. The averaged cost per hour for each employee is calculated at $45 per hour or $0.75 per minute. The cost of locating information manually is:

0.75/hr. x 2 min. = 1.50 x 3500 = $5,250 per day

$5,250/day x 252 work days = $1,323,000 per year

Based on our information from testing an intranet search engine, we believe that we can save each user one minute in finding their information—resulting in a savings of $661,500 per year ($1,323,000/2 = $661,500). The intranet search engine under consideration costs $400,000 for software and implementation. The cost to our IT department for adding one person ($60,000/yr.), plus associated implementation costs, is $200,000. Total first-year cost for implementing this search engine is $600,000, resulting in a payback of just 12 months. Annual savings thereafter are about $600,000, deducting for the additional salary of $60,000.

As you can see, this all sounds very good and the numbers look impressive—especially if you think that many people will be using the intranet more than once per day, and that as they find it easier to navigate, more users will take advantage of it, and blah, blah, blah—goes the sales pitch.

However, putting this into deeper perspective, we might wonder: Does saving one user one minute in an eight-hour day (480 minutes) really make a difference? Is one minute a unit of time that even remotely provides any gains in efficiency? Can one person effectively use that one minute to do other work?

This type of soft-dollar savings argument is made every day to corporate management and is successfully used to get approval to purchase products.

Cost Justification Analysis (CJA) Process

The cost justification process is a method of gathering data from current operational processes and comparing that data against a proposed system's processes and costs. The projected differences are viewed over a period of time, with the result telling you whether your new system is a good or bad investment.

For example, think of all the improvements companies have made because of one simple tool—the spreadsheet. In years past, it may have taken hundreds of hours, and several people, including a special typist and specialized typewriter, to create a complex company spreadsheet. Today, similar work may take several hours and the result is actually better and more accurate. Hence, you not only save time and resources, but you get a better product. This is the Holy Grail of cost justifications.

The cost benefit analysis needs to be carried out with as much accuracy as possible. It is the financial foundation upon which your project is built, and will become the basis for long-term evaluation of the project.

Figure A-1 diagrams the basic cost justification process. It starts with analyzing current operations to determine what work functions are performed and ends with the derived cost-benefit analysis.

Figure A-1. *Cost Justification Process*

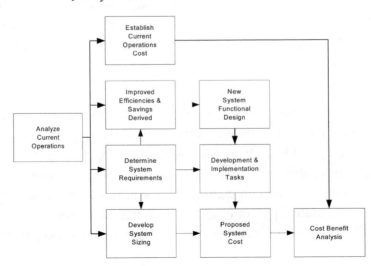

Current Operations

The baseline for all CJA work hinges on establishing an accurate accounting of current operations. Considerations include

- number of personnel.
- salary and benefits.
- facilities costs.
- resources cost (mainframe computer usage).
- other miscellaneous costs (identifiable) that will be associated with the work that is going to be improved upon.

Once the cost aspects of a department have been determined, the real challenge is to document and understand each step in the work process that is going to be the subject of the study.

Let's use an insurance-claims processing group as a model for our study. In a typical claims process, the claim may be received via mail, courier, fax, or even be posted to a database automatically. Once a claim is received, it has to be processed—that is, it is not automatically paid but is reviewed by certain people who may approve or question the claim and the amount.

One of the keys to understanding current operations is interviewing the people who perform the work. For each person who works with the claim, the following information must be documented:

- Each step in the work they do to resolve a claim
- The amount of time for each step
- Resources (mainframe) and consumables used

In the example below, the current time spent on a function is compared to the projected time for doing the same work with a new "system" that makes the work faster, better, and cheaper. For example, a customer-service clerk might have the following duties:

Tasks	Current percent of time spent on task	Projected percent of time spent on task
Organize new claims and file	25%	15%
Respond to customer questions	25%	10%
Photocopy and pass information to adjusters	40%	15%
General support	10%	10%
Total	100	50

For this clerk, we would then try to envision how the reengineered system would affect his work. For Task 1, for example, some file organization would still be needed, but a significant amount could be accomplished by the new system. We may then estimate that 40 percent of Task 1 can be automated, reducing the percentage of time spent on that task from 25 percent to 15 percent. For Task 2, we could assume that the new system will reduce the number of calls (claims are paid faster), commensurately reducing the amount of time spent answering those calls. Therefore, we can reduce Task 2 by 60 percent. This process should be repeated for each work task.

It may be deduced from this study that if there were eight clerks in the current operation, their working time would be reduced by 50 percent. This result may be viewed in one of two ways. If the new system were implemented, the number of clerks could be reduced by 50 percent, with the remaining four clerks able to handle the present volume of work. The second view is that for companies undergoing high growth, the current number of clerks would be able to handle approximately 50 percent more work before additional clerks needed to be hired (an "aversion cost" item).

Being able to calculate gains and efficiencies requires a thorough understanding of the new system, and the potential ability to reengineer a process: some steps in a process may never be eliminated—for political or marketing reasons—while others can be totally eliminated. For example, a company could have an automated voice-response system for all calls and yet choose to maintain a live operator who answers the phone and transfers calls to call-messaging for people who are unavailable.

Strawman System Architecture—System Sizing
Once the basic work has been documented, and the reengineering possibilities are becoming evident, the next step is to begin to establish the components of the new system. This is typically called "strawman architecture" because it lets you identify and list all system hardware, software, and application software that is needed for the new system. From this strawman, you also begin to build your "estimated" budget for the project.

The system architecture is determined by the information that results from the first step. Based on the reengineered processes and workflows, the basic number of workstations and other components can be derived. In the above insurance example, we were able to reduce the clerical headcount from eight to four. This means that we can reduce all system expenses from eight to four for such concomitants as computer workstations, software, and perhaps even the size of the server if significant processing reductions are being made.

This kind of thinking enables the team to accurately develop the equipment list and system software. Once this list is compiled, pricing estimates can be assigned to the equipment.

Equipment Pricing
Pricing is a straightforward exercise in working with established vendors or asking selected vendors to provide system pricing. Several vendors should be polled and an average price developed. For example, data servers, workstations, scanners, and printers all have multiple sources.

It will be harder to obtain an average price for the system software since software vendors' pricing has a wider range than the hardware vendors'. However, by contacting potential vendors and using the information from the operations analysis, the application software supplier should be able to provide pricing. Again, these prices should be averaged, if possible, and the average price used in the model.

Estimating the amount of development time needed to build the application will be the most difficult part of this pricing effort. Software vendors and system integrators typically provide this service, or the project team may elect to assume this role. If the development is to be done in-house, then additional costs such as training may need to be developed. *This component of the cost model should not be ignored because it can equal or surpass the cost of the equipment.*

System implementation involves facilities costs, hardware/software, and the software application that results in faster, better, and cheaper training, documentation, maintenance and support, and projected long-term costs for consumable supplies.

Financial Indicators
Once all of the above information has been developed and estimated, then all of the numbers can be totaled and a financial analysis performed. The most commonly used indicators for capital-acquisition projects follow:

- *Payback period.* The payback period is the time required to recoup the initial investment in the system. For example, if the system cost is $500,000 and the system provides a financial benefit of $250,000 per year, the system would have a payback of two years. From a strictly financial point of view, the sooner the payback, the better the value of the project. Projects are not decided solely based on payback, however, because it does not take into account the value of the investment over time.

- *Net present value (NPV)*. NPV is expressed in dollars as the difference between the present value of cash inflows (savings) over the life of the project (typically three or five years are used, depending on the type of project) and the initial investment. The general rule is that if the NPV is positive, the investment is sound. (But remember, other competing projects may have a better NPV and ROI than your project.)
- *Internal Rate of Return (IRR)*. IRR is a formula that calculates a percentage that equates to an interest rate. Generally, the IRR of the project is compared to the company's required internal rate of return on its capital. The general rule is that if the IRR is equal to or greater than the internal cost of money, then the project is sound.

Your CFO might also ask to see the projected cash flow, the average annual savings, or other internal measurements that are normally used to evaluate a project.

After the cost justification study has been completed, it is possible to develop and test a number of possibilities. For example, what if the justification turned out negative? Using the work performed, the project team should be able to pinpoint any area that was not providing a positive return; the team could then project what would be needed to make the returns positive for that deficient area, and to make the overall project positive.

In addition to providing a sound financial foundation for the project, the cost justification model provides two essential numbers needed to proceed to the next phase of the project, which is to develop and write an RFP.

The first essential number is the project budget. The CJA study will give you an overall estimated budget for the project. As a bonus, if the budget is too high, you have all the information needed to determine where project costs can be reduced. Alternately, you also have all the materials to convince your CFO that even though the projected budget is too high, the project will pay for itself and, therefore, should be approved.

The second essential number is the estimated cost of individual materials (hardware, software, etc.) and time (development and implementation) for the project. Thus, when reviewing vendor price proposals, you are reviewing them with an established set of figures by which to judge whether their prices are reasonable. If prices are out of line in the submitted proposals, the project team should be able to identify where the discrepancies are and to question those areas with the vendor.

CJA Summary

The areas of budget analysis/cost justification, process reengineering, and equipment identification are critical considerations when developing the requirements for a system RFP. All three are somewhat intertwined and need to be looked at together. The work done in the cost justification process will help the team understand whether simple or complex reengineering will be financially sound. Reengineering and conversion must be accomplished to some degree, but how far should the project team go, and on what basis do they make a decision? Performing the cost justification analysis will help the team understand these issues and develop a sound and defensible position.

These interrelated issues hinge on many variables that might not be intuitively obvious to the project team. The company's financial position, the team's experience, the project's complexity, and the technology must all be considered. Thought should also be given to the "accuracy" of the project analysis. For example, the CJA may be considered to be accurate plus or minus 20 percent. Therefore, there is a certain amount of risk involved in going with the project.

Once the analysis has been accomplished and you are satisfied that you have worked at a level of detail that will satisfy your management team, the data can be manipulated and a number of what-if scenarios can be prepared. For example, what if the development software costs are off by a factor of 35 percent? How will that affect the investment? What if hardware prices and quantities are underestimated? How much incremental change can the model stand before the investment turns negative? Or, what will it take to turn a negative analysis into a positive analysis?

Beyond ROI, Measuring Project Results

Part of the life cycle for a system project should be the continuous measurement of gains and efficiencies achieved. In many cases, a reengineering project will be approved based on some anticipated gains in business efficiency, and these gains provide the return on investment (ROI) that pays for the system costs. If the project began by analyzing the potential benefits of reengineering a business process, then at some point after installation, those gains should be measurable.

If the project is based on a positive cost justification analysis, then the groundwork for the postimplementation study is already laid and the tools for measuring results are already available. If the project is not based on a cost justification analysis, then it may be difficult to measure gains because there is no benchmark to measure against.

The easy answer is to review the new system against the original cost justification and the projected savings. Was the 35,000 square feet of floor space recovered? Were 20 FTEs (full-time equivalents) released or reassigned as predicted? Is paper usage down from 500,000 sheets per month to 10,000? Are business processes completed faster, such as resolving a claim in three working days instead of 15? Can you process a contract in one day instead of three days? Have you received fewer customer complaints since the new system was brought on board? Have you started to reduce the rate of customer attrition?

The answers to these questions are relatively easy to determine and will provide part of the answer—or at least an indication that the newly installed system is working as expected. However, what if your system purchase is not based on retrieving floor space, or cutting printing costs, or eliminating FTEs? What if your system purchase is based on soft-dollar benefits, such as improving customer service or providing new work processes? What if the new system is not based on previous processes?

Intangible benefits are difficult to prove or disprove and even harder to measure. How do you know that employee morale has improved as a result of the new system and is responsible for an 8 percent decrease in employee absenteeism? How do you measure customer satisfaction in dollars and, more so, how can you be sure that any increase (or decrease) is attributable to the new processes and systems?

Measuring the life cycle benefits of a system must be planned for as part of the overall cost justification process.

The results of installing a new system may not become evident for at least a year and possibly longer. If a complete overhaul of the business is undertaken, the changes will provoke a short-term increase in problems, which may cause a temporary spike in the work of a department. If the measurement is undertaken before the "electronic dust" has settled, the conclusions will be false.

For example, if the current company benefits system is replaced by a new and improved system, people who are the "customers" of the system may respond with increased questions about benefits (perhaps reminded of a question previously forgotten), confusion about new forms and procedures, or simple inquisitiveness about the change.

This increased activity should not be calculated as a general increase in questions (work), from 100 per day to 150 per day. The increase is temporary and due to change; when the new processes begin to work, the actual number of questions should drop, based on having better procedures and systems in place. If the number of questions does not drop or actually rises, the new system should be reviewed to determine why—but at least you have the benchmark to know where you are starting from.

A second outcome may show gains, attributable to increased customer satisfaction. This type of gain or loss may only be calculated after years of continuous monitoring, and must be based on a previous understanding of customer satisfaction. For example, customer turnover may have been previously established at 30 percent per year by reviewing the past five years' records. Turnover may have been traced, in part, to poor customer services, such as lack of response, poor response times, and low-quality responses. A new turnover-percentage calculation may require as many as two years or more before customer turnover can be analyzed, due to annual contract renewals and other factors. And perhaps only after several years can it be established that customer turnover has been affected (reduced) by the new system.

Measurement of results should be planned as part of the original project. A proper baseline must be established and the original figures maintained and available for several years; appropriate resources must also be dedicated to maintaining the information needed for a new analysis. A side benefit to revisiting the cost benefit analysis is that midcourse corrections may be made based on new data, and further process improvement may occur.

Conclusion

This brief explanation of the cost justification process provides you with an overview of both the process itself and the benefits derived from this work. We suggest that prior to starting your analysis, you consult with your financial department and explain what you are going to do and what will be the intended result. It is entirely possible that your CFO has additional ROI indicators that should be looked at and prepared for at the conclusion of the study. Certain other information will be needed from the financial people, such as your company's cost of money, depreciation method, and depreciation time.

If you are undertaking a project that is based on long-term improvements, be prepared to assign someone to ensuring that measurements are conducted at the proper intervals, and that the results of the measurements are considered in some meaningful way.

This work will provide you with an insight into your company's operations that perhaps few managers will share. Based on this knowledge, and the benefits that can be derived through new technology or systems, the detailed data behind the numbers will become a solid foundation for your system request.

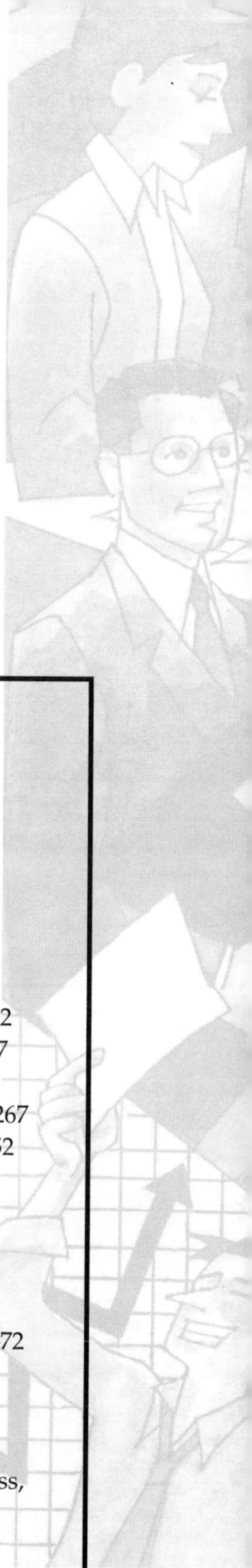

INDEX

A

Abbreviations
  and acronyms, sample style guide,
    Figure 5-14
  list, Figure 5-8, 113
Activities, proposal, 34–38
Alternate proposals, 49–51
Appendices
  for this book, 293–326
  for your proposal, 173–175
Art Log, Figure 11-6, 289
Artwork, numbering and indexing,
  287–289
Assembly, final, 228–229
Assumptions, Figure 6-2, 150

B

Best and final offer (BAFO), 205–207
Best value, 3
Best-case RFP scenario, 62
Bid/no-bid decision, 72–78, 79
  checklist, Appendix H, 305–307
  sample of no-bid letter, Figure 3-2,
    77
  when not to bid, 76–78
  when to bid, 74–76

Bidders' conference, transcript of
  exchange at, 66
Binder tabs, 216–219
  Figures 9-2 and 9-3, 217
  order, Figure 10-3, 241
  ordering, Figure 9-4, 218
Binding, types of, 223–226
Boilerplate files
  developing, 232–236
  illustration, Figure 10-7, 251–252
  library, maintenance of, 265–267
  material, 156–158
  preparing and managing, 231–267
  previous proposals into, 251–252
  summary, 267
  text, 236–252
  using, 260–262
Bonds, 115–116
Brochure-ware proposals, 3–4
Budget, determining project's, 70–72
Buy USA Statement, 116
Buyer, qualifying the, 65–72

C

Clarity of content and completeness,
  importance of, 4

Clip art, sources of, 279–280
Company services provided, 239–242
Compliance matrix, Figure 5-9, 114
Contract negotiation, 207–208
Corporate
    and project management descriptions, 242–245
    capabilities and facilities, 250–251
Cost Justification Whitepaper, Appendix J, 315–326
Cover
    artwork and illustrations, 260
    design, Figure 9-1, 214–216
    illustration, 277
    letter, 105–108
    letter, Figure 5-3, 106
    printing, 214–216
    proposal, 101–104
    proposal, Figures 5-1 and 5-2, 103

D

Data, avoiding non-essential, 4
Delivery
    conditions, 186
    method, 187–188
    requirements, following, 184–188
    summary, 188
Developing and writing your proposal, 123–176
    fundamental steps for a winning, 57–59
    summary, 175–176
Disposition activities, proposal, 47–49
Dissemination of material, 264–265

E

Evaluation, proposal, 81–99
    "confessions" of a proposal reviewer, 84
    checklist, Appendix E, 301–302
    checklist, figure 4-2, 93
    criteria, 84–85, 89–92
    customer, 94–98

determining areas of importance to customer, 85–86
    guidelines, Figure 4-1, 91–92
    helping the evaluation, determining what can be done, 86
    in-house, 87–94
    in-house team, forming, 92–94
    potential strong/weak points vs. competition, 86–87
    readers, 84
    summary, 99
    typical customer team, Figure 4-3, 97
Exceptions list, Figure 5-10, 115
Excess, eliminating, 5
Executive summary, components of, 124–141
Expectations, avoiding inflated, 6
Extension, request for, Figure 2-5, 45

F

Facilities, illustration of, 256–257
Features, benefits and needs, clarifying service or product, 24–26
Figure and table numbers, 284
Figure caption placement of, Figure 11-1, 271
Flow chart for typical proposal, Figure 3-1, 64
Format, proposal, 101–122
Front matter
    additional, 114–116
    order of, 105–113

H

Headquarters organization, illustration of, 257–259

I

Illustration
    boilerplate files, 252–260
    consistency and orientation, 285–286
    file, master proposal, 289–290
    formats, 280–282
    references, two rules of, 284

standards, 282–286
Illustrations
    art of, 270–280
    "boxing," 283
    developing for your proposal,
        269–292
    in-house boilerplate graphics from
        technical illustrations depart-
        ment, 279
    organization of, 287–290
    sample of computer-generated,
        Figure 11-4, 278
    sources of ready-to-use, 278–280
    storage of, 290–291
    summary, 291–292
    types of, 271–280
In-house review and sign off of proposal,
    39–42
In-text graphics, 281–282
Indexing files, 262–264
    illustrations, 263
    written, 262–263
Instructions, following the RFPs, 5

K

Kickoff meeting, 21–22, 29–32
    activities, 30–32
    agenda, Figure 2-5, 31
    materials, 29–30

L

Landscape *vs.* portrait orientation, 281
Layout instructions, Figure 5-12, 118
Leader's responsibilities, proposal, 34
Letter of transmittal, 105–108
Line art, 271–272
Line weights, 283–284
Losing proposals, examining, 55–57

M

Maintenance response time, Figure 10-2,
    240
Management organization charts, illus-
    tration, Figure 10-8, 258

Management section, 153–163
Manager, proposal, 33, 63
Minority Business Enterprise
    Requirements (MSWVBE form), 116

O

Online meetings, 20–22
Opportunity, qualifying the, 61–79
    getting started, 63–65
    summary of steps, 78–79
Organization,
    of illustrations, 286–290
    proposal, 117–118
Organizational chart, Figure 6-4, 162

P

Pain quotient as representing business
    reason for RFP, 71–72
Photographs, 272–275
Post delivery considerations, 189–194
Post proposal
    activities, organizing, 46–47, 189–211
    checklist, Appendix G, 304
    data, interpreting, 208–209
Pre-contract steps, 194–211
    summary, 210–211
Preproposal checklist, Appendix A, 294
Presubmission checklist, Appendix C,
    298–299
Presentation, proposal, 196–200
Price, considerations other than, 2–3
Pricing
    cost information, illustrating, 259–260
    for PCs, Figure 6-6, 169
    outline, Figure 6-5, 168
    section, 163–173
    strategies, 169–172
Printer
    preparing instructions for, 219–220
    selecting a, 226–228
Printers dummy
    Figure 9-5, 221
    preparing the, 220–223

Printing
    and delivering proposal, 213–229
    checklist, Appendix D, 300
    methods, 213–214
    specialty, 214–219
Product
    demonstration, 200–203
    pitches *vs.* business solutions, 4
Products
    or equipment, illustrating, 255–256
    or services, descriptions of, 236–239
Project management schedule, Figure 6-3, 150–151
Project plan, Figure 10-4, 246
Proposal
    definition and overview of, 1–5
    developing a winning, 17–59
    outlining your, 27–29
    schedule, 42–46
    status and tracking, Figure 2-4, 29
    status sheet, Appendix I, 308–314
    submission checklist, Appendix F, 303
    team, 17–18, 19
    team, Figure 2-1, 19
    writing checklist, Appendix B, 296–297
    writing schedule, Figure 2-3, 28
    writing your, 123–176
Proprietary Notice, Figure 5-5, 110–111
Punctuation, 285

Q
Qualifying the RFP and buyer, 65–72
Question-and-answer period, 195–196

R
Red Team review (in-house evaluation), 39–42, 94
    virtual, 42
Reference account
    descriptions, 245–250
    Figure 10-6, 249
    illustrating, 259

References, checking, 203–205
Reproduction shop, selecting a, 226–228
Request for information (RFI), definition of, 9–12
Request for proposal (RFP)
    bank, example of, 71
    best-case scenario, 62
    business reason for, 71–72
    definition of and response to, 5–16
    instructions, importance of following, 5
    project cycle, Figure 1-1, 15
    qualifying, 65–72
    questions, developing, 34–38
    requirements of, 4
    sample questions, 38–39
    specifications, Figure 10-1, 238
    wiring the, 68–70
    worst-case scenario, 61–62
Requirement/response format, Figure 6-1, 146
Resume, Figure 10-5, 247
Resumes, personnel, illustrating, 257
Road map, proposal, Figure 5-11, 117

S
Sales pitch, clarity of, 24–26
Schedule, proposal, 42–46
Software
    collaborative, 21
    illustration, 253–255
    proposal-writing, 20
Strategy, winning, 22–24
Style sheet
    Figure 5-13, 118–121
    proposal, 33–34
Submission
    criteria, 178–180
    general criteria, 180–182
    requirements, following, 177–188
    specific criteria, non-standard, 182–184
    summary, 188

T

Table and callouts, Figure 11-2, 276

Table of contents (TOC), Figures 5-6 and 5-7, 111–113

Tables, 276

Tabular information presented as a chart, Figure 11-3, 277

Technical illustrations department, in-house, 279

Technical section, components of, 141–152

Teleconferencing, 22

Themes, "win," 22–24

Title page, 106–110
    Figure 5-4, 109

Titles and captions, 284–285
    Figure 11-5, 284–285

Type styles, 283

W

War Room, 18–22
    designating a "virtual," 20–22

Winning proposal process, developing a, 17–59

Wiring the RFP, 68–70

Work area, designating a, 19–20

Work assignments, 32–33

Work space, 18–22

Worst-case RFP scenario, 61–62

Writing levels, technical, marketing and business detail in proposal, 51–55

Writing your proposal, 123–176
    summary, 175–176